2000 TIPS for Trainers & Staff Developers

2000 TIPS for Trainers & Staff Developers

edited by PHIL RACE

KOGAN PAGE

First Indian Edition 2003
Reprinted 2008

Kogan Page India Private Limited
4737/23 Ansari Road,
Daryaganj
New Delhi 110 002

This edition is for sale in Indian subcontinent only. Not for export elsewhere.

ISBN-10: 81-7554-196-2
ISBN-13: 978-81-7554-196-2

Published by Vinod Vasishtha for Kogan Page India Private Limited,
4737/23 Ansari Road, Daryaganj, New Delhi 110 002.

Printed and bound at Raj Press, R-3 Inderpuri, New Delhi - 110 012.

Contents

Preface

This book is for busy trainers, who have not the time (or even the inclination, perhaps) to wade through the tomes of theoretical knowledge underpinning the design of effective training programmes. The tips in this book aim to provide you with practical suggestions you can try out straight away in your own work. It is not the sort of book that is meant to be read through from cover to cover. It is meant to be a companion to you, to dip into wherever and whenever you can draw something useful to you from it.

The origins of the book started way back in 1994, when with Brenda Smith I wrote *500 Tips for Trainers*, which has since established itself in both the UK and the USA. Then more recently, with Steve McDowell, I wrote *500 Computing Tips for Trainers*. Also, two other tips books I wrote myself have strong links to the world of training, namely *500 Tips on Open and Flexible Learning* and *500 Tips on Group Learning*. The present book is my attempt to draw from these sources the most relevant of the suggestions they contain, and structure them into a logical compendium for trainers. This compendium also includes some bits and pieces I have adapted from other things I have published, including relevant extracts from *2000 Tips for Lecturers*.

Chapter 1, 'Face-to-face training', is in effect the heart of this compendium, addressing in turn planning, preparing, giving presentations, creating your learning environment, getting events off to a good start, keeping them going and (last but not least) looking after yourself!

Chapter 2, 'Group-based training', is about people learning together, with or without the presence of a trainer or facilitator. Several things relating to group learning are also included in various parts of Chapter 1, but in Chapter 2 is more depth about how learning happens in groups, and tips on addressing the behaviours that can damage the effectiveness of group work.

Chapter 3, 'Resource-based training', is about selecting, adapting or designing learning resource materials that can enable at least some of your trainees' learning to be done under their own steam. This chapter starts with suggestions to help you to work out which parts of your training may lend themselves to flexible learning, and how to select, adopt or adapt flexible learning resource materials. The chapter ends with suggestions about how (if you choose to do so) you may go about designing new flexible learning materials of your own.

Chapter 4, 'Computer-based training', starts with advice about how you yourself may get into the world of computers and technology, should you not already be there. Next follow suggestions on how to help your trainees get into using computers. This is followed by a section on online learning, including using communications technologies, e-mail, computer conferencing and the Internet in training. The chapter ends with some advice on keeping your own stress levels down when working with training technologies, followed by a 'jargon-busting' glossary, which is intended to be both informative and amusing!

Chapter 5, 'Evaluating your training', ends the compendium, with suggestions on a range of ways of finding out how your training is going, and not just 'happy sheets'.

I hope that you will find things in this compendium that you can put into practice straight away, and others that you can ponder about and develop in your own way. More important, I hope you will recognize throughout using this book things you are already doing really well, and suggestions that you are already exceeding in your own work.

Acknowledgements

I am grateful to Brenda Smith and Steve McDowell, my co-authors for two of the four principal sources of this compendium, for their help in updating and improving the content of many parts of this book. Steve McDowell's eagle eye also caught many of my grammatical and punctuation errors, and he taught me to use the 'tracking changes' features of my word-processing package as an editing resource. I am grateful to Steve Higgins for permission to adapt and include his glossary on the terminology of computing and electronic communications.

I am also grateful to Jonathan Simpson of Kogan Page, who helped to shape the idea represented by this book, and encouraged me along the way. Finally, I am pleased to thank Helen Moss, whose copy-editing unearthed a variety of things that needed putting right.

Chapter 1

Face-to-face training

Planning and preparation

1. *What's your training ethos?*
2. *Designing a new training programme*
3. *Setting training event objectives*
4. *Where can learning outcomes be useful to trainees?*
5. *Fine-tuning and communicating learning outcomes*
6. *Getting the content right*
7. *Timetabling your training event*
8. *Tips when using visiting trainers*
9. *Designing pre-event tasks*
10. *Behind the scenes*
11. *Refreshments*
12. *Getting your bits and bobs ready*
13. *Planning for distant venues*
14. *Tips for international trainers*

Preparing and giving presentations

15. *Do you really want to give presentations?*
16. *Preparing your first presentations*
17. *Giving presentations*
18. *Designing and using handouts*
19. *Using overhead projectors*
20. *Why use computer-aided presentations?*
21. *Some don'ts for presentation managers*
22. *Helping trainees to learn from computer-aided presentations*

The tips in this chapter are about planning and delivering training events. Some of the tips apply particularly to designing one-off training events for particular purposes, perhaps for 'away ground' rather than your normal workplace, and others apply to regular day-to-day training in your regular working environment.

The chapter starts with tips on **planning and preparation**, bringing together quite a mixture of agendas, from organizing refreshments to taking your show on the road internationally. However, the suggestions on designing your training outcomes or objectives apply to most training scenarios.

There then follow tips on **giving presentations**, both for trainers who have not yet done much in the way of giving presentations, and for old hands too. In particular, there are suggestions for using computer-aided presentation packages to support your presentations.

The chapter moves on to **creating your training environment**, and addresses some of the other things you may use in your work, including whiteboards or chalkboards, and video machines.

The section on **getting training events off to a good start** includes a wide range of tips on process, and how to deal with different sorts of trainees in different contexts.

There is a broad range of further suggestions on process, including tips on handling difficult situations or people, in the section on **keeping the show going**.

The chapter ends with tips on looking after yourself: some suggestions on handling your own overall workload, and making it that bit more manageable.

1. What's your training ethos?

Here are some general indicators of what could be regarded as a productive training ethos. Good training is about helping trainees to learn and to participate:

- **A training event should be an active occasion for participants, not just for us!** It's well worth building your training event programmes around the things that participants will do during the sessions. People tend to remember more when they are actively involved – and having fun!

- **Plan each training event like a journey, with a beginning, a middle and a goal.** This helps you to ensure that training events are a coherent learning experience for participants, and that participants know where they are at each stage.

- **Participants need to know where they're going.** Make the purposes of each training event as clear as possible, for example by spelling out intended learning outcomes or training event objectives.

- **Participants want to know why they should be going.** Express the intended learning outcomes in terms that participants will find relevant to their work situations, and attractive targets for them personally.

- **Participants like to know how they will get there.** Share with participants information about the sorts of processes they will engage in during the various stages of a training event – doing so may help to dispel any anxieties.

- **Regard the experience of your participants as your greatest training event resource.** Whenever possible, allow participants to tell you things, rather than you telling them things that some of them may already know. Give participants credit for what they already know whenever possible.

- **Build in interaction whenever possible.** A good training event is mainly interactive, and uses only a very limited amount of 'direct input' from trainers. The input does not have to be in presentation format, but can take the form of learning resources such as handouts, displays and case studies.

- **Allow for ongoing feedback from participants.** It is far better to abandon your original plans when something unexpected but important crops up, than to try to soldier on and stick to a pre-planned schedule of what should be covered in a training event. However, don't abandon coffee breaks!

- **Anticipate what you would like participants to say about a training event.** Try to plan your training events along lines that will be both enjoyable and productive from the point of view of participants.

- **Regard each training event as a new learning experience for yourself.** The day you think you've got a training event 'exactly right', you've got a problem! If that day comes, design some different training events, and keep on learning.

2. Designing a new training programme

Designing a new area of training is an exciting but complex task, requiring the integration of a whole range of interdependent elements. The following tips, in sequence, are designed to help you do so in a systematic way. These are most likely to be of use to you if you are (or will be) in the role of leader for the new programme:

- **Identify the market for your programme.** Few new programmes these days are offered to a captive, predetermined market of potential trainees. You will need therefore to have good evidence of a real demand for your proposed programme. It will be useful to identify the competition – other institutions offering a similar programme. Can you show that either the market is sufficiently large or that you can offer something very different to attract a sufficient number of trainees? Your institution will require you to show how your programme will sit within the existing course portfolio.

- **Clarify the rationale for the new programme.** You need to be sure of your reasons for its particular flavour and its ultimate viability. Can you run it with the human and physical resources you can get? Can you provide for a sufficiently large number of trainees? Specifically consider: the unique characteristics of the group it is aimed at; the programme's aims, intended learning outcomes and the qualification or accreditation that it will lead to.

- **Clarify how it will be costed and funded.** This is a daunting process if it's your first time, and we advise you to gather know-how from other colleagues in your institution who have already planned and implemented a new programme. There may well be formal institutional checklists and guidelines for you to follow.

- **Decide upon a time-frame.** Curriculum design is a complex and time-consuming process. Mistakes are made if the process is rushed. If a programme is to be designed from scratch, sufficient time should be allowed to negotiate and incorporate internal as well as external quality assurance processes. Time is also needed to market the course effectively. Be realistic about a start date!

- **Expect to become involved in the recruitment of trainees.** It is often found, particularly with new programmes, that trainees receive inappropriate guidance and advice, and can end up taking a course for which they are not suited. Retention statistics are increasingly under the spotlight in institutional review procedures. A useful part of planning a new programme is to look at how trainees will be guided before they enrol, and the kinds of follow-up support they are most likely to need after enrolment. Such guidance has been found to be an essential factor in ensuring that trainees don't drop out of new programmes.

- **Map out the intended learning outcomes.** You will need to design these carefully, based on the programme rationale and its target trainee group, so that they are specific, measurable, achievable, realistic and time-specified, and in parallel with the standards and benchmarks that may already exist in the subject area concerned. More detailed suggestions on doing this are provided later.

- **Decide on how the outcomes are to be described.** It can often be useful in planning the delivery of learning outcomes to use the terminology of the UK's vocational qualification framework: performance criteria, evidence indicators and range statements. If these are translated into simple, jargon-free language, you will find that both your trainees and fellow trainers will be really clear about what is required of them.

- **Consider appropriate teaching and learning strategies.** You will need to decide to what extent you will use traditional teaching methods, resource-based learning, flexible learning pathways and communications technologies in the delivery of your programme.

- **Think about who will deliver it.** You may need to assemble a team to deliver the programme. It is not a good idea to design a programme that is too dependent on the particular qualifications or expertise of individual colleagues. Typically they will leave or drop out in due course. This requires you to identify a pool of appropriate colleagues to whom you can turn. It's a good idea therefore to assemble a collection of CVs of the colleagues who are likely to contribute.

- **Think carefully about the people, facilities and resources you will need to run the programme effectively.** These may include training staff, support staff, library and information technology resources. You may also need to budget for laboratory, workshop or studio facilities, specialized equipment, printing and photocopying. Do not assume that institutional resources and facilities will be automatically available to you just because the programme is approved.

- **Consider the staff development the team may need to deliver the programme effectively.** There will be training needs associated with any new programme, be it in using unfamiliar delivery methods, standardizing assessment procedures, content updating or simply team building.

- **Decide how the learning outcomes will be assessed.** It is common to express the content of a programme in terms of what trainees will be able to do or know. Good decisions on how best to assess whether the specified learning outcomes have been achieved are crucial. There is a real danger of assessing only some of the learning outcomes and then only partially. For this reason, put assessment (and quality assurance) at the top of your list of things to get right.

- **Think about the values that underpin your programme.** For example, your underpinning philosophies about how trainees learn need to be explicit, agreed and shared by the course team.

- **Plan into the structure of the programme a process of continuous quality review and improvement.** It is critical that you look at how you will monitor the success of your programme. This will include trainee satisfaction, peer review, retention and completion rates, and assessment reliability.

3. Setting training event objectives

People like to know where they're heading. They like to know what they may expect to be able to do at the end of the training session that they can't do already, or that they may like to do better. They also like to know how the things they can already do relate to the agenda for the session. It is therefore crucial to be clear about the intended learning outcomes of training sessions. The intended learning outcomes are the most important starting-point for any training programme. Learning outcomes give details of syllabus content. They can be expressed in terms of the objectives that trainees should be able to *show* they have achieved, in terms of knowledge, understanding, skills and even attitudes. They are written as descriptors of ways that trainees will be expected to demonstrate the results of their learning. The links between learning outcomes and assessment criteria need to be clear and direct. Learning outcomes indicate the standards of courses and modules:

- **Look for likely 'training needs'.** In pre-event planning, talk to anyone who can help you focus on to the real issues that you should attempt to cover during the forthcoming training session.

- **Start with some 'provisional' objectives.** Prepare a slide or two, or overhead transparency (or handout sheet) listing some relatively broad 'intended outcomes' of your training session.

- **Ask participants, 'What do you want?'** Asking participants to identify their own personal wishes helps you to find out the 'real agenda' that may lie behind the training session. A good way of doing this is to give out small pieces of acetate (or Post-its) and ask participants to write down what they 'hope for most' from the forthcoming session.

- **Treat participants' wishes seriously.** If you have gone to the trouble of collecting participants' expectations, don't waste them. Stick them up on a flipchart where they can remain visible throughout the training session. As often as possible, return to particular participants' expectations as the session progresses.

- **Get the wording right.** Make sure that the words used to express training objectives or intended learning outcomes mean the same to everyone. Ask 'What do we really mean by this?' and adjust the wording so that the objectives are understood and shared by all present.

- **Feel free to jettison some of your own objectives.** When the real agenda (as determined from participants) differs from the agenda you prepared in your planning for a training session, it is important to be seen to be willing to favour participants' wishes, even at the expense of some training event objectives that you yourself feel are really valuable.

- **Try getting participants to prioritize objectives or outcomes.** For example, suppose there are six possible objectives. Ask participants to give each of the objectives a 'star rating', for example 'three stars for crucial', 'two stars for useful', 'one star for interesting', 'zero stars for irrelevant'. Collect up the 'stars' on a flipchart or overhead transparency listing the objectives, and take your priorities from the result.

- **Return to the objectives or intended outcomes.** Link training event activities to the objectives, so that your participants can see exactly why they are being asked to do particular things during the training session.

- **At the end, review the objectives or intended outcomes.** Feel free to admit those that have not been achieved by the session. Confirm those that you know have been addressed successfully.

- **At the very end, return to your participants' expectations.** Give them the opportunity to confirm which of their expectations have been realized during the training session – and which still remain as 'outstanding'. It is often possible to harness the 'outstanding' expectations as the basis for a follow-up training session.

4. Where can learning outcomes be useful to trainees?

Learning outcomes should not just reside in course validation documentation (though they need to be there in any case). They should also underpin everyday teaching–learning situations. They can be put to good use in the following places and occasions:

- **In handbooks**, so that trainees can see the way that the whole course or module is broken down into manageable elements of intended achievement, and set their own targets accordingly.
- **At the start of each presentation**, for example on a slide or transparency, so that trainees are informed of the particular purposes of the occasion.
- **At the end of each presentation**, so that trainees can estimate the extent to which they have travelled towards being able to achieve the intended outcomes associated with the presentation.
- **At suitable points in the briefing of trainees for longer elements of their learning**, including projects, group tasks, practical work and fieldwork.
- **On each element of handout material** issued before, during or after presentations, to reinforce the links between the content of the handout and trainees' intended learning.
- **On tasks and exercises, and briefings to further reading**, so that trainees can see the purpose of the work they are intended to do.
- **On the first few screens of each computer-based learning programme** that trainees study independently (or in groups).
- **At the beginning of self-study or flexible learning packages**, so that trainees can estimate their own achievement as they work through the materials.

5. Fine-tuning and communicating learning outcomes

- **Work out exactly what you want trainees to be able to do by the end of each defined learning element.** Even when you're working with syllabus content that is already expressed in terms of learning outcomes, it is often worth thinking again about your exact intentions, and working out how these connect together for different parts of trainees' learning.

- **Don't use the word 'trainees' in your outcomes** – except in dry course documentation. It is much better to use the word 'you' when addressing trainees. 'When we've completed this presentation, you should be able to compare and contrast particle and wave models of radiation' is better than stating 'The expected learning outcome of this presentation is that trainees will...' Similarly, use the word 'you' when expressing learning outcomes in trainee handbooks, handouts, laboratory briefing sheets and so on. Trainees need to feel that learning outcomes belong to them, not just to other people.

- **Work imaginatively with existing learning outcomes.** There may already be externally defined learning outcomes, or they may have been prescribed some time ago when the course or programme was designed or accredited. These may, however, be written in language that is not user-friendly or clear to trainees, and that is more connected with the teaching of the subject than the learning process. You should be able to translate these outcomes, so that they will be more useful to your trainees.

- **Match your wording to your trainees.** The learning outcomes as expressed in course documentation may be off-putting and jargonistic, and may not match the intellectual or language skills of your trainees. By developing the skills to translate learning outcomes precisely into plain English, you will help the outcomes to be more useful to them, and at the same time it will be easier for you to design your teaching strategy.

- **Your intended learning outcomes should serve as a map to your training programme.** Trainees and others will look at the outcomes to see if the programme is going to be relevant to their needs or intentions. The level and standards associated with your course will be judged by reference to the stated learning outcomes.

- **Remember that many trainees will have achieved at least some of your intended outcomes already.** When introducing the intended learning outcomes, give credit for existing experience, and confirm that it is useful if some members of the group already have some experience and expertise that they can share with others.

- **Be ready for the question, 'Why?'** It is only natural for trainees to want to know why a particular learning outcome is being addressed. Be prepared to illustrate each outcome with some words about the purpose of including it.

- **Be ready for the reaction, 'So what?'** When trainees, colleagues or external reviewers still can't see the point of a learning outcome, they are likely to need some further explanation before they will be ready to take it seriously.

- **Work out your answers to 'What's in this for me?'** When trainees can see the short-term and long-term benefits of gaining a particular skill or competence, they are much more likely to try to achieve it.

- **Don't promise what you can't deliver.** It is tempting to design learning outcomes that seem to be the answers to everyone's dreams. However, the real test for your teaching will be whether it is seen to enable trainees to achieve the outcomes. It's important to be able to link each learning outcome to an assessable activity or assignment.

- **Don't use words such as 'understand' or 'know'.** While it is easy to write (or say) 'When you have completed this module successfully, you will understand the third law of thermodynamics', it is much more helpful to step back and address the questions, 'How will we know that they have understood it?', 'How will they themselves know they have understood it?' and 'What will they be able to do to *show* that they have understood it?' Replies to the last of these questions lead to much more useful ways of expressing the relevant learning outcomes.

- **Don't start at the beginning.** It is often much harder to write the outcomes that will be associated with the beginning of a course, and it is best to leave attempting this until you have got into your stride regarding writing outcomes. In addition, it is often much easier to work out what the 'early' outcomes actually should be once you have established where these outcomes are leading trainees.

- **Think ahead to assessment.** A well-designed set of learning outcomes should automatically become the framework for the design of assessed tasks. It is worth asking yourself 'How can I measure this?' for each draft learning outcome. If it is easy to think of how it will be measured, you can normally go ahead and design the outcome. If it is much harder to think of how it could be measured, it is usually a signal that you may need to think further about the outcome and try to relate it more firmly to tangible evidence that could be assessed.

- **Keep sentences short.** It is important that your trainees will be able to get the gist of each learning outcome without having to reread it several times, or ponder on what it really means.

- **Consider illustrating your outcomes with 'for example...' descriptions.** If necessary, such extra details could be added in smaller print, or in brackets. Such additional detail can be invaluable to trainees in giving them a better idea about what their achievement of the outcomes may actually amount to in practice.

- **Test-run your learning outcome statements.** Ask target-audience trainees 'What do your think this really means?', to check that your intentions are being communicated clearly. Also test out your outcomes statements on colleagues, and ask them whether you have missed anything important, or whether they can suggest any changes to your wording.

- **Aim to provide trainees with the whole picture.** Put the trainee-centred language descriptions of learning outcomes and assessment criteria into trainee handbooks, or turn them into a short self-contained leaflet to give to trainees at the beginning of the course. Ensure that trainees don't feel swamped by the magnitude of the whole picture! Trainees need to be guided carefully through the picture in ways that allow them to feel confident that they will be able to succeed a step at a time.

- **Don't get hung up too much on performance, standards and conditions** when expressing learning outcomes. For example, don't feel that such phrases as 'on your own', 'without recourse to a calculator or computer', 'under exam conditions' or 'with the aid of a list of standard integrals' need to be included in every well-expressed learning outcome. Such clarifications are extremely valuable elsewhere, in published assessment criteria. Don't dilute the primary purpose of a learning outcome with administrative detail.

- **Don't be trivial!** Trivial learning outcomes support criticisms of reductionism. One of the main objections to the use of learning outcomes is that there can be far too many of them, only some of which are really important.

- **Don't try to teach something if you can't think of any intended learning outcome associated with it.** This seems obvious, but it can be surprising how often a teaching agenda can be streamlined and focused by checking that there is some important learning content associated with each element in it, and removing or shortening the rest.

- **Don't confuse learning outcomes and assessment criteria.** It is best not to cloud the learning outcomes with the detail of performance criteria and standards until trainees know enough about the subject to understand the language of such criteria. In other words, the assessment criteria are best read by trainees *after* they have started to learn the topic, rather than at the outset (but make sure that the links will be clear in due course).

- **Don't write any learning outcomes that can't (or won't) be assessed.** If it's important enough to propose as an intended learning outcome, it should be worthy of being measured in some way, and it should be *possible* to measure.

- **Don't design any assessment task or question that is not related to the stated learning outcomes.** If it's important enough to measure, it is only fair to let trainees know that it is on their learning agenda.

- **Don't state learning outcomes at the beginning, and fail to return to them.** It's important to come back to them at the end of each teaching–learning element, such as presentation, self-study package, element of practical work and so on. Turn them into checklists for trainees, for example along the lines 'Check now that you feel able to…' or 'Now you should be in a position to…'.

6. Getting the content right

Many of the suggestions in this book are about *how* to conduct training events, rather than about *what* to cover in them. Of course, the content itself is important too. The following ideas may help you to focus the content:

- **Link the content of your training event directly to the advertised aims or objectives.** Of every component of your planned training event, ask yourself, 'How exactly does this relate to the intended outcomes?' If the link is tenuous, the element concerned may be an optional extra.

- **Remember that most activities take longer than we imagine they will.** This is particularly important when devising new activities that you haven't tried out before. It is better to allow 45 minutes for such an activity and then fill in with something else if it only takes 30 minutes, than vice versa.

- **Don't ride hobby-horses too hard!** When we've got a strong belief in something, it's all to easy for us to plug it so hard that it becomes difficult for participants to take – particularly if they have views rather different to ours.

- **Research how relevant and useful each part of your training event feels to participants.** In follow-up questionnaires or interviews, ask which parts of the training event content were most useful, and ask which things could be left out if necessary.

- **Give participants your content rather than tell them it.** It can save a great deal of time to have the main principles of your training event wrapped up in handout materials or summaries, so that participants can spend their time with you exploring the issues rather than trying to write them down.

- **Check that your content is authoritative, up to date and correct.** It is very useful to find trusted colleagues elsewhere who will be willing to look at your handout materials and overheads with a supportive but critical eye, and give you feedback about anything that may need to be adjusted.

- **Remember that content changes.** Participants will consider your training event to be as up to date as the most recent developments you refer to during the session. Make sure you have some new references as well as well-established ones. A handout sheet listing these is very much appreciated.

- **Let participants help you to develop your content.** Next month's repeat session can benefit a lot by incorporating questions and answers that emerge from your present training event. A sheet collecting together such questions and answers is very useful as handout material for future training events.

- **Focus on what participants will do during your training event.** The activities you devise will be the most important aspect of your participants' view of the content of your training event.

- **Have plenty of spare content up your sleeve!** You never know when an activity will take only half the time you allowed for it (for example, when everyone already knows a lot about the subject). Sometimes, you'll have to drop a training event element entirely because you find out at the last minute that everyone has already covered it elsewhere. Have ready a range of alternative things that you can use to fill participants' time usefully.

7. Timetabling your training event

If you can manage time, you can manage everything else. Timetabling a training event is an important element of designing it. We've gathered the following ideas by trial and error (mostly by error!):

- **Start with coffee (and tea, and juice).** For example, you're much more likely to achieve a prompt 10.15 start if the advertised programme starts with 'Coffee and informal introductions' at 9.45.

- **Start on time anyway.** Even if participants are still drifting in for an assortment of wonderful reasons, it does no harm to be seen to be already under way at the advertised start time. You can choose to do things that aren't particularly important until everyone has arrived. If you delay the start, participants who have made the effort to be punctual can feel very cheated.

- **Stop on time (or even ahead of time) for coffee breaks or meal breaks.** It may come as a great disappointment to you that most participants are actually rather pleased when a coffee break starts five minutes early!

- **Don't say, 'Come back in 20 minutes.'** No one will know when the 20 minutes started! It's more effective to say, 'Please can we resume at 11.23?' (An odd time tends to stick in people's memories, and usually works surprisingly well.)

- **Plan a reasonable amount of time for coffee breaks.** As well as consuming a drink and a biscuit, participants will probably want to pay a call – or make a call. Also, the conversations that participants get into during breaks are not only interesting but useful. It's better to have a prompt start after a 25-minute break than a laboured start after an attempt at a 15-minute break.

- **Sometimes avoid breaks, but still have coffee.** Where refreshments are available in the room, it is then possible to give five minutes for everyone to equip themselves with refreshments, and enter into (for example) a plenary discussion or syndicate task where participants can consume their refreshments as they work.

- **Don't underestimate how long it takes for everyone to get lunch.** Even when running training events in hotels, there may be slow table-service, or queues at the buffet table. (Pull out the buffet table from the wall that it always seems to be placed against, so that participants have twice the opportunity of serving themselves.)

- **In case lunch is fast, ensure that participants don't have a boring wait.** One way of doing this is to combine lunch with a lunchtime task or an exhibition of materials, so that participants can use any spare time without feeling held up.

- **Have a clearly advertised finishing time.** This helps participants plan round the other things in their lives, including transport home or picking up kids from school. Always finish on (or ahead of) this time. You can of course stay on for informal chats with those participants who are not in any hurry after 'closing time'.

- **Don't try to do everything you've prepared for.** When a training event gets behind your personal schedule, feel free to drop inputs or activities that are not crucial, and aim to give every appearance of sticking to the planned timetable. Remember, participants find the words 'I don't think we need to spend any further time on this – we've already explored it quite fully this morning' music to their ears!

8. Tips when using visiting trainers

It is always a good idea to introduce variety and change by inviting outside trainers or speakers. However famous and well respected these people are, a few precautions can be vital:

- **Agree things in writing.** A friendly conversation over the telephone may be difficult to recall months or even weeks later. It is useful therefore to put pen to paper and send a summary of your conversation to visiting trainers.

- **Check the understanding of the title.** The same words can all too easily mean different things to different people at different times. Try to check out exactly what the title means to you, and to the visiting trainer. Talk things over in advance.

- **Discuss in some detail the areas to be covered.** Have you had an experience where you thought you had agreed something, only to find the other person doing or saying something completely different? It can be embarrassing, especially when you see the looks on other people's faces. Talk through exactly what you both understand about the topics to be covered. Examples can be very useful.

- **Prepare guidance notes about overhead transparencies.** How many times have we all been at training events where we cannot read what is shown on the overhead projector (OHP)? A few guidance notes on general layout and size of print can save much embarrassment later. Prepare a standard checklist form to send to all visiting speakers – this could help maintain the quality of your training provision.

- **Ensure that enough copies of handouts are available for distribution.** Ask presenters to bring along copies of their overhead transparencies, or send them before the event, so that you can produce copies. Suggest shrinking overheads to four or six on a page, and photocopy both sides of the paper to save forests.

- **Check when your presenter wants to distribute material.** If handouts are supplied in advance, check whether it is intended that they should be issued at the start, or at particular stages during the session.

- **Check what facilities the presenter will need.** Ask how the room should be set out. Are tables needed for materials? Is a remote control for the video essential or not? Presenters who wish to stop and start a video frequently while adding comments could be rather thrown if they have to sit in front of the machine and jump up and down at each appropriate moment.

- **Send a good map, well in advance.** There is nothing more frustrating than trying to find a venue with a poorly constructed map, especially when doing so as a visiting presenter. Ensure the map is printed large enough to read without a magnifying glass, and that appropriate buildings and streets are clearly marked. It is a good idea to indicate which way the map should be held, by relating it to marked buildings or landmarks – and always include a compass pointer that shows which way north is at least, otherwise it is all to easy to hold a map upside down!

- **Don't be afraid to interject when necessary.** If you can see that the audience has completely switched off, try to bring the session back on track. To throw in a question can help to steer things in another direction when necessary, or can help the audience to understand better. Alternatively, a quick and friendly chat to the visiting trainer over coffee can often save the day.

- **Follow up with a thank-you note.** However experienced we are, it is always good to receive such notes. It may also be appropriate to send on any evaluation comments you receive.

9. Designing pre-event tasks

You haven t always the chance to set participants tasks to do in preparation for a training event –

but when such an opportunity is available, you can use it to your advantage, and your participants can benefit considerably too. Here are some suggestions:

- **Make sure the tasks reach everyone in good time.** One way of checking that all your participants have received the tasks is for the same mailing to include something they need to send back to you before the training event, for example a registration form or a car-parking permit request.

- **Don't make the tasks too demanding.** Short, specific tasks are best. Ideally, you want all participants to have spent approximately equal time on the tasks, rather than have some participants who have spent a great deal of effort on them while others have only thought about them lightly.

- **Include pro formas.** For example, if one of your tasks is 'Work out a list of 10 questions that you think we should address during the course of the training event', providing a page with 10 boxes can help to make sure that participants bring their lists ready. The lists can then be displayed during the training event, and an agenda for discussion can be made from the most common questions.

- **Make the tasks quite definite.** It's little use just asking participants to read through some handout material as preparation for the training event. It is better to give them something definite to do while they read, such as 'Find five advantages of the approach described in the handout, and also find five drawbacks of the approach.'

- **Use the tasks to bring participants up to an appropriate 'starting level'.** It can save a lot of valuable time if those participants who are starting from scratch have an opportunity to gain familiarity with the basics of the topic from tasks they do using handout materials before they come to the event itself.

- **Use pre-event tasks to prioritize training event objectives or outcomes.** Simply asking participants to give a rating showing which objectives or outcomes they can already achieve is useful. This can help you avoid wasting time on things that your participants can already do.

- **Don't depend on all participants having done your pre-event tasks.** With the best will in the world, things won't always go your way. You may end up with one or two substitute-participants who were told to attend your training event at the last minute – and of course, they won't even know about the pre-event tasks.

- **Don't leave a task unattended.** When people have spent time doing some preparation, they are naturally quite upset if their work goes unrecognized. Make sure that each pre-event task is debriefed at least briefly during the training event.

- **Encourage participants to bring along to the training event materials they think may be useful or relevant.** Setting a pre-event task along these lines may help you track down valuable resource materials that you would not have come across otherwise, and such tasks place value on participants' existing knowledge and experience.

- **Print your pre-event task sheets on coloured paper.** This can help you recognize at once the things that participants have already done in preparation – and helps participants themselves to avoid losing the task sheets in a mass of white papers.

10. Behind the scenes

It's vital that you make due preparations before your training event takes place, so that everyone is at ease during the session – and to save you from last-minute panics:

- **Get your venue details right – and send them out.** Send each participant relevant details, including travel directions if needed, about 10 days ahead of the event. Remember that some participants may be travelling directly from some other event or location, so give time for the details to be redirected to them if necessary.

- **Show the way.** Prepare large direction signs for the event and venue – enough for all possible entrances to the building. Remember how creative people can be when it comes to finding their way into a building they do not know!

- **Prepare name badges for everyone (including yourself).** These are best prepared using big lettering (18- or 24-point on desktop-publishing programmes) so that names can be seen without an intimate inspection of the upper body! Double-check your spelling of people's names – no one likes to be misnamed.

- **Feed bodies as well as minds.** Check that catering arrangements are in place and that you have catered for diverse needs or tastes as far as you can. If you want to keep your group awake in the afternoon, fresh fruit works rather better than syrup sponge and custard. However, oranges (except mandarins) are not a good idea, as participants don't really want to be seen with juice dripping down their fronts!

- **Prepare evaluation sheets.** Make these specific to the event you're going to run, so that you can gather detailed feedback on which of the aims have been achieved successfully, and find out any expectations that have not been met.

- **Check your equipment.** Make sure that you are familiar with the projector, video machine or TV sets that you may want to use during your session.

- **Get your ambience sorted out.** For example, if you wish to play suitable music during the minutes while participants are arriving and settling in, check that suitable playback equipment is available – it's often worth bringing your own anyway (a small portable tape or disc machine will do).

- **Have more than enough handouts.** Check that they are stapled in the correct order, or filed in piles so that you can give them out in the right order as your session proceeds. Photocopy or print back-to-back wherever possible, to save trees.

- **Get your own act together in advance.** Get your overheads and notes assembled into the right order, so that you don't have to scrabble around looking for particular resources as you proceed.

- **Know who is supposed to be coming.** Get your list of expected participants ready, and have copies available for everyone. When participants are coming from around the country, it can be useful to circulate lists in advance, including contact phone numbers, so that participants can help each other with travel arrangements. It is amazing how often participants can travel to your session from the same site and organization, without knowing of each other's attendance till they arrive.

11. Refreshments

Think back to the last conference you attended. Whatever else you've forgotten about it, you'll probably remember whether the food was superb or terrible! The following suggestions may help you to ensure that your own participants don't have sad memories about the refreshments during your sessions:

- **Provide drinks on arrival.** People may have travelled a long way and usually welcome a top-up of caffeine, tannin and so on. Try to arrange that the drinks are available some time before the advertised start of the session, so that people who arrive early have their own reward.

- **Allow people to make choices.** Provide tea (including herbal, raspberry, orange, passion fruit), coffee, orange juice, hot water, cold water, fizzy water and plain water. People feel better when they have choices to make. This is your first step towards empowering your participants. Making such choices is also a good way of participants getting to know you and each other.

- **Don't forget the late arrivals.** Make sure that the drinks are still available 30 minutes after the start of your programme. Anything could have happened that morning – failed alarm clock, flat tyre, mother-in-law called just before departure, late train and so on. It's not always people's fault when they're late. (In your case, of course, it's your fault!)

- **Provide lots of refreshments.** Regular breaks help the brain to function more effectively, and it's amazing what some people will tell you over a cup of coffee!

- **Provide a table for the refreshments.** Those with bad backs will find difficulty bending down to floor level to pick up their cup of tea. A table also acts as a central focus for conversation. It somehow gives stability to strangers, and if anyone finds conversation difficult they can always eat a biscuit and talk about the advantages of wholemeal ones.

- **Place the table in a suitable part of the room.** If the refreshments are to be topped up throughout the event, try to avoid the catering staff having to fight their way through people, chairs, flipcharts and video cameras. Place the table somewhere where it is easily accessible, and not blocking anyone's view. If your group is large, it helps to place the table so that people can get to all sides of it – this helps to avoid queues.

- **Watch the budget.** It is really impressive to serve fresh salmon and strawberries, followed by afternoon tea! However, you may be unable to provide seminars later in the year, or people may not be able to afford to come. Simple, wholesome food also helps to keep people awake.

- **Variety is the spice of life.** Isn't it amazing how different we all are? Have you ever tried cooking a meal for six children! In your group you will probably have people who eat most things, vegetarians of different kinds, people who can't eat pork, eggs, caviar, cucumber and so on. Play safe and provide a mixture of food.

- **Provide earplugs or play lively music!** Have you ever wondered why catering staff never go on training courses that teach them how to lay out cups and saucers quietly? Try and be flexible so that while stocks are being replenished you can provide a change in activity that does not require quiet contemplation.

- **Allow lots of time for eating.** Evaluations often state that the most valuable part of the session was talking to colleagues. Therefore a way of improving your ratings with clients is to provide lots of opportunity for this interaction to occur. How often have you had to leave a lovely, sticky dessert because the afternoon session was about to begin?

12. Getting your bits and bobs ready

Carry your case of bits and bobs with you at all times. Being prepared is the motto of the effective trainer. How many times have you asked for materials to be available only to find they were not provided?

- **Get a box!** Invest in a creative box, carry-case or container that you can take anywhere.

- **Get the size right!** If you're travelling mostly by car, you can afford to take with you a bigger box than you may be able to carry on trains or on foot.
- **Be secure!** Think about the best way to keep your bits and pieces from getting mixed up in transit. Make sure that separate things can be kept in separate parts of your kit. Have you noticed how inconvenient it is when Blu-tack, pens and pencils become intimate in your kit?
- **Label everything.** Make sure that all your bits and pieces have your name, work address and phone/fax number on them. This way, you're likely to get back the things you leave behind in the hurry of departure.
- **Have everything with you.** This can profitably include Blu-tack, OHP pens, flipchart pens, scissors, spare paper, paper clips, drawing pins, tissues (you may make some participants cry!), string, sticky labels, a clock, pins, sunglasses (for when the group adjourns to the lawn on a hot day), safety pins (you never know when you – or a participant – will really need one), a toothbrush, an eraser, peppermints, headache tablets, chalk, blank transparencies, Sellotape, even a set of jump leads and a complete rail timetable. Don't forget also how useful a couple of screwdrivers can turn out to be, including a Phillips one.
- **Make a checklist.** For each event, make a list of the things you know you may need, and tick them off as you check you've got them in your box. You can also use this list to check that you've collected everything back at the end of your session.
- **Avoid rummaging.** When searching for a particular item from your kit, choose a moment when participants are busy, rather than watching you search.
- **Add to your inventory.** There will always be *something* that you wished you'd brought with you. Next time, you can.
- **Actions speak louder than words.** Always have one or two exercises that you can give participants to do when you need to gather your own thoughts. Have handouts or briefings for such activities included in your kit.
- **Never leave home without one!** As you build up your experience, keep a bag packed with all the things that *you* (not your participants) find you may need on an away trip of a couple of days or a week. Look after yourself, and you'll look after your participants all the better.

13. Planning for distant venues

It's worth spending a bit of time planning how you will look after yourself both on the way to your session, and while running it. Trainers often have to travel for their work, and getting the arrangements right can make all the difference to your training events. The following tips are gleaned from the hard school of experience (often getting things wrong!):

- **Research your travel arrangements carefully.** Fix start and finish times of training events to fit in with your travel plans. Being able to catch the 5.05 train may make your life much easier than travelling just 10 minutes later. Book your taxi at lunchtime for the homeward journey.

- **Avoid travelling to the venue on the actual day when possible.** Travelling the night before can reduce undue stress on the day itself.

- **Travel light.** Stick to a good smart suit or jacket and ring the changes with a variety of blouses/shirts when you are away for several days.

- **Wear really comfortable shoes.** You may be on your feet for long periods of the day and it does not help if they are aching.

- **Specify really clearly to your client what you expect to be available in the training room.** Don't expect everything to be there without question. Put your requirements in writing – don't just rely on telephoned reassurances.

- **Allow enough time at the beginning of the session to check equipment and materials.** Give yourself the comfort that you will have time to ask for further supplies if necessary. Have a checklist ready, including such things as overhead projector, blank transparencies, OHP pens, video playback equipment, audiotape machine, slide projector, flipchart and plenty of flipchart paper, flipchart pens, whiteboard pens and wiper, drawing paper, Blu-tack, masking tape, Sellotape, chalk, scissors, index cards and so on. (In another set of tips we've suggested items for your own basic portable kit too.)

- **Specify in writing (or check) the times for lunch, tea and coffee.** Double-check these times on arrival – nothing messes up your timings as much as late refreshment breaks. If your client doesn't supply lunch for you, research your own arrangements (or take your own lunch).

- **Keep a supply of mints and/or throat pastilles with you.** This can save you the embarrassment of voice problems during your training event. Ensuring you have a drink of water available also helps. Other useful emergency aids include aspirin, tissues, spare tights (if appropriate), a spare tie (if appropriate) and a dram for the journey home (often very appropriate!).

- **Pace yourself.** When your participants are 'on task', sit down and wait for them to ask for help. Don't pace about and interrupt their tasks too much. Save your energy for the parts where you need to be dynamic.

- **Keep your stress levels down.** Don't let yourself get flustered by people who arrive late, disappear for parts of your session, leave early, or are obviously upset or worried by things outside your training event or your control. Stay calm and concentrate on the training session.

14. Tips for international trainers

Trainers who travel abroad frequently need to be especially well organized and prepared. The following suggestions, gleaned from hard experience, may be helpful to you:

- **Always carry your main training materials in your hand luggage** – even if they are quite bulky. You just can't afford for them to go missing in a lost suitcase. This is particularly true of your collection of overhead transparencies or laptop computer.

- **Send out as much as you can in advance.** Send out handouts, books and overhead transparencies, and get your client to fax you an acknowledgement of their receipt, allowing yourself time to take out replacements if they don't arrive. Couriers are often only a little more expensive than the postal system, and can get things to most places within five working days.

- **Carry one of everything important anyway.** Even when you've sent out copies of handouts or transparencies, always have enough with you to be able to generate new copies from scratch in an emergency.

- **Think carefully about your equipment needs.** Have contingency plans in case something you ask for is not available. Even overhead projectors are not universal, and flipchart paper is unknown in some countries (newsprint makes an acceptable alternative and is widely available).

- **Check that any electrical equipment you take is compatible with local supplies.** This particularly applies to any projection or computer equipment you may want to take with you.

- **Remember that hot countries often have air-conditioned training facilities.** This can make your training room quite cool, so dress accordingly. It is a strange experience to be shivery while working in a tropical country!

- **Check out local dress codes with your client.** It is almost as embarrassing to be over-formally dressed in a relaxed context as it is to be underdressed in a formal one. You will need to consider carefully whether your clothing might offend local beliefs or customs in some countries.

- **Be careful with acronyms.** Those familiar in your own country may be unknown in others. For example, familiar education acronyms in the UK such as SEDA, IPD or HESDA may well mean nothing to people in other countries. Spell all acronyms out if you need to refer to (for example) the Staff and Educational Development Association.

- **Mind your language.** In countries where the first language is not English, frame your language appropriately, avoiding excessive use of unusual or jargon words. Even audiences in English-speaking countries may find elements of what you say incomprehensible to them.

- **Don't expect it to be a holiday automatically.** An international training trip can be stressful and very tiring. Don't expect to do too much sightseeing alongside your work (unless you can build in some extra days just for this).

- **Take plenty of business cards with you.** People often want to keep contact with you after a training event – and this can develop into further opportunities for follow-up trips.

- **On long-haul flights, don't expect to do too much work.** If you want to minimize the effects of jet lag, you need to rest and relax on the flight. Avoid too much alcohol – this in conjunction with cabin air-conditioning can be very dehydrating. Dress comfortably and in layers to cope with changing temperatures (planes can be quite cool), and exercise regularly (in the confines of the loo if necessary).

- **Keep your emergency medical kit in your hand luggage**. This could include aspirin, diarrhoea remedies and so on. It is frustrating to feel ill when all your medicines are safely stowed in the plane's hold!

- **Travel as light as possible.** You need fewer clothes than most people think, and laundry facilities exist throughout the world. Take clothes that travel well and don't mind being crushed in a suitcase.

- **Take something to eat and drink in your hand luggage.** This can be a life-saver if you are delayed for hours, maybe at an airport with no catering facilities.

- **Think carefully about taking your laptop computer.** Check that your insurance covers international travel, and also check whether there will be suitable power supplies for it. It may be possible for you to arrange for your client to loan you a computer for the duration of your visit.

- **Allow plenty of time in your schedule for delays.** It is not unknown for you to arrive at your destination 24 hours late on long trips involving several connections. Build in appropriate leeway in your travel schedule.

- **Double-check passport and visa requirements.** Find out, for example, whether you need a work permit for what you are doing. Immigration controls can be strict and draconian.

- **Don't carry everything you're given back with you.** If you're given lots of reports, brochures, papers and so on by your client or by your participants, post them home (along with any of your own training materials that you're sure you have finished with) rather than struggling to fit them all into your luggage. But don't post anything that you could need urgently.

- **Remember that faxes and e-mail are cheaper than phones** (and don't depend on the person you're contacting being 'in'). Leave your colleagues and loved ones with details of where they can contact you and when. You may be surprised how well you can remain in touch at the other side of the world. However, the phone is always worth it for that very special person!

- **Take two watches.** If your journey is taking you to several different time zones, it is handy to have one watch permanently set to home time. This can help ensure that you know when to catch anyone you may need to ring up back at home. And you never know when your main watch may drop off in Singapore – a back-up can be very useful.

- **Don't drink Nile water.** When in countries where the public water supply may contain things your metabolism is not geared up to, stick to cool drinks from bottles or cans. Don't forget that ice cubes can be contaminated by things your system won't cope with happily. The whisky may be fine, but the knocks can come from the rocks!

15. Do you really want to give presentations?

Before going on to offer you some tips on ways of making your presentations effective, it is useful to start by addressing the question, 'Are presentations really so good as a training process?' How much have *you* learnt by being talked at? How many of the presentations or lectures *you* have attended were riveting, life changing and real learning experiences? The usual answer is 'Few'. Here are some ways of making sure that you don't do to your trainees what has often been done to you:

- **Have a very clear purpose for any presentation you give.** Make the aims clear at the start, and sum them up again at the finish.

- **Remember how short concentration spans are.** Members of your audience can concentrate for a few minutes now and then – but no one can concentrate for as long as you (or your author!) sometimes like to speak. Build in 'brain breaks' at least hourly.

- **Put it in print.** Giving your audience handout copies of the main ideas you wish to share with them can help you avoid going into too much detail. In fact, it is often better to give them the print, and then turn the presentation slot into a question-and-answer session, rather than just to amplify the facts as a presentation.

- **Sometimes participants want to sit and listen.** Yes indeed, but often as a work-avoidance strategy! After all, it is easier (if more boring) to sit and listen to a presentation than to do some real learning.

- **Remember that it's up to them.** You may see your role as delivering a training event – but the real measure of success is how much your participants learn during it. Just doing 'your bit' doesn't necessarily mean they do 'their bit'.

- **Watch yourself presenting.** There are few things more sobering or salutary than seeing ourselves on video giving a presentation. Make sure that at least once a year you arrange to see yourself as others see you. This can reduce the urge to give presentations quite significantly.

- **Value the experience around you.** Often, the combined experience of participants at your training events will be very great. Don't tell people things they already know – give them the chance to tell each other what they know.

- **Make presentations active learning experiences.** There are all sorts of ways of involving your audience in what you're presenting. The most useful tool is a good list of questions to which you can draw answers from your audience. This gives them the ownership of success.

- **Capture your best presentations.** When you know you've got a short presentation off to a fine art, make a video of it. You can then use the video as a training event tool, and additionally be there as 'expert witness' to address questions arising from the content of the video. This can also give you a chance to recover your voice during an extended training event.

- **Get other people to do short presentations, instead of you.** If you're working over several days with participants, a change of presenter will be a relief to them (no disrespect!). Also, you can ensure that other people introduce elements to your training event that you intend to address.

16. Preparing your first presentations

The suggestions below are for *new* trainers, about to step on to the rostrum for the first time. Please skip these if you're already practised:

- **Find out where your topics fit into the syllabus.** The more you know about what trainees will have learnt already, the easier it is to avoid boring them by repeating things they already know. Look at the syllabus and see where your bit fits in. Borrow copies of the most central texts on the topics. Make brief notes of the most important parts, and remember to keep references to the sections you will ask trainees to consult.

- **Find out more about the trainees.** Talk to colleagues who are already working with them. Ask them what sort of class it seems to be. Ask about any aspects of teaching that seem to be working particularly well with them.

- **Get yourself used to the presentation room.** Go in some evening when it's empty and find out where the lighting controls are, how the overhead projector works and how it feels to 'talk to the seats' for a while.

- **Decide not to imitate the trainers who taught you.** It's worth trying to emulate the good things you remember, but there's no need to do some of the more boring things you'll also remember. Your trainees will think more of you if you simply are yourself.

- **Build in plenty of lead-in time.** Preparing and giving presentations at the last minute is not a good idea – even for experienced trainers! It can easily take 10 hours or much more to prepare a new 1-hour presentation. It may take even longer if you're planning to prepare handouts and overheads to support your presentation.

- **Go to some more presentations.** Most of the presentations you will have been to will have been occasions when you were trying to capture the gist of the presentation. It's worth going to a few more just to observe the good (and bad) ways that different trainers approach the task of working with a group of trainees. Make notes of how they do it.

- **Remember what it was like when you were a learner.** You will probably have learnt a great deal about your subject since you were lectured to on it. And even then, you were probably a 'high-flier' – that's why you're lecturing yourself now. Think of the average trainee, and plan to pitch your presentation to such trainees.

- **Do a dry run before your first presentation.** If possible, get some friends in to role-play the audience. Even better, try to get someone to make a video of you doing your dry run. You can learn a great deal about how you're coming across from watching yourself perform.

- **Think about your pace.** Some of the worst disasters that happen in presentations are associated with going either far too fast or (more commonly) devastatingly slowly. The most difficult job of all when starting to teach is to gauge how long a new presentation will take; this remains problematic even for very experienced trainers, but you won't notice it when you watch them, as they will have developed coping strategies. Try to build in some flexibility so you can say more or less, depending on how fast you are covering the material.

- **Think about your delivery.** Find out more about how you can project your voice. If the room is very large, you may need a microphone (and should ask for one). Otherwise you can help your voice to carry by standing up, breathing slightly more deeply than normal, using the walls of the room to help your audibility, addressing the trainee most distant from you, and just relaxing. Never shout.

- **You may not need to start with the 'first' presentation.** If you're going to do a series of presentations, it may be preferable to start with a topic you feel confident to give a presentation on, or where you've got interesting visual back-up to support your talk. Getting off to a good start with your trainees helps you (and them) to feel better about the rest of your series.

- **Prepare some handout material to support your presentation.** Handout materials are particularly useful if you're feeling nervous, as you can refer trainees to things in the materials when you need all eyes to be off you for a moment or two.

- **Think about making your handouts 'interactive'.** For example, include in your handouts tasks for trainees to do (individually or in twos and threes) during the presentation, with space for them to write down their ideas.

- **Prepare overhead transparencies or presentation-manager slides to support your presentation.** Don't put too much on any transparency – bullet point lists of main headings are usually enough.

- **Build up your store of 'interesting things'.** Trainees often remember the anecdotes better than the main points of a presentation. Try to collect several points that are amusing or memorable, and that will also help to capture trainees' attention at key points in your presentations.

- **Don't over-prepare.** Everyone seems to prepare far more for their first few presentations than they can ever get through. Be modest in your expectations of how much you will cover.

17. Giving presentations

Presentations can be turned into memorable learning experiences for trainees. Also, presentations constitute one of the most 'public' forms of training, and therefore may be high on your quality assurance agenda. These tips are designed to optimize the learning potential of presentations, and to remind you of ways that such sessions can pay real dividends to trainees:

- **Make the most of opportunities when you have the whole group together.** There are useful benefits of whole-group shared experiences, especially for setting the scene in a new subject and talking trainees through known problem areas. Use these as sessions to develop whole-group cohesion, as well as to give briefings, provide introductions, introduce keynote speakers and hold practical demonstrations.

- **Make sure that presentations are not just 'transmit-receive' occasions**. Little is learnt by trainees just writing down what the trainer says, or copying down information from screens or boards. There are more efficient ways of providing trainees with the information they need for their learning, including the use of handout materials, textbooks and other learning resource materials.

- **Be punctual, even if some of your trainees are late**. Chat to the nearest trainees while people are settling in. Ask them, 'How's the course going for you so far?', for example. Ask them, 'What's your favourite topic so far?' or 'What are the trickiest bits so far?'

- **When you're ready to start, capture trainees' attention.** It's often easier to do this by dimming the lights and showing your first overhead than by trying to quieten down the pre-presentation chatter by talking loudly. Do your best to ignore latecomers. Respect the courtesy of punctuality of those already present, and talk to them.

- **Make good use of your specific intended learning outcomes for each presentation**. Find out how many trainees think they can already achieve some of these – and adjust your approach accordingly. Explaining the outcomes at the start of the session, or including them in handout materials given out to trainees, can help them to know exactly what they should be getting out of the presentation, serving as an agenda against which they can track their individual progress during the minutes that follow.

- **Help trainees to place the presentation in context.** Refer back to previous material (ideally with a short summary of the previous presentation at the beginning) and give them forewarning of how this will relate to material they will cover later.

- **Use handout material to spare trainees from copying down lots of information.** It's better to spend time discussing and elaborating on information that trainees can read for themselves.

- **Face the class when using an overhead projector.** Practise in a presentation room using transparencies as an agenda, and talking about each point listed on them. By placing a pen on the transparency you can draw attention to the particular point on which you are elaborating, maintaining vital eye contact with your trainees.

- **Work out some questions that the session will address.** Showing these questions as an overhead at the beginning of the session is a way of helping trainees to see the nature and scope of the specific learning outcomes they should be able to address progressively as the session proceeds.

- **Give your trainees some practice at note making (rather than just note taking).** Trainees learn very little just from copying out bits of what they see or hear, and may need quite a lot of help towards summarizing, prioritizing and making their notes their own individual learning tools.

- **Get trainees learning-by-doing, even during presentations.** Just about all trainees get bored listening for a full hour, so break the session up with small tasks such as problems for trainees to work out themselves, applying what you've told them, reading extracts from their handout material, or discussing a question or issue with the trainees nearest to them. Even in a crowded, tiered lecture theatre, trainees can be given things to do independently for a few minutes at a time, followed by a suitable debriefing, so that they can compare views and find out whether they were on the right track.

- **Variety is the spice of presentations.** Make sure that you build into large group presentations a variety of activities for trainees, which might include writing, listening, looking, making notes, copying diagrams, undertaking small discussion tasks, asking questions, answering questions, giving feedback to you, solving problems, doing calculations, putting things in order of importance and so on.

- **Ask the trainees how you are doing.** From time to time ask, 'How many of you can hear me clearly enough?', 'Am I going too fast?' or 'Is this making sense to you?' Listen to the answers and try to respond accordingly.

- **Use presentations to start trainees learning from each other.** Getting trainees to work in small groups in a presentation environment can allow them to discuss and debate the relative merits of different options in multiple-choice tasks, or put things in order of importance, or brainstorm possible solutions to problems. After they have engaged with each other on such tasks, the trainer can draw conclusions from some of the groups and give expert-witness feedback when needed.

- **Use presentations to help trainees make sense of things they have already learnt.** It is valuable to make full use of the times when all trainees are together to give them things to do to allow them to check out whether they can still do the things they covered in previous sessions.

- **Use presentations to help shape trainees' attitudes.** The elements of tone of voice, facial expression, body language and so on can be used by trainers to bring greater clarity and direction to the attitude-forming shared experiences that help trainees set their own scene for a topic or theme in a subject.

- **Genuinely solicit trainees' questions.** Don't just ask 'Any questions?' as you are picking up your papers at the end of a class. Treat trainees' questions with courtesy even if they seem very basic to you. Repeat the question so all trainees can hear, and then answer in a way that doesn't make the questioner feel stupid.

- **Don't waffle when stuck.** Don't try to bluff your way out of it when you don't know the answers to some of the questions trainees may ask. Tell the questioners that you'll find out the answers to their questions before your next presentation with them – they'll respect you more for this than for trying to invent an answer.

- **Use some presentation time to draw feedback from trainees.** Large-group sessions can be used to provide a useful barometer of how their learning is going. Trainees can be asked to write on slips of paper (or Post-its) questions that they would like you to address at a future session.

- **Use whole-class time to explain carefully the briefings for assessment tasks.** It is essential that all trainees have a full, shared knowledge of exactly what is expected of them in such tasks, so that no one is disadvantaged by any differentials in their understanding of the performance criteria or assessment schemes associated with the tasks.

- **Show trainees how the assessor's mind works.** This can be done by devising class sessions around the analysis of how past examples of trainees' work were assessed, as well as by going through in detail the way that assessment criteria were applied to work that the class members themselves have done.

- **Record yourself on video every now and then.** Review the video to help you see your own strengths and weaknesses, and look for ways to improve your performance. Your keenest critic is likely to be yourself, so don't try to resolve every little habit or mannerism at once, but just tackle the ones that you think are most important, little by little. It may also be useful for a group of colleagues together to look at each other's videos, and offer each other constructive comments. This is excellent practice for inspection or other quality assessment procedures.

- **Use all opportunities to observe other people's presentations.** You can do this not only in your own department but also at external conferences and seminars. Watching other people helps you to learn both from what is done well that you might wish to emulate and from awful sessions that lead you to resolve never to do anything similar in your own classes.

- **Put energy and effort into making your presentations interesting and stimulating.** A well-paced presentation that has visual impact and in which ideas are clearly communicated can be a motivating shared experience for trainees. Become comfortable using overhead projectors and audio-visual equipment in imaginative ways.

- **Watch the body language of your audience.** You'll soon learn to recognize the symptoms of 'eyes glazing over' when trainees are becoming passive recipients rather than active participants. That may signal the time for one of your prepared anecdotes or, better, for a task for trainees to tackle.

- **Don't tolerate poor behaviour.** You don't have to put up with trainees talking, eating or fooling around in your presentations. Ask them firmly but courteously to desist or, as a last resort, ask them to leave. If they do not do so, you should leave yourself for a short period to give them a cooling-down period.

- **Don't feel you've got to keep going for the full hour.** Sometimes you will have said all you need to say, and still have 10 or 15 minutes in hand. Don't feel you have to waffle on. It may come as a surprise to you, but your trainees may be quite pleased to finish early occasionally.

- **Don't feel that you have to get through all of your material.** Even very experienced trainers, when preparing a new presentation, often overestimate what they can cover in an hour. It is better to cover part of your material well than to try to rush through all of it. You can adjust future sessions to balance out the content.

- **Use large-group sessions to identify and answer trainees' questions.** This can be much more effective, and fairer, than just attempting to answer their questions individually and privately. When one trainee asks a question in a large-group session, there are often many other trainees who only then realize that they too need to hear the answer.

- **Help the shy or retiring trainees to have equal opportunity to contribute.** Asking trainees in large groups to write questions, or ideas, on Post-its helps to ensure that the contributions you receive are not just from those trainees who aren't afraid to ask in public. It can be comforting for trainees to preserve their anonymity in asking questions, as they are often afraid that their questions may be regarded as silly or trivial.

- **Come to a timely conclusion.** A large-group session must not just fizzle out, but should come to a definite and robust ending. It is also important not to overrun. It is better to come to a good stopping place a few minutes early than to end up rushing through something important right at the end of the session.

18. Designing and using handouts

Handout materials are often very important in terms of participants' learning from a training event. It is these materials that participants can refer to again and again, at their own pace. Such materials can also help you make best use of the face-to-face opportunities that a training event provides. With modern developments in desktop publishing, coupled to the ready availability of photocopiers and offset litho printing, the use of handout materials has escalated dramatically. There is still, however, the danger that handout material is simply filed by trainees and not used for active learning. Some ways round this are suggested below:

- **Plan to use handouts to save having to tell participants things.** Some participants may already know them. It's much quicker for everyone to scan a handout than to listen to you explaining everything in person. When part of your training event is intended to tell participants things, see how much you can put into handout materials, so that you no longer have to spend time telling people things (which many of them could already know anyway).

- **Use the start of a handout to remind trainees what its purposes are.** It can be useful to state on each handout the intended learning outcomes of the particular element of work involved.

- **Use plenty of headings.** There's little more off-putting than a solid page of unbroken text. Where possible, make headings stand out, by using bold print or large-size print. When a glance at a handout gives information about the structure of its contents, it has already started to help people learn.

- **Make sure you have sufficient copies.** There are often a couple of unexpected participants – and some may want to have an extra copy to give to an absent colleague. It pays to be ready to give anyone or everyone copies of anything that is relevant to the aims or objectives of your training event.

- **Make handouts look attractive.** Use desktop publishing software to give your handouts that look of professionalism and style. The medium is the message – scrappy handouts (however good their content) will devalue your messages. Graphics can also help to make your handouts look better and more memorable.

- **Make handouts interactive.** Build in tasks and activities, so that anyone looking again at your handouts can relive the experience of being at your training event. The most important dimension is what participants may do when trying the tasks and activities you build into your handout materials.

- **Use handout material in advance.** When you can, send participants handouts containing the things that your training event is going to be based upon, so that when they arrive to participate they are all at a similar level of knowledge or expertise.

- **Include space for participants to make the handouts their own.** When participants write their own comments, reactions or answers to questions on to their own copies of the handout materials, they immediately gain a sense of ownership of the materials. The handouts are no longer just pieces of paper they were given during a training event.

- **Specify the aims and objectives of your training events on handouts.** This helps participants to link your agenda to theirs, and to know exactly what the purpose of your training events may be.

- **Include a 'feedback sheet' in your handouts.** A simple questionnaire can give you a range of ideas to incorporate into the next issue of each handout. Don't forget to ask 'What's missing?' from any edition of a handout.

- **Include 'committed space' for trainees to do things in handouts.** Structured tasks are best, such as 'Think of six reasons why the economy is in recession and list them below.' The fact that space has been provided for trainees' answers helps persuade them (often subconsciously) to have a try at the tasks rather than simply skip them.

- **Use tasks as chances for trainees to learn-by-doing, and to learn by getting things wrong.** Multiple-choice questions are useful for this. The handout can serve as a useful reminder of 'wrong' options chosen, as well as a pleasant reminder of 'correct' choices.

- **Use handouts to get trainees making notes, not just taking notes.** Use handouts to avoid the wasteful process of trainees simply writing down things you say, or transcribing things they see on the screen or board. Copying things down is a low-level learning activity. Having such information already in handout form allows you to spend face-to-face time getting your trainees probing into the meaning of the information, interpreting it, questioning it, extrapolating from it, analysing it and so on.

- **Work out what you intend trainees to add to the handout during your session.** For example, leave spaces for individual 'brainstorms' (such as 'List five symptoms of anaemia') and for the products of buzz-group discussions (such as putting some factors in order of importance). The aim should be that the handout trainees take away at the end of the session is much more valuable than the blank one they were given at the start.

- **Include annotated bibliographies in handout materials.** A few words about what to look for in each particular source can make a big difference to the ways in which trainees follow up references.

- **Where possible, store your handout materials on disk.** Go for small print runs. It is then easy to make considerable adjustments and additions to handouts each successive time you use them. Avoid the waste associated with piles of handouts that you've subsequently replaced with updated, improved versions.

19. Using overhead projectors

One of the most common devices at our disposal in our training sessions is the overhead projector. Making good use of projectors can make all the difference between a professionally run training event and a shambles. The following suggestions may help you to get the most out of your OHP:

- **Know your machine.** If you're working on home ground, this is not an issue. However, if you're working in a new training room, it's well worth your time to take steps to become familiar with the particular machine you're going to work with. Most machines have a focus control, but this is located differently on different types of projector. Most machines also have a red–blue adjustment lever (or fringe control). Don't be afraid to move the machine to get it into good focus, across the whole of the screen area. When you can, adjust the height and positioning of the projector to avoid 'keystoning' (the top of the image being a different width from the bottom).

- **Ensure that your transparencies will fit any projector.** Many projectors have a plate of approximately A4 size (and can usually be arranged for vertical or lateral display). Some projectors have square screens, wider but less deep than A4 size.

- **Get the machine position right.** The aim is to ensure that all your trainees can see the screen without anything obstructing their vision (particularly you!). Put on a slide, and sit in various seats in the room (before the trainees are there) so that you know that the screen is clearly visible, and that the average overhead will be easily seen.

- **Be ready for problems.** If the bulb should suddenly go, is there a 'switchable' spare? If there is, check that this works. Alternatively, have a spare projector (which you know works) sitting inconspicuously in a corner of the room.

- **When all else fails...** Have one or two exercises up your sleeve that do not depend on the availability of an overhead projector. Plan these so that while your trainees are engaged on them you give yourself the time to arrange a new projector.

- **'The medium is the message.'** Good-quality overheads can add credibility to your messages. It's worth using desktop-publishing programs to make your principal overhead transparencies look professional and believable. With inkjet and laser colour printers, it's nowadays relatively easy to produce coloured transparencies with graphics.

- **Be careful with coloured print or writing.** Some colours, especially red, are harder than you might imagine to see from the back of a large room. Throw away any orange or yellow ones from your set of overhead pens – unless you're using them for colouring in blocks on diagrams or flow charts, for example.

- **Don't use typewritten overheads.** To be clearly visible, most fonts need to be at sizes 18, 24 or larger – considerably bigger and bolder than typical typewritten materials. Make sure that each transparency you prepare will be visible from the back of the largest room you are likely to use, even by someone without perfect eyesight.

- **Keep the number of words down.** A good overhead transparency only needs to contain the main ideas, not the details. You can add the details as you discuss the main points on the transparencies. Your own 'crib' notes can then be written on to a paper copy of each transparency.

- **Use landscape rather than portrait orientation.** This helps you to make the best use of the top half of the screen, which is usually more easily visible to most of your audience.

- **Watch trainees' eyes.** As soon as you notice trainees having to move their head positions to see something on one of your transparencies, it's worth trying to move that part up so that they can see it without moving their gaze.

- **Get your transparencies into the right order before your presentation.** There's nothing worse than watching a trainer sifting and sorting to try and find the right overhead. It's sometimes worth arranging them into two sets: ones you will *definitely* use, and ones you *might* wish to use if time permits or if anticipated questions arise.

- **Use the top half of the screen.** By sliding your transparencies up, you can normally make the most important pieces of information appear towards the top of the screen – more easily visible by trainees at your sessions.

- **Try not to read out your overheads.** Your trainees can read much faster than you can speak. People don't like having things read out to them that they can read for themselves.

- **Give people time to take notes if they wish.** Sometimes, you may have copies of your transparencies in handout materials you issue to trainees. Otherwise, expect that at least some trainees will want to jot down the main points they see on the screen, and make sure that they've done this before you move on to another transparency.

- **Minimize passive transcribing by trainees.** Copying down words from transparencies is not the most productive of learning activities. Where possible, issue handout materials that already contain the wording from your principal overhead transparencies.

- **Don't point at the screen itself.** This would mean losing eye contact with your trainees. Use a pen or pencil to rest on the transparency, indicating the part you're talking about.

- **Be prepared to add things to your transparencies during discussions.** This ability to edit slides 'live' is an advantage of overhead projectors over computer-based presentation managers, and can help your trainees to feel that their comments are important and valued. With transparencies produced from inkjet printers, however, don't write on your original: put a blank sheet of acetate over it!

- **Don't overuse 'progressive reveal' techniques** (showing transparencies a bit at a time by gradually moving a masking sheet of paper). Some trainees feel manipulated if they are continually 'controlled' in this way. It can be better to build up a complex overhead using multiple overlays.

- **Make your own masking sheet.** Tape a pen or short ruler to what will be the top edge, or stick a piece of Blu-tack there. The extra weight will help to ensure that the sheet does not slip off your transparencies prematurely revealing your last line or two (which may be punch-lines!).

- **Remember to switch the projector off.** Most overhead projectors make at least some noise. When you're not actually showing something, it's important both visually and auditorily that you are not distracting your trainees.

20. Why use computer-aided presentations?

The package most commonly used is Microsoft PowerPoint. The suggestions that follow relate to this program, but apply to most other presentation managers. Trainers choose to use computer-aided presentations for different reasons. Interrogate your own reasons against those listed below:

- **Because you want to make a good impression on your audience.** Some people may think that if you are using just old-fashioned ways of giving presentations in your teaching that your message itself may be outdated. However, the quality of your use of the medium is actually more important than simply choosing an up-to-date medium.

- **Because you want to be able to edit your presentation easily and frequently.** Computer-generated presentations are very easy (and very inexpensive) to edit, even to restructure completely. It is much easier to adjust a computer-delivered presentation after every experience of giving it than it would be to prepare a new set of overhead transparencies each time.

- **Because you want your handout material to relate directly to your presentation.** In PowerPoint presentations, for example, you can print off handout pages containing multiple slides. You can also annotate individual slides to make handouts with additional notes and background information. The strongest advantage of printing out your slides as handout materials is that your trainees then don't need to do menial tasks such as simply copying your slides into their own notes, but can do more active things such as writing their own notes on to their print-outs of your slides.

- **Because you want to show things that can't be shown using traditional methods.** For example, if you want to show your trainees pictures, moving images or graphics, which would be difficult or impossible to do using overhead transparencies, you can be fairly sure that you are justified in making your presentations computer-aided.

- **Because you want to be able to have *all* of your teaching presentations available.** A single floppy disk can carry hundreds of slides of presentation material; a CD ROM can carry many thousands. If your teaching repertoire is wide and varied, it might be impossible to carry it all around with you on overheads or handouts. Carrying a few disks or a CD ROM is much more feasible, and you can customize a new presentation from your repertoire quite easily once you have had some practice at editing, and print off those handouts you need locally.

- **Because you want your trainees to be able to have another look at your presentation later.** You can give trainees your computer-managed presentation on disk, to work through at a machine in the resources centre or at home. You can e-mail the presentation to trainees at a distance, or place it in a virtual library or conference area on your computer network.

21. Some don'ts for presentation managers

Any presentation medium can be used well or badly. The following suggestions should help you to avoid some of the most common pitfalls with presentation managers:

- **Don't just use computer-aided presentations because everyone else seems to be using them.** This may be a reason for making at least some of your presentation computer-aided, but it is worth thinking hard about whether computers provide the best medium for the exact purposes of each element of your presentations. It is better to mix and match, rather than to switch blindly to a different way of supporting your presentations.

- **Don't just use computer-aided presentations because the equipment happens to be there.** Some institutions lay on computer-delivered presentation systems as a matter of routine. It is still possible to use overhead projectors, whiteboards and flipcharts too! Sometimes, these may be pushed out of sight to make room for the computer and projector, but they are usually not far away.

- **Don't cause 'death by bullet point'!** Even though computer-aided presentation packages can introduce bullet points to slides in a variety of ways (fly from left, dissolve and so on), bullet points can quickly become tiresome to an audience. It is worth having a good reason for building any slide step by step.

- **Don't underestimate the problems that can arise.** You may not be able to get the room dark enough for trainees to see your presentation properly. There may be compatibility problems between the software version you have used to create your presentation, and the version on the computer through which you wish to show it. The image size on your laptop may not be compatible with that required by the data projector. The resolution of the projection equipment may not be sufficient to show fine details of images that you carefully placed into your presentation.

- **Don't overdo the special effects.** Doing the whole presentation in a single format becomes boring for your audience, but programming a random sequence of slide builds tends to be irritating for you as presenter, as you don't know what build sequence will be produced when you move to your next slide. Similarly, don't go overboard on the snazzy changes from one slide to the next.

- **Don't use it just like an overhead projector substitute.** Simply transferring the contents of your overhead transparencies into a computer-delivered presentation does not make full use of the medium. Try to do *other* things with computer-aided presentations, for example making good use of the possibilities of moving images, graphics and so on.

- **Don't forget that it's not that bright.** Most computer-aided presentation packages rely on projection equipment that is not nearly as bright as a good overhead projector. This means that you may need to take particular care with room lighting, daylight from windows and (worst of all) direct sunlight. If you use a liquid crystal display tablet, it isn't a good idea to place it on top of an ordinary overhead projector; you need a high-powered one (1,000 watts or more) for reasonable visibility.

- **Don't forget to check the focus before you start.** Some projection systems are fine for video projection, but turn out to be too fuzzy for computer-managed presentation projection. Modern systems have easy ways of adjusting the focus, but older systems may need to be set up in considerable detail before an acceptable image quality is produced, or may just not be capable of producing clear still images. Looking for any length of time at fuzzy images can give some members of your audience headaches, as their eyes try in vain to compensate for the fuzziness.

- **Don't forget the conditions appropriate for human sleep!** Turning down the lights, sitting comfortably in the same place for more than a few minutes and listening to the sound of your voice may be just the right conditions for your audience to drop off, particularly if the images are unclear.

- **Don't forget that sunlight moves.** If you're setting up a teaching room first thing in the morning, you may need to plan ahead for where any sunlight may be later in the day.

- **Don't put too much on any slide.** There still seem to be few computer-aided presentations where *all* of the slides are perfectly readable from the back of the room. It is better to have twice as many slides, rather than to cram lots of information on to each slide. It usually takes two or more slides to project the same amount of information as with one overhead transparency.

- **Don't put important text in the lower half of slides.** Unless all members of your audience have an uninterrupted view of the screen, people sitting at the back may have to peer around their nearer neighbours to read any text at the bottom of the screen. Unlike overhead projection, you can't simply move a transparency up to make the final points visible to people at the back.

- **Don't use portrait layout.** You will usually have the choice between landscape and portrait, so use landscape to make the most of the top part of the screen. You may already have found that the same applies to overhead transparencies.

- **Don't import tables or text files.** The fact that you *can* import such files into a computer-managed presentation package leads many into temptation. These are very often the slides that can't be read from the back (or even from the front). It is normally better to give trainees such information as handouts, rather than try to show it on screen.

- **Don't use the wrong colours.** Colours that look good on a computer screen don't always show up so well when they are projected. If most of your presentations will be in rooms with natural daylight, it is usually best to stick to dark colours for text, and light (or even white) backgrounds. If you know you're going to be working in a lecture theatre where you have full control of the lighting, you can then be more adventurous and use light lettering against dark backgrounds (not forgetting that you may be lulling your audience to sleep when you turn down the lights).

- **Don't use the same slide format for all of your slides.** Computer-managed presentation packages may allow you to switch your whole presentation into different pre-prepared styles, but the result can be that your slides all look too similar to have an optimum learning pay-off for your viewers. Vary the layout, colours and backgrounds, so that each new slide makes its own impact.

- **Don't leave a slide on when you've moved on to talk about something else.** It is better to switch the projection off, rather than to leave up information that people have already thought about. If you're within reach of the computer keyboard, pressing 'B' on some systems causes the display to go black, and pressing 'B' again brings the display back. This is far simpler and safer than switching the projector to standby and risking having to wait for it to warm up again when you want to project your next slide. An alternative is to insert a 'black' slide, where you wish to stop your audience from looking at the screen. Don't, however, forget where you've placed these and panic about where your display has gone!

- **Don't talk to the screen.** With overhead projectors, it's easy to develop good habits, including looking at the transparency rather than at the screen, and avoiding turning your back on your audience. With projected images, you may have no alternative but to watch the screen, but you need to make sure that you talk to your audience. If you can arrange things so that you can look at a computer screen rather than the projection screen, the problem can be partly solved.

- **Don't go backwards for too long.** If you need to return to a slide you showed much earlier, it is better to switch the display off and find the slide you want without your audience seeing every step. The same applies to returning to your original place in your presentation.

- **Don't forget to rehearse your presentation.** With overhead transparencies you always know what is coming next; with presentation managers it is all too possible to forget. If *you* look surprised when your next slide appears, it does not do much for your credibility with your audience.

- **Don't underestimate the potential of remote controls surprising you.** Many systems allow you to change slides with a remote control connected to your computer or to the projection equipment. Pressing the wrong button on this can switch the system to something quite different (for example, video input), and can mean that you can find yourself unable to get back to your presentation without losing your cool. It is best to find out in advance which buttons *not* to press, and possibly to place some adhesive tape over them to reduce the possibility of pressing them.

- **Don't forget to check your spelling.** PowerPoint, for example, can do this for you, but you have to instruct the software appropriately. Be careful not to let the software replace words automatically, or you will get some strange slides if you are using unfamiliar words.

- **Don't fail to get feedback on your presentation before you run it.** It is really useful to get someone else to watch your slides, and to ask about anything that isn't clear or point out anything that could irritate an audience. It's also useful to check your timing, and the overall length of your presentation in practice.

- **Don't miss out on seeing your presentation on paper.** Consider printing out your slides, for example six per page. This helps you to get an overview of your presentation, and can sometimes alert you to where to insert an additional slide or two. It is also useful to have such pages in front of you as you present, so that you can easily remind yourself of what's on the next slide.

- **Don't neglect to adjust and improve your slides.** It is so easy to alter a set of slides that there's no real excuse for not editing your presentation frequently so that it is always finely tuned to the particular audience and context. The most beneficial additions are often new slides inserted to address frequently asked questions in advance.

- **Don't stop watching other people's technique.** This is one of the fastest ways of improving your own presentations. Look for things that work well for other people, find out how the effects were achieved and then emulate them. More importantly, look for things that don't work, and make sure that you avoid them.

- **Don't forget your overheads.** It is still useful to have at least some of your computer slides on traditional acetate. Computers can go down. More likely, you can press the wrong button on a remote control and switch your projector on to video or off altogether. At such times, it can seem life-saving to be able to go to an overhead projector, at least temporarily.

22. Helping trainees to learn from computer-aided presentations

- **Remember that people don't actually remember a great deal of what they see.** Keep your computer-aided presentations down to relatively small, self-contained episodes, and intersperse them with activities that involve your trainees in learning-by-doing, or other activities such as discussing, prioritizing or summarizing.

- **Get your trainees to formulate some questions before you start your computer-aided presentation.** For example, ask groups of trainees to decide what they want to find out about the topic you're going to cover, and to write down some questions that they hope will be covered. When they have already got questions in their minds, they are much more receptive to the answers when your presentation addresses the questions.

- **Help your trainees to *make* notes.** This is much more productive than merely *taking* notes, such as when they copy down things they see on the screen or write down verbatim things that you say. When you give your trainees copies of your computer-projected slides, you can encourage them to annotate these, adding in thoughts of their own and questions that arise in group discussion.

- **Build tasks into your computer-aided presentation.** Get your trainees to *do* things with the information that is presented on-screen, rather than just watch it. Use your computer slides to pose questions and then answer them, rather than just present the answers alone. Get your trainees to work out which are the most important points from an on-screen list, or to work out the consequences of changing the conditions in a scenario.

- **Include questions to trainees in your presentations.** For example, pose a question on-screen, and then pick a trainee at random to try to answer it. Don't make the trainee too uncomfortable if an answer is not immediately forthcoming, however. When trainees become accustomed to being put in the position of having to try to answer a question at short notice, they naturally become more attentive, as no one likes to be found lacking an answer.

- **Consider making your presentation available to trainees, to consult individually, after the group has seen it.** It is normally straightforward to install your presentation on to a computer, where your trainees can have the chance to refresh their memories of it when they choose to. Alternatively, if your trainees have their own computers or regular access to computers, you could consider giving them copies of your presentation on floppy disk or CD ROM. You may be wise to make such copies 'read-only' and have your name clearly as a footer on each slide, to prevent anyone from pirating your expertise.

- **Stop and switch the presentation off every now and then.** Design tasks to get your trainees recalling and consolidating what they have just seen and heard. Think about short tasks that they can do in twos or threes where they are sitting, so that they can be reminded of the main things that you wish them to remember from the episode of presentation that they have just seen.

- **Consider turning a presentation into a question-and-answer session.** You can brief trainees with the questions on-screen, and then turn off the presentation while they try to work out (or guess) answers to the questions. When you resume the presentation they will be more receptive to the answers that your presentation already contains than if they had not been trying to answer the questions themselves for a while.

23. Seating, tables and workspace

Participants can become very bored if they are always sitting in the same chair in the same place and with the same neighbours – even in a training event lasting just a day, let alone an extended residential course:

- **Try to find rooms that lend themselves to variety.** Training rooms where chairs and tables can be moved around easily are best. Tiered lecture theatres and boardrooms with heavy tables are worst.
- **Don't encourage participants to hide behind tables.** When there is a table between them and you, it is somehow easier for them to sit passively, lean on the table and even fall asleep. With nothing to lean on, people are more attentive and involved. Having tables scattered around the edge of the room is better.
- **Be kind to bottoms.** Use your own experience to decide what sorts of chairs are best. Remember that participants will be sitting down for longer periods that you will. Concentration spans are less to do with brains, and more to do with bottoms!
- **Don't have too many chairs.** Have only two or three spare chairs; stack up any others in a secluded corner – or, better still, get them out of the room altogether. Spare chairs often become a no-go zone near the trainer (people sit at the back if there's a back to sit at). Alternatively, spare chairs get occupied by coats, bags or briefcases.
- **Avoid straight lines or rows of chairs.** A circle of chairs, or a U-shape, works better for an introductory plenary session (with any tables behind the chairs). Try to arrange the chairs so that all participants have an uninterrupted view of you, and of the projector screen and flipchart. Don't be afraid to move chairs.
- **Help ensure that participants can see each other's faces.** Again, circles and U-shapes work best. When participants can observe each other easily, they get to know each other better and more quickly, and feel more involved in your training event right from the start.
- **Have no safe hiding place.** Have you noticed that in rectangular table layouts, the most awkward participants always seem to establish themselves in one or other of the back corners? If there aren't any corners to start with, this can't happen. (However, when you set out your circle or U-shape, make sure that there are no chairs anywhere near any tables that are in the back corners!)
- **Weigh up the need for note taking in plenary**. Decide whether to use handout materials to save participants having to copy things down passively, or whether the act of making notes will help them to remember the material in their own ways.

- **Now find a table!** When you give participants individual or group tasks to do, invite them to move their chairs to any of the tables round the edge of the room (and not the tables to their chairs). This also helps you to be able to circulate freely, and speak to them in groups or individually as necessary.

- **Make full use of any other rooms you have available.** Having additional rooms for syndicate work gives participants a change. Make sure that the same syndicate isn't stuck in the same syndicate room for session after session – ring the changes and give everyone some variety. Move the plenary location around too if there is more than one room big enough.

24. Using flipcharts yourself

Flipcharts are among the most common of visual media used by trainers. The following suggestions may help you make your use of this medium professional and trouble-free:

- **Set it up before you start.** Some flipchart stands have a will of their own, and seem to come provided with three legs of unequal length. Don't allow your participants to see you struggle with the thing!

- **Bring your own pens.** There's nothing more frustrating than a flipchart without proper pens. Overhead projector pens will do in a crisis, but your lettering will look spidery and may be hard to read at the back of the room.

- **Don't put too much on a flipchart.** It's best to 'write big' and use broad pens, so that everyone can see all the words without difficulty. Unless your handwriting is unusually good, you may find it best to print upper-case letters when writing on flipcharts. But remember too many upper-case letters tend to generate eye fatigue.

- **Don't forget your Blu-tack.** You may often want to display several flipcharts at the same time, so make sure you've got that essential means of sticking flipcharts to doors, walls and even windows. Be careful, however, if walls are wallpapered – with care it's still possible to stick flipcharts to such walls as long as you develop the knack of using Blu-tack sparingly, and gently peel off the chart with the Blu-tack still sticking to the chart rather than to the wallpaper.

- **Make it easy to tear off successive flipcharts.** With pads of perforated flipchart paper, this is straightforward. However, usually you will have to make your own arrangements for removing sheets. Often, it helps simply to unscrew the two knobs that secure the chart to the easel, allowing you to make clean, neat tear-offs at the very top of the pad.

- **A sharp knife can be useful.** For example, there are small collapsible razor-knives. With these, you can (with practice) score along the top of a chart neatly and tear it off leaving a straight edge at the top. Be careful not to cut more than one sheet at a time though!

- **Decide when 'live' flipcharting really is a sensible choice.** Don't end up writing long sentences dictated by participants. Flipcharts work best for keywords, for example in brainstorming sessions.

- **Prepare important flipcharts in advance.** For example, if you're going to use flipcharts to write up tasks for participants to do in your training event, it's useful to be able to turn straight to a ready-made flipchart rather than write it all out with them watching.

- **Get participants to use flipcharts.** For example, giving a syndicate a flipchart as a means of reporting back on the task they are doing can help concentrate their minds on the task in hand, rather than engaging in sophisticated work-avoidance strategies!

- **Always have some rubber bands.** Often, you'll want to take away the flipcharts produced at a training event, so you can write up a report on the event, or collate and distribute the products of the event. An armful of loose flipcharts is not an easy package to carry away – but rolled up tightly with a couple of rubber bands is much more manageable.

25. Planning Post-its and flipcharts into group work

Getting things down on paper is often a vital element in keeping group learning going. The largest common size of paper is the A1 flipchart, and the smallest the Post-it (which comes in various sizes, of course). The following suggestions may help you to decide which medium to use for which purposes:

- **Use Post-its for private brainstorming.** When all members of the group are intended to think in parallel, before putting together their ideas, it is useful to give everyone one or more Post-its, on which they can write their individual ideas, views or questions.

- **Use Post-its to overcome 'blank sheet fright'.** Faced with a whole sheet of paper on which to jot down ideas, trainees often become inhibited and don't know quite where to start. A Post-it is much smaller and less challenging, and helps trainees to make that first step, getting at least one idea down in words.

- **Use Post-its for individual named contributions.** Getting everyone in a group to write their names on each Post-it along with their contribution allows ownership of ideas to be kept track of. This can, however, inhibit free brainstorming of ideas, so it is important to use names only when there is a good reason for doing so.

- **Use Post-its as an equal opportunity medium.** One of the problems with oral brainstorming is that it can so easily become dominated by the most extrovert or confident members of the group. Writing ideas on Post-its overcomes the inhibitions of the less forthcoming members of the group.

- **Use Post-its to save time transcribing ideas to a flipchart.** It can be painfully slow for a facilitator or group scribe to write up all the ideas on to a flipchart. It is much faster to simply stick the Post-its on to a flipchart, to present a visual display of all of the ideas generated. Also, transcription tends to be unfaithful, and people's meanings often become distorted by the words chosen by the transcriber, causing a loss in the sense of ownership individuals have regarding their ideas.

- **Use Post-its for prioritization.** When everyone in a group has written some ideas on to Post-its, it is much easier for the whole group to attempt to prioritize the ideas in order of importance (or practicability, likely pay-off and so on). This can be done by rearranging and readjusting the Post-it display on a flipchart, with the most crucial ideas at the top, and the less important ones further down. It can be very productive to get groups to choose and prioritize only the top nine ideas, using a 'diamond-9' formation on the flipchart.

- **Use flipcharts to create something that can be shown to other groups.** A display of Post-its stuck to a flipchart is fine for the group that created the ideas, but is less suitable for sharing with other groups, because of the size of handwriting. It is worth summarizing the ideas that may have been generated on Post-its on to a freshly drawn flipchart, using broad marker pens and colour to emphasize importance and links between ideas.

- **Use flipcharts to exchange between groups.** A very productive way of exchanging ideas between groups, without tedious repetitive report-back stages, is for one member to cross over to another group, bearing the flipchart product from the previous group, and talk the new group through the thinking behind the flipchart. It is then useful to get the new groups to add further ideas to the flipcharts, by asking them to extend the original task in specified directions.

- **Use flipcharts for exhibitions.** This is especially useful when different groups have been tackling different issues relating to an overall theme. Pasting the flipcharts to a wall and allowing all group members to circulate round them can be more interesting than listening to a series of report-backs from each group. This can be further enhanced when one member of the group that created each flipchart stands by the exhibit to explain it as necessary to visitors.

- **Details on flipcharts can be captured and circulated.** This is of course possible when electronic flipcharts are available, allowing a print-out of the contents of a 'chart' to be made and copied to all members of the group. However, it is becoming more attractive to have a digital camera and snap each chart, loading the contents into a computer and printing them out, if necessary with editing or explanations added. Once such equipment is available, the running costs are almost negligible.

26. Using whiteboards or chalkboards

It's often assumed that anyone can use these things well. One thing is often forgotten – why use them? To use them wisely, there has to be an intended learning pay-off for participants. The following suggestions combine ideas for good reasons for using such visual aids, with techniques for using them professionally:

- **Have a clear purpose in mind.** For example, participants may be expected to note down what you write, or the visual display may be intended to be there for a while to provide focus for subsequent participant activity and discussion.
- **Don't write too small.** Your writing needs to be visible from the furthest point in the room – this determines the minimum size of your writing on whiteboards or chalkboards.
- **Consider other ways of disseminating information.** It is often better to issue a handout containing information than to write it up yourself for participants to note down. The use of whiteboards or chalkboards is probably best restricted to things that emerge during a session, rather than the basic information on which the session is based.
- **Use whiteboards or chalkboards to capture matters arising.** When ideas emerge during a session, 'get them on the wall' where they can safely reside until such time as they can be adequately dealt with. This is particularly useful for defusing confrontational situations, and is much better than trying to pretend that there is no cause to debate the matters arising.
- **Normal handwriting is usually not suitable.** Unless you have a (fast) naturally attractive script, it's probably better to use upper-case letters rather than 'joined-up writing' when using chalkboards or whiteboards. Lower-case script on prepared overheads may indeed be easier to read than capitals, but the same does not seem to apply to handwriting on boards.
- **Use bullet points rather than whole sentences.** The time it takes to write long sentences can be irritating to participants – especially if they're also trying to note the sentences down themselves.
- **Squeaky chalk is painful!** Most of us remember this from our schooldays. Breaking a stick of chalk in two usually yields a chalk surface that writes more freely.
- **On whiteboards, use the right pens.** Pens need to be non-permanent and erasable. Also, the thickness of the pens needs to be appropriate for the size of the room and the maximum distance from participants' positions.
- **Use colours wisely.** A single colour soon becomes monotonous. Separate colours can help different points to stand out from a list. Colour can be used to prioritize and to show what's really important.

- **Don't erase too soon.** Participants can feel manipulated if you remove information from their view before they've had the chance to note it down themselves, or at least complete their thinking about it.

27. Using video machines

It's normally possible to arrange for a video player and monitor to be available at a training event – many training rooms have such things as standard equipment. The following suggestions may help you (and your participants) get the most from video, especially when you're running a session on 'away ground':

- **Arrive early.** You may think you know everything there is about video players, but this location will certainly have a different one. And you'll need to find who went off after the last session with the remote control.

- **Know your machine.** One video player looks much like another, but they all have their ways. A couple of minutes trying to get it to start up can seem like an hour with all eyes on our efforts! Get a certificate in video handling! Why can't manufacturers standardize all those machines? Try and practise on as many different machines as you can – or ensure that there is a six-year-old in your group who will quickly make any machine do anything you want.

- **Make friends with the local technician.** Suddenly you will realize that you need an extension lead, or the machine is locked up, or the colour or sound will go off for no reason, or the machine won't start at all. 'I've got a problem, I'm afraid, and I'd be really grateful if you could help me out' is a much better opening sentence than 'Are you the person in charge of this awful video?'

- **Check the blackout facilities (or arrange suitable weather!).** It is really frustrating being a member of the audience with the sun shining in your eyes or on the screen. Work out where the sun will be when you plan to show your video. If no blackout facilities are available and it's the middle of summer, you may need to be flexible and reschedule your video till the sun has moved round a bit.

- **Check visibility.** Before the training event or during a break, check whether the most distant participants will still have a reasonable view of the television set. Try to place the set on a high table if participants' heads may obscure the view of those sitting further back. If necessary, rearrange the chairs for the slot where you're going to use video.

- **Time your showing.** Try not to guess how long the interview on tape lasts. Time it and tell your participants. You may be able to play a really good video that lasts 30 minutes, but it does help participants' mindset to know how long they will have to sit and watch it. Don't be afraid to stop and start the tape and allow discussion in between – watch participants' body language for signs of boredom.

- **Check that the security tab has been removed.** This stops the children, the next-door neighbour or the technician recording *Top of the Pops* or *Who Wants to be a Millionaire* over your £600 videotape.

- **Check the 'X' rating.** Do make sure that you bring the correct tape along and that the children have not put the wrong cover on it – or the wrong label. Particularly make sure that it's not something that came from the back room of the video hire shop! Check for potential offence. Even innocuous training videos can contain things that can offend people. Apply your equal opportunities checklist to the video. Watch for bad language, gender inequality or racial inequality, all of which can easily offend.

- **Know the content of your videotape.** It's easy to think that just because you saw the tape last year you can remember everything on it. Try and view it a couple of times before the event, making notes. You could find this really useful if you arrive at the venue to find there's not a remote control, or the number-counter measures metres of tape rather than minutes. Then you'll be depending on your memory as you fast-forward or fast-reverse. Now did that interview with Daxa come before or after the view of the castle...?

- **Fix an electronic tab to your tape that bleeps if you leave it behind.** In your haste to get away at the end of an event it's easy to leave the tape behind. Also, if you forget to take it out of the machine after you've shown it, it's not very easy to see. I was once 10 miles out of town before realizing that the video was still in the machine (and had been promised to someone else that night for use the next day).

- **Plan an alternative.** 'The best laid schemes o' mice an' humans gang aft a-gley' (Burns, after applying equal opportunities). It can be really embarrassing after you've geared-up your group to watch this really important video to find it does not work – and yes, you did arrive early, and it was working then! Just have one or two alternatives up your sleeve.

- **Are you getting past it?** A favourite video that you used often and to great effect five years ago may have been really good then, but could be quite dated for now. When you watch an old video carefully, you may be surprised how fast times move on. If the video looks 'dated', your whole message could be undermined.

- **Have the tape at the right place to start.** If you're trying to locate a particular part of a programme using fast-forward and fast-reverse while everyone watches and waits, you may find that you simply can't find the bit you want at all!

- **Remember people's attitudes to television.** We're conditioned to forget quite quickly most of what we see on our small screens. We're also conditioned to use television as a medium for relaxation rather than a learning resource. If you want television to serve a useful learning function during your training events, you will need to overcome such conditioning.

28. Maximizing learning pay-off from video

Video recordings play valuable roles in helping to show trainees things that they would not be in a position to explore on their own. You may already use video extracts in your teaching, or give trainees video materials from which to learn selected elements of their programme. With computer-based training, there are often video sequences embedded in multimedia programs. However, the act of watching material on a television screen is not one of the most powerful ways through which trainees actually learn, unless the video extracts are carefully planned into the learning programme. The following suggestions may help you help your trainees to make the most of video:

- **Decide what the intended learning outcomes directly associated with the video extracts will be.** It is important that any video extracts are not just seen as an optional extra by your trainees. The best way to prevent this from happening is to tell them exactly what they are intended to gain from each extract of video material.

- **Decide why video is the best medium for your purposes.** Ask yourself, 'What is this video extract doing that could not be done just in print?' Video extracts can be invaluable for showing all sorts of things that trainees could not experience directly, as well as for conveying the subtleties that go with body language, facial expression, tone of voice and interpersonal interactions, skills and techniques.

- **Have a definite purpose for using video.** Work out exactly what you intend your participants to gain from viewing a video, and make the aims clear to them before you use the programme. Where possible, use video to help participants achieve things they could not have achieved using any other medium. For example, video can help to bring to the forefront such dimensions as body language, tone of voice and facial expression – all of which can be more powerful than printed words.

- **Decide *how* the video material is planned to help your trainees to learn.** Is it primarily intended to whet their appetites and stimulate their motivation? Is it designed to help them to make sense of some important ideas or concepts that are hard to learn without seeing things? Is it designed to give them useful briefings about things they themselves are intended to do after watching the material?

- **Remember that concentration spans are short.** It is often better to plan to use a few selected clips than to try to show a programme lasting half an hour. The most useful control on the video machine is the pause button! Use short extracts at a time. People are conditioned to watch quite long episodes of television, but to do so in a relatively passive way. Make sure that your trainees approach video extracts in a different way from the one they normally adopt for watching television. It is better to split up a 30-minute video into half a dozen or so separate episodes if there are several different things you wish your trainees to get out of the material.

- **Prepare an agenda in advance.** With participants, if possible, make a list of questions or issues that you wish to gain information on by means of the video. Where participants are watching a video with some definite intentions, there is much more chance that their watching will be attentive.

- **Follow each clip by a discussion session.** Help participants to reflect on what they've learnt from the video – or to use ideas from the video to promote deeper debates.

- **Consider whether your trainees will need further access to the video.** If they are intended to watch the video a number of times, you may be able to arrange that the materials can be viewed on demand in a resources centre. If so, make sure that there are mechanisms enabling trainees to book a time slot when they can see the video material.

- **Decide what your trainees will take away after watching the video.** One of the dangers with video extracts is the 'now you see it, then it's gone' situation. If the video is serving important purposes for your trainees, they will need to have something more permanent to remind them of what they learnt from it.

- **Work out what (if anything) will be assessed.** If the video is just 'icing on the cake' and there is nothing arising from the video material that will be directly involved in any form of assessment, tell your trainees that this is the case. When things they derive from using the video elements *are* involved in their assessment, explain this to them, to help them give the video materials appropriate attention.

- **Set the agenda for your trainees before each episode of video.** Ensure that your trainees are set up with questions in their minds, to which the video extracts will provide answers.

- **Consider giving your trainees things to do while they view the video extracts.** You could brief them to note down particular observations, or to make particular decisions, or to extract and record specific facts or figures.

- **Consider asking your trainees to do things after they've watched each extract.** This can help them to consolidate what they have gained from watching the extracts. It can also prompt them to have a further look at any extract where they may have slipped into passive viewing mode and missed important points.

- **Don't underestimate the importance of printed support materials.** To make the most of video elements, trainees need something in another medium to remind them about what they should be getting out of the video, and where it fits into the overall picture of their learning. Video recordings often work best when supported by a printed workbook, into which trainees write their observations and their interpretations of what they see. Their learning from such workbooks can be reviewed by looking again at them, even without looking again at the recording.

- **Keep the video available.** Some participants may want to have another look at things they've seen, and it may be possible for them to do this in breaks in your programme.

- **Remember to collect feedback on the usefulness (or otherwise) of the video.** Include questions about the video in your evaluation questionnaire.

29. Using audiotapes in your training

Audiotape is so commonplace and cheap that its potential in teaching contexts is easily overlooked. In subject disciplines such as music, where sound is all-important, the use of audiotapes as a learning medium is already well developed. In multimedia packages, sound and images are often combined to good effect, yet audiotape can sometimes play a similar role at much less cost. The following suggestions may inspire you to put simple audiotape to good use to support your trainees:

- **Have good reasons for using audiotapes.** Always be in a position to explain to your trainees *why* an audiotape is being used alongside their other resource materials. Share with them information on what they should be getting out of using the audiotape.

- **Most trainees have access to audiotape.** Many trainees have portable cassette players, and may use these when travelling on public transport, jogging, driving and in all sorts of circumstances. When elements of learning packages are available as audiotapes, there is the possibility that you will extend their learning to times when they would not otherwise be attempting to study.

- **Label audiotapes informatively.** People who listen to tapes tend to accumulate lots of them, and it is easy for audiocassettes accompanying learning programmes to get lost amid those used for entertainment.

- **Keep audiotape extracts short and sharp.** When there are specific intentions about what trainees should get out of listening to audiotapes, extracts should normally last for a few minutes rather than quarters of an hour! It is worth starting each extract with a recorded 'name' such as 'Extract 3, to go with Section 1, Part 2', and to have the same voice reminding trainees when they have reached the 'End of Extract 3, going with Section 1, Part 2', and so on.

- **Use audiotape where tone of voice is important.** It can be particularly useful for trainees to hear messages, where the emphasis that you place on key words or phrases helps them to make sense of material that would be harder to interpret from a printed page or from a computer screen.

- **Sound can help trainees into subject-related jargon.** When there is new terminology, for example, it can be hard to tell how to pronounce a word just by seeing it in print, and it can be humiliating for trainees to find only when talking to a trainer that they have got their pronunciation wrong! Audiotapes can introduce the vocabulary of a subject to trainees.

- **Use audiotapes to bring learning to life.** Audiotapes can be invaluable for giving trainees the chance to hear people talking, discussing, debating, arguing, persuading, counselling and criticizing, and can capture and pass on to them many experiences and processes that would be difficult to capture in print.

- **Clarify exactly when a recorded episode should be used.** If you are using audiotape alongside printed materials, it can be useful to have a visual 'flag' to indicate to your trainees when they should listen to a recorded extract.

- **Turn trainees' listening into an active process.** Listening can all too easily be a passive process. Avoid this by setting your trainees things to think about before listening to a tape extract. Prime them with a few questions, so that they will be searching for the answers from what they hear.

- **Consider using audiotape to give trainees feedback on their assignments.** It can be quicker to talk for a few minutes into a tape recorder than to write down all of your feedback on your trainees' written assignments, or even to key in your feedback for e-mail transmission. The added intimacy of tone of voice can help you to deliver critical feedback in a more acceptable form. Trainees can also play the tape again and again, until they have understood each part of your recorded feedback. Always try to begin and end with something positive, just as you would do with written feedback.

- **Combine audio and visual learning.** It can be useful to use audiotape to talk trainees through things that they are looking at in their resource materials. For example, complex diagrams or derivations in printed materials, or graphics, tables and spreadsheets shown on-screen in computer-based materials can be brought to life by the sound of a human voice explaining what to look for in them.

30. First impressions count

There is no second chance to make a good first impression! When people first arrive at a training event they are often feeling a little bit apprehensive. Anything you can do to put them at their ease helps:

- **Tell people where to go.** Make sure participants know which room the session will be in, and where the toilets are. Put up signs around the building, and be prepared for some participants to arrive via side doors.

- **Welcome participants.** Putting up a 'welcome' overhead slide or a 'welcome' message on the flipchart can help participants to settle in comfortably.

- **Be there as participants arrive.** Smile and welcome them individually – this is a good time to start your task of learning their names. Resist any temptation to sit there finishing your preparations or reading the newspaper (however desperate you are to catch up on the news!).

- **Feed your participants.** Have refreshments waiting – not just tea and coffee, but also orange juice.

- **Chat to participants informally as they arrive.** There's plenty to chat about, including the weather, late trains, burst tyres, British Rail coffee and the effect of the climate on gardens. Don't declare your political sympathies yet, however!

- **Move around and address participants by name.** Check that they have their name badges on (and maybe also supply name cards so everyone can see each other's names at a considerable distance). Ensure that first names can be seen easily, and try to encourage Mr A G Jones to relax enough for everyone to be able to call him 'Archie'!

- **Be comfortable yourself.** Choose your own clothes so that you can look comfortable and confident (even though your knees may be shaking!). Check in advance your buttons or zips – otherwise people who notice any discrepancies may stare at you unmercifully!

- **Get the venue ambience right.** A bowl or vase of flowers can make a stark training room look homely. However, check that participants can see past such artefacts – and place them where you're not going to send them flying as you make a gesture of emphasis.

- **Make the venue sound interesting.** Having baroque or mood music playing softly in the background can help participants relax and settle in.

- **Keep your cool (or warm!).** Check that the temperature of the room is moderate, and find out how to control it. Be prepared to monitor and adjust the room temperature throughout your session. Remember to ask participants now and then whether they feel it is too stuffy or too cool and so on.

31. Introducing yourself

Whenever working with a new group of participants, you need to introduce yourself in one way or another. The following suggestions may help you decide how to do this on particular occasions:

- **Circulate a brief CV beforehand.** This can list your areas of experience and also give details of the particular aspects of training that you're normally involved in. It's worth making this sort of CV friendly rather than intimidating – a bit about your likes and dislikes does no harm.

- **Prepare an overhead to introduce you.** This can give brief details of your background or experience, and alert your participants to some aspects of the style in which you will conduct the course. Be careful, however, not to read out to participants word for word things they can see on the screen. Elaborate on one or two points where appropriate.

- **Tell it all verbally.** This is probably the option I recommend least! Not many participants really enjoy hearing the life history of their facilitators. However, there may be times when you find that you should choose this option. Don't forget, though, that participants won't actually remember much of something they simply hear – they will only remember the impression (or lack of one) that the words made.

- **Make it clear through pre-event documentation.** Including things you have already written or published in pre-event papers can be a useful way of alerting participants to your track record in the field.

- **Be interviewed by participants.** This can be an interesting way for participants to find out more about you (and for you to find out a great deal about them). Suggest that groups of participants spend a few minutes formulating questions about you, your background and your experience, and then stand ready to deliver answers to their questions.

- **Get yourself introduced.** Sometimes, your client may be willing to provide an introduction to the person who is about to facilitate a training session. You may well need to provide your client with succinct briefing notes to keep this introduction to the areas that you wish to be covered. Alternatively, you may be lucky enough to be quite embarrassed by the eloquence of such an introduction.

- **Make little introduction at all.** Sometimes it is best to let participants get to know you as your course unfolds, and to make no claims regarding experience or expertise (particularly if you have a lot of either).

- **Get everyone to introduce themselves.** You can then join in along with the rest, giving a few choice words about your background and experience.

- **Don't do a hard sell.** If you're famous in your field, there's no benefit in advertising your latest books during the introduction! In fact, advertising your own work at the beginning of a training event can alienate participants irrevocably. If you're so famous, everyone will already know of your work.

- **Concentrate on beliefs or values.** Get everyone to introduce themselves in terms of what they believe in or value, and join in with them.

32. Mind your body language

Whether you are talking to 200 people in a large lecture room or training a small group of people, it is important to consider your use of body language. Watching your participants carefully can give you some very useful indications of how they are feeling and can help you to think about how you are coming across to them in terms of your own body language:

- **Maintain eye contact with your group.** This helps to establish a positive relationship with participants. Looking people in the eye along with a smile can help to relax folk as they enter your room. Remember, some may be feeling apprehensive, not knowing quite what to expect.

- **Avoid looking over people's heads.** They will start to turn round to see what is on the back wall. Equally, don't spent too much time watching the floor; some participants may begin to feel left out – or to think that the carpet is magic!

- **Avoid looking at the same person all the time** (even when that person has a friendly face). It is only too easy to focus your attention on the person directly in front of you. It is easy to miss out people sitting on your far left or far right, and occasionally you may need to position your body directly towards these groups so that they don't feel left out.

- **Watch your hands.** Swinging them around your body with great enthusiasm can be distracting to some. Holding them firmly clasped behind your back can indicate a 'royal stance'! If you are feeling nervous, it is only too easy to clasp your hands in front of you as though they are about to drop off. Remember that those in the front row see the close-up view. If your hands shake when you're nervous, try not to write directly on to the OHP, where shakes are magnified tenfold.

- **Avoid hiding hands in pockets** (especially when the pockets contain coins or keys). It is amazing the sounds you can create – but which you don't hear yourself – when you are busy thinking of the next thing you are going to say. By the time you have finished saying it, someone will have worked out exactly how much money is in your pocket!

- **Think about what you are wearing.** You may think that your patched jeans and 'holey' T-shirt are the latest in fashion – but others may perceive them differently. Think carefully about the culture of the organization where you're working. In some, casual wear is the norm, but in others it may be perceived as not paying respect to tradition.

- **Video yourself, and reflect on your body language.** Do you move around too much, or stand glued to the floor? It is sobering (and often painful) to see ourselves as others see us. It is always useful. It is valuable to gather feedback from your group too.

- **Avoid standing too close to any one person.** Remember there are social distance zones. If we encroach too far into these zones, people will back off or misinterpret our intentions. Be aware of different cultural norms. What is considered a normal body distance zone in one culture can be a threatening one in another culture.

- **Watch the position of your body.** Turning sideways when talking to someone may give the message that you're not really interested in the conversation. Folding your arms may be perceived as being defensive. Walking up and down the room too much could indicate you're nervous (or have an attack of pins and needles!).
- **Interpret the body language of others with caution.** Fiddling with cuffs or collars may not necessarily indicate nervousness – it could be a case of a button that is about to fall off. Crossed arms can be a comfortable position for many – only take care when they are accompanied by crossed legs and a frown!

33. Introducing participants

How participants at your training events first get to know each other can make a big difference to the progress of your sessions. Later in this book there's a whole section on 'ice-breakers'; meanwhile, here are some first ideas about ensuring that participants learn about each other. Obviously, don't go overboard on such activities, and choose the one or two that you will use on the basis of the sorts of people you believe you are likely to be working with:

- **Keep introductions in perspective.** For example, when starting off a five-day training event, extended introductions can be worthwhile, but in a half-day event (for example) it's very important to keep them short.
- **Do a round of 'who I am, and what I believe in'.** This can give participants the chance not only to explain their background, but also to express their points of view regarding the theme of the session.
- **Get participants to interview each other in pairs.** Then ask everyone to give a brief introduction of the person they have just interviewed. This has the benefit of allowing participants' achievements to be aired by someone else, and preserves modesty.
- **Devise a pro forma.** Ask all participants to fill in details of their background, views and experience, and then ask all to display their pro formas on a wall.
- **'One thing I really like' (or 'one thing I really hate' – or both).** Ask all participants to identify such things and to say a few words about themselves in the context of whatever they choose to reveal about themselves under this category.

- **'What I really want from this course and why.'** This is a way of letting participants state their personal expectations, and also giving some details of the circumstances surrounding their expectations of your course.

- **'Four things in common.'** Provide a checklist covering a range of interests, hobbies, beliefs and values. Ask participants to tick up to six things that apply to them individually. Then ask them to compare their responses to other people's and identify fellow participants where (say) four things are 'in common' on their lists. This can help to bring together kindred spirits at the start of a course.

- **Introduce a treasure hunt.** For example, devise a sheet asking group members to find someone else in the room with (say):

  the same colour eyes;
  a talent for singing in the bath;
  blue as a favourite colour;
  a cat;
  a penchant for pasta;
  a liking for walking over open fields;
  roses as favourite flowers;
  a liking for talking books;
  a wish to holiday in the Caribbean.

  Each person 'discovered' is asked to place his or her name on the lists alongside the appropriate preferences.

- **Draw a poster.** Put participants in pairs, and ask them to share their likes and dislikes (and anything else they don't mind sharing with the rest of the group). Then ask them to draw a poster together depicting some information they have just shared. See if the rest of the group can identify which person is depicted in which part of each poster.

- **Take some instant photos.** Obtain an instamatic camera or a digital one and, as participants arrive, ask their permission and take their photos. Display the photos around the wall, with a blank sheet of paper alongside each. Then ask each person to write up one positive feature they can identify through the photos of at least one other person. As the course progresses, ask participants to write further good points alongside photos as appropriate (but only *good* points).

34. Working with mature trainees

It is important to treat mature trainees appropriately, and that they feel comfortable even when in groups where they are working alongside much younger trainees. The following suggestions may alert you to some of the principal issues that arise when working with mature trainees:

- **Consider designing a self-profiling questionnaire for all of your trainees.** This can give you an accurate picture of where the skills and competences of your mature trainees and their younger colleagues overlap or diverge.

- **Check out the expectations of your mature trainees.** Ask them why they have chosen to study your subject, and how they believe it will fit into their future careers or how it may feed into their plans for further studying. They will often have more definite answers to these questions than younger trainees who are simply taking your subject because it's part of their whole course.

- **Be aware of the anxieties that mature trainees often have when first returning to studying.** They may have negative memories of their last experiences in education, and things may have changed a great deal since they were last trainees. Try not to allow them to feel vulnerable or exposed until they have had sufficient time to gain confidence.

- **Remember that mature trainees may know a lot.** Their work experience could well have equipped them with knowledge of how some of the topics they are studying relate to the real world, and it's worth giving them the chance to share this experience. This can do a lot to increase their confidence in the group, especially in contexts where their younger counterparts are ahead of them in other ways, such as a familiarity with computers and electronic communication.

- **Some mature trainees tend to be demanding.** This can be a serious problem with trainees on assessed credit-rated programmes of study. Such trainees often take their studying a lot more seriously than some of their younger counterparts, one reason being that they are often footing the bill themselves or are being invested in by their employers.

- **Remember that mature trainees don't know everything – or may be 'rusty'.** Just because mature trainees look older doesn't automatically mean that they have picked up some of the things that their younger counterparts have learnt. There will be gaps, so ensure that mature trainees find out about these gaps with minimum embarrassment. Specifically designed study support or learning-skills induction programmes for mature trainees can be most valuable to them and much appreciated by them.

- **Take care about assumptions.** Some mature trainees will have covered ground you might never have expected them to have covered, and others won't have experienced things you would have expected them to have experienced. It's well worth spending a little time finding out a bit more about mature trainees' views of their own strengths and weaknesses.

- **Treat mature trainees appropriately.** They do not like being treated like children, but of course neither do younger trainees – or children themselves! It is worth reminding yourself that at least some mature trainees who are just learners in your training room are likely to be experienced professionals like yourself in other places. Be sensitive about the different focus that mature trainees need regarding their early days on a course.

- **Help mature trainees to save face.** Mature people often don't like to be seen to get things wrong, especially when seen by younger people. Watch out for occasions when feedback from assessments may raise this issue. Be sensitive to mature trainees' feelings when they make contributions in the group; if their comments or questions are shown to be 'silly' or inappropriate, it can be a serious blow to their confidence.

- **Give mature trainees the chance to interact well with the rest of the group.** When choosing groups for tasks or projects, it is often worth trying to get a good mix regarding age and background, to allow exchange of knowledge and experience in as many directions as possible.

- **Be realistic about other demands on mature trainees' time and energy.** They normally have abundant motivation and drive, but sometimes other pressures in their lives can affect the possibility of them meeting deadlines or targets.

- **Be a mature trainee yourself!** It is always useful to put yourself in a position similar to that of your trainees. Even if the course or topic you're studying is a minor part of your life, being a learner again will alert you to ways of refreshing your own teaching practice. It can be particularly helpful to take an assessed course yourself, as this will remind you what it feels like to prepare yourself for a tutor to look critically at your work. This can help you to remain sensitive to the feelings of your trainees.

35. Working with international trainees

The suggestions below aim to alert you to some of the particular help that may be needed by this particular cross-section of your trainee population. Trainees from other countries or from a different ethnic background to the majority of your trainees may need additional support in various ways and at different stages of their studying. The suggestions below aim to help you minimize the disadvantages that such trainees can experience:

- **Arrange specialist induction provision for international trainees.** Pre-sessional courses addressing aspects of cultural acclimatization and study-skills good practice can be of enormous benefit in helping such trainees start off their studies without being disadvantaged.

- **Produce clear information for international trainees.** Try to ensure that they receive this information before they arrive. Ideally we should be producing clear information for all trainees, such as by using course handbooks, but it is particularly important that international trainees should receive good documentation about their courses, as well as about the institution and its environs. International trainees are more likely to need to revisit such information again and again until they have tuned in to their new situation, and they can often do this more successfully when the information is in print rather than in easy-to-forget face-to-face formats.

- **Help them to understand what is expected of them in training sessions.** Many international trainees come from cultures with particularly formal methods of education, and find it hard to cope with the more interactive modes of teaching. Trainees from some cultures can find it a shock to encounter the full and frank debates between trainees and tutors that are regarded as healthy indicators of a seminar. This may explain their own reluctance to become involved, and they will need patient encouragement to adopt the roles that they are expected to play in their new setting.

- **Search for ways of lessening the isolation of international trainees.** Encourage them out of the institution, so they can absorb more of the local culture and make new contacts and friends, without putting them under any pressure to break their normal links with fellow trainees from the same background.

- **Be sensitive on issues of religion.** Some religions require followers to pray at specific times and in particular settings. This can be a problem for trainees required to fit in with tight timetabling, and sensitive flexibility needs to be shown regarding their needs and rights.

- **Help trainees with special food requirements.** Coping with a new culture is enough of a hurdle for trainees from different backgrounds and cultures, without imposing the additional burden of having to cope with new food habits. Gather feedback on what would be acceptable alternatives that could be built into menus and catering provision. Advise those arranging catering at induction events to be especially sensitive about labelling food, so that international trainees don't become anxious about what they can and cannot eat.

- **Consider getting previous trainees from each country to write an introductory guide to the idiosyncrasies of the British!** It can be useful for new trainees from overseas, and for staff and trainees not from abroad, to get the chance to see themselves through the eyes of people from other cultures or countries.

- **Recognize cultural differences regarding attitudes to alcohol.** Significant groups of staff and trainees come from cultures where alcohol may be forbidden on religious grounds. Sensitivity regarding attitudes to alcohol means recognizing that some trainees will be in a difficult position if field trips or visits include a stop on the way back at a suitable pub! It also means recognizing that group discussions of alcohol marketing strategies or pub social behaviours will be offensive or alien to trainees (or staff) whose culture forbids alcohol.

- **Consider the special facilities needed by trainees from other countries.** For example, toilet and washing facilities need to accommodate the different practices that are involved in some cultures or religions. When such trainees attempt to make use of unaccommodating facilities, their actions are in danger of being misunderstood.

- **Consider the accommodation needs of trainees from other cultures.** Trainees from some countries, when booking their place at an institution in the UK, may not know what is meant by 'hall of residence', 'single study-bedroom' or 'shared apartment'. Accommodation literature needs to be written or supplemented so that all trainees know what each category of accommodation entails.

- **Offer language support at appropriate levels.** Trainees studying in English as a second or other language will need different kinds of language support as they continue their studies. At first, they may need help in getting started in English, but later the help they need may be more connected to how they should use written language in assessed work, and spoken English in interviews with tutors or in oral examinations. If you are using computers, the layout of the keyboard and the characters available could be a source of difficulty.

- **Help them to communicate with home, especially in emergencies.** International telephone or fax charges are high, and trainees may not have access to locations where they can use such communications in relative privacy. The costs, both financial and academic, of trainees having to make emergency visits home are more serious, and ways need to be found of helping trainees sort out some of the problems that could lead them into such costs.

36. Working with trainees with special needs

Training providers have a responsibility to provide the best possible educational opportunities within their remit for all trainees. Open-access policies, together with statutory requirements, mean that we need to take into account the requirements of trainees with special needs when planning our training programmes. These suggestions are designed to help you think about how best to approach this:

- **Adopt a positive action approach.** Trainees with special needs should not be regarded as a problem to be dealt with, but rather as a constituency of users whose needs must be taken into account.

- **Involve the trainees in managing the support you offer.** The people who are most affected are usually the best to advise you on appropriate support strategies. They should be consulted alongside specialist external advisers when designing your provision.

- **Think carefully about the language you use.** The term 'handicapped' can cause offence, since it is derived from those who came 'cap in hand' to ask for help. 'Disability' can also be seen as a derogatory term, suggesting something of less value than ability. People with special needs usually prefer to be regarded as people first and last, rather than being categorized by what they can't do.

- **Don't assume that people with mobility problems are wheelchair bound.** Most people entitled to use the UK orange badge on their vehicles are not, in fact, users of wheelchairs. They may, however, experience difficulties in walking long distances, climbing stairs or undertaking other strenuous activities. Be aware of hidden disabilities, such as asthma and heart problems.

- **Don't use difficult buildings as an excuse to exclude people with special needs.** It can be expensive and difficult to install lifts, automatic doors and ramps, especially into old buildings, but lateral thinking can work miracles. Careful timetabling can permit the holding of sessions including someone with mobility problems in ground-floor or easy-access rooms. In the UK, government funds are often available to improve access when a need has been clearly identified.

- **Help people with visual impairments.** Institutions can do much to help trainees who don't see well to study effectively. Allowing trainees to tape-record classes and making recording equipment available on loan can help considerably. Visual impairment is frequently not total, and trainers can do their bit by using large font sizes on overhead transparencies, and making material available to trainees who find it difficult to copy from the board or screen. The mobility of people with visual impairments can be improved moderately easily by such means as Braille signing, tactile strips on corridor floors and 'talking' lifts. If you are using computers, think about how the technology could help those with visual problems. At its simplest, this could involve using larger type or different colours; at a more sophisticated level, computers can 'speak' the screen contents or even provide Braille output.

- **Help trainees with hearing difficulties.** Many institutions now have audio loop systems, which enable trainees to amplify sound. These can be supplemented by individual trainers ensuring that trainees who don't hear well can have their choice of seats. Trainers can facilitate audibility, by speaking clearly, and provide back-up material on request.

- **Make provision for trainees with learning difficulties.** These trainees cope well, especially when given additional targeted support as required, and can fully contribute to the life of the institution. Learning resources centres can be especially helpful in providing a range of resources to support the learning of these trainees.

- **Provide support for trainees with, or recovering from, mental illness.** Individual counselling and guidance can be enormously beneficial in enabling these trainees to use their training course as part of a programme of personal recovery and development.

- **Be aware of the problems that computers can cause for people with special needs.** These problems can include co-ordination difficulties, which may make mouse or keyboard operation difficult. Some people may find computers easier to use if they are at a different height from usual. Flickering screens can trigger epilepsy in some susceptible people.

- **Keep in mind health and safety requirements for trainees with special needs.** Procedures for fire or bomb-threat evacuation need to take account of those people who cannot move fast, who may not hear or see warnings, or who may be unduly alarmed by emergency situations. Ensure that your strategies for coping with emergencies of all kinds take account of the special needs of all of your trainees.

37. Gathering and using trainees' expectations

As trainers we sometimes feel we have to give participants what we know they need. However, we should never do this at the expense of missing an opportunity to find out what they *want* – and making the most of common ground between their needs and wishes:

- **Make your own provisional agenda clear first.** Show participants the intended outcomes of the training event, and say a few words about how you plan to go about achieving these outcomes. Make it clear, however, that you are about to enter into fine-tuning to meet participants' expectations.
- **Ask participants, 'What do you personally most wish to get out of this programme?'** Give them time to think, and don't ask them for verbal replies – the first few replies could divert the ideas of participants who are slower to reply.
- **Get participants to *write* their personal expectations.** This can be done by giving everyone a small piece of acetate (a quarter of an A4 sheet is usually enough) and an overhead projector pen. Ask them to add their names to their expectations (this helps you keep track of who is wanting what).
- **If necessary, put participants into small groups to discuss and decide their expectations.** This can be useful if you sense that there are several participants who don't really have any clear expectations yet. 'Group expectations' are also useful if you've got more than (say) 24 participants, when it could be too time-consuming to look at all their individual expectations.
- **Share their expectations in plenary session.** Put their acetate slips in turn on the overhead projector. Invite particular participants to clarify or expand on any expectations that seem to need this. Seeing their own handwriting up on the screen helps participants to feel a sense of ownership of the fine-tuning you are making to your training event.
- **Show their expectations in random order.** This is better than collecting them in a particular order and sticking to this order. Random order helps keep participants' attention focused – at least until their own acetates have been shown.
- **If useful, let participants introduce themselves briefly while their expectations are on-screen.** This is useful if they don't already know each other, and can save the time of having

a purely introductions round. You can keep introductions to a reasonable time when necessary by removing one acetate and pressing on with the next.

- **Keep your replies to their expectations brief.** It's useful to say now and then 'Yes, we'll certainly be dealing with this later in today's programme', but don't make a detailed argument concerning why you're *not* intending to address particular expectations.

- **Keep the expectations in common view.** This is easily done by gently pasting the backs of the acetate slips with a glue stick and sticking them lightly on a flipchart. This helps participants feel that you are taking their expectations seriously.

- **Return to particular expectations as your training event develops.** Link things you intended to do anyway to particular requests from participants – give them the credit of thinking of sensible issues to address.

- **Return to the expectations towards the close of your training event.** If the acetate slips have been pasted lightly enough, you can remove them from the flipchart again and display them once more, asking whether each participant is satisfied.

38. Maximizing learning pay-off

One of the most important factors that predetermines trainees' success in learning is confidence. We need to give our trainees every chance to develop this confidence, and one of the best ways of us helping them to do this is to assist them to gain greater ownership of, and control over, the processes they apply during their learning. In this way, their learning pay-off can be maximized. The suggestions below summarize how you can address the key factors about how people learn in group situations, discussed in more detail later in this book:

- **Help trainees to want to learn.** They may need to be helped to increase their motivation by showing them what the benefits are for them arising from the achievement of their intended learning outcomes. When possible, enhance their motivation by making learning fun, interesting and rewarding. Don't mistake lack of confidence for lack of motivation.

- **Needing to learn something can be almost as productive as wanting to learn it.** When trainees know *why* something will be useful to them, even if they find it difficult, they are more likely to maintain their efforts till they have succeeded.

- **Provide trainees with learning-by-doing opportunities.** Most learning happens when trainees practise things, have a go, and learn by making mistakes and finding out why. Care needs to be taken to ensure that learning-by-doing is focused on practising useful, important things, and not just anything to keep trainees busy.

- **Look for ways of giving trainees as much feedback as is reasonably possible.** Trainees need to find out how their learning is actually going. Feedback from trainers is very useful, but trainers can also facilitate trainees getting feedback from each other and from various kinds of learning resource materials. It follows too that feedback must be timely for it to be of optimum use to trainees.

- **Help trainees to set out to make sense of what they are learning.** It is of little value learning things by rote, or becoming able to do things without knowing why or how. Getting trainees to think about how their learning is happening is one step towards helping them to develop a sense of ownership of their progress. Learning is not just a matter of storing up further knowledge; it is about being able to apply what has been learnt, not just to familiar situations but also to new contexts.

- **Provide trainees with clues about how they are expected to learn from the ways in which we teach them.** If we simply concentrate on supplying them with information, they are likely simply to try to store it. If we structure our teaching so that they are practising, applying, extending, comparing, contrasting, evaluating and other higher-level processes, they are likely to see these processes as central to the ways they should be learning.

- **Use assessment to drive learning productively.** Trainees are often quite strategic in structuring their learning to be able to do the best they can in the contexts in which their learning is to be assessed. Assessment formats and instruments can be used to help trainees to structure their learning effectively, as well as to give them appropriate timescales within which to organize their learning.

- **Encourage trainees to learn from each other.** While much can be learnt by trainees working on their own with handouts, books and learning resource materials, trainees can also learn a great deal by talking to each other, and attempting tasks and activities jointly.

39. Establishing ground rules

Ground rules can be very useful indeed in group work contexts. Below are some starting-points from which practical ground rules can be developed:

- **Create ownership of the ground rules.** The various ground rules agendas suggested below should only be regarded as starting-points for each group to adopt or adapt and prioritize.

- **Be truthful.** Successful group work relies on honesty. It is as dishonest to 'put up with' something you don't agree about, or can't live with, as to speak untruthfully.

- **You don't have to like people to work with them.** In group work, as in professional life, people work with the team they are in, and matters of personal conflict need to be managed so they don't get in the way of the progress of the group as a whole.

- **Affirm collective responsibility.** Once issues have been aired and group decisions have been made as fully as possible, the convention of collective responsibility is applied, where everyone lives with the group decisions and refrains from articulating personal reservations outside the group.

- **Develop and practise listening skills.** Every voice deserves to be heard, even if you don't initially agree with the point of view.

- **Participate fully.** Group work relies on multiple perspectives. Don't hold back from putting forward your view.

- **Everyone takes a fair share of the work.** This does not mean that everyone has to do the same thing. It is best when the members of the group have agreed how the tasks will be allocated among members.

- **Working to strengths can benefit the group.** The work of the group can be achieved efficiently when tasks are allocated according to the experience and expertise of each member of the group.

- **Don't always work to strengths, however!** Activities in groups can be developmental in purpose, so task allocation may be an ideal opportunity to allow group members to build on areas of weakness or inexperience.

- **Keep good records.** There needs to be an output to look back upon. This can take the form of planning notes, minutes or other kinds of evidence of the progress of the work of the group. Rotate the responsibility for summing up the position of the group regarding the tasks in hand, and recording this.

- **Group deadlines are sacrosanct.** The principle, 'You can let yourself down, but it's not OK to let the group down', underpins successful group work.

- **Cultivate philanthropy.** Group work sometimes requires people to make personal needs and wishes subordinate to the goal of the group.

- **Value creativity and off-the-wall ideas.** Don't allow these to be quelled out of a desire to keep the group on task. Strike a fair balance between progress and creativity.

- **Work systematically.** Establishing a regular programme of meetings, task report-backs and task allocation is likely to lead to effective and productive group performance.

- **Regard ground rules as a continuing agenda.** It can be productive to review and renegotiate the ground rules from time to time, creating new ones as solutions to unanticipated problems that might have arisen. It is important, however, not to forget or abandon those ground rules that proved useful in practice but were not consciously applied.

40. Following up pre-event tasks

There is nothing worse for participants than having done some preparation for a training event, only to find that what they did is never mentioned again. Here are some ways of ensuring that the efforts participants put in to preparing for your training events are recognized, valued and used:

- **Don't forget what you asked participants to do before attending.** Keep the exact wording of your pre-event tasks in sight.
- **Ask participants for any problems they encountered in the tasks.** If they have not attempted them, they will be very quiet at this stage. However, those participants who did have a go at them will have their chance to bring any problems to the surface, and will feel pleased to be able to do so.
- **Where possible, set tasks so that participants can bring their 'product' along to your training event.** It will be clear that some participants have tried the task and that others have not. It is useful then to put participants into small groups, asking them to summarize their products for discussion at the next plenary session.
- **Don't leave any pre-event task cold.** Anyone who has invested time and effort into having a go at such a task will feel devalued if you never refer to the task again. Make sure that all pre-event tasks are built into your programme in one way or another.
- **Give participants time to catch up on what they should have done!** For all sorts of reasons, some participants will not have attempted your pre-event tasks, or will not even have received the instructions. Allow short but reasonable amounts of time for participants individually (or in groups) to make up for what they have not yet attempted.
- **Have some examples to hand.** It can often be useful to show participants at your training events the sorts of things that 'past' participants did with your pre-event tasks. Sometimes, the main message will be how much better your present participants have tackled the tasks than anyone has ever done before – this makes for happy training events!
- **'Here is one I cooked earlier.'** Your own answer to a pre-event task is particularly useful when you know it will be (or already has been) surpassed by the work of your participants. Conversely, resist the temptation to show them the one you 'cooked earlier' when their work is not up to the standard you expected.

- **Consider setting a choice of tasks.** This can allow different participants to have attempted different things – helping you to make the most of the possibilities of them giving feedback to each other.

- **Ask participants, 'What pre-event tasks should I set next time?'** You will usually find that you learn a lot from this, and can use it next time to advantage.

- **Monitor the outcomes of pre-event tasks.** The main benefit you can derive may be simply to adjust the wording of the task instructions ready for next time, so that you can confidently expect everyone to try to do what you really want them to try to do.

41. Brainstorming

'Brainstorming' should be a quick way of gaining a lot of ideas, without any restrictions on the validity of the ideas that may emerge. Here are some suggested ways of ensuring that brainstorming sessions work well and productively:

- **Suggest that all ideas are welcome.** One of the fundamental principles of brainstorming is 'free thought', and it is important in the early phases that no ideas are subject to criticism or rebuke.

- **Allow anyone to 'pass'.** It is important that participants feel that, if at the time they have no new ideas to offer, they are not regarded as inferior.

- **Get participants to write their ideas on Post-its.** Their Post-its can subsequently be stuck to a flipchart (or wall) in any order, and the order rearranged as the shape of the general flow of ideas emerges.

- **Use small bits of overhead transparency for brainstorming now and then.** The advantage of this is that participants' own words, in their own handwriting, can appear for all to see on the screen. This can be time-saving compared to writing up their words on a flipchart.

- **Sometimes, put participants into groups to brainstorm.** This is particularly useful when you know that some participants are new to the area to be explored and may not have particular experience to offer. Ask the groups to prioritize the suggestions that emerge in their discussions.

- **Continue till there are no more new ideas.** Sometimes, you may feel that all the useful ideas have already been contributed, but it is important to wait until all your participants have had their say. This is a way of giving them ownership over the whole range of ideas that will be subsequently explored and developed.

- **Establish participants' view of the relative importance of ideas.** For example, number the principal ideas (say) from 1 to 12, and ask them to vote for the 6 most important and record their votes alongside each idea.

- **Invite any further ideas.** Often, after a brainstorm, participants may be able to think of further ideas (or better ideas) that have not already surfaced.

- **Ask 'How should we best approach this idea?' in turn.** This helps to establish participants' ownership over the processes whereby your training event will address each item on the agenda that they have identified.

- **Keep the products of brainstorms in view.** For example, stick up flipcharts to the walls. Show that you value the results of brainstorming sessions by referring to these flipcharts when appropriate as the training event progresses, and remember that it is never too late to add further ideas to flipcharts produced earlier.

42. Maximize 'learning-by-doing'

Most people learn far more by having a go at things themselves than from listening to someone who can already do them talking about them. Make your training events active learning experiences:

- **Remind participants how they really learn.** Ask them to think of something they know they are good at (but not to write it down). Then ask them to write down how they became good at whatever it was – Post-it slips are suitable for this. Then point out to them how most of their successful learning has been by practising, having a go and so on.

- **Value 'getting things wrong' as a way of learning.** When participants feel there is no shame in making mistakes, they will be more willing to try anything – and they will be more tolerant of trainers' mistakes too! It's worth reminding participants that there should be no such thing as 'failure' – only feedback.

- **Plan your training events around things for participants to do.** These ingredients are more important than things you wish to tell them. A successful training event is often a series of participant activities, linked together by very small briefing and discussion episodes.

- **Make the task instructions clear and simple.** If everyone – trainers and participants – knows exactly what they are trying to do, there is much more chance that they will do it well. It can be a great help to have tasks written down on overhead transparencies, so everyone can see them clearly and if necessary for long enough really to understand them.

- **Be ready to negotiate tasks.** Where the task you had planned turns out to be not entirely relevant to participants' needs or expectations, be prepared to adjust the task briefing with their help to make it more suitable.

- **Give participants time.** While it is good practice to set a time limit for each task, use your eyes and ears to discover whether participants have sufficient time. If they are given too much time they can become impatient to press on. If they are in the middle of a useful learning experience when 'time is up', it is well worth extending the deadline.

- **Value the things participants do.** Even when they get things wrong, don't make them feel their efforts were in vain. Celebrate their successes when they do things correctly or well.

- **Have a go at your own tasks.** 'Here is one I prepared earlier' is not the same as having a fresh attempt at a task. Even better, extol how much better your participants' attempts are than the one you've just made.

- **Provide escape routes.** When you are using a task that will be very difficult for some participants, think of using the option to work in groups rather than individually. Alternatively, think of some more-straightforward tasks to set those who have not the experience to attempt the hard ones.

- **Let participants set *you* tasks.** Show that you yourself are willing to have a go at things you've not tried to do before. Better still, let participants tell you how you could have gone about it more successfully.

43. Avoiding alienation

People are all different, but they don't like being made to *feel* different. The following suggestions show some ways of avoiding turning particular participants into deadly enemies:

- **Get to know all names, not just some.** It's almost like an insult when someone doesn't know your name, but knows other people's names. Using place cards or (large) lapel badges helps you to get to know names in a group (and also helps the group members to get to know each other).

- **Get names right.** If you call someone by the wrong name, or spell names incorrectly, you risk making enemies (or at least losing friends!). There's no better way of checking the spelling of people's names than getting them to write their own names on place cards or badges. That way, you'll find out whether Jonathan prefers to be called Jon (and not John), and whether Victoria prefers to be called Vikki – or Vicky.

- **Avoid racism.** Even with a group of the same ethnic origin, some people will be sensitive to even the slightest hint of prejudice. With multiracial groups, be particularly careful to treat every member equally. This includes making it your business to be able to pronounce names you have not come across before correctly – 'How exactly do I pronounce your name?' is a useful way of showing you care about equality.

- **Avoid sexism.** This is particularly important with mixed groups. The main offending words tend to be 'he', 'his' and 'him' – especially when talking of situations that are equally applicable to women and men. 'S/he' is clumsy and unsatisfactory. 'He or she' only draws attention to the issue. Plurals are usually much safer – there are few problems with 'they', 'them' and 'their'.

- **Treat people equally.** You can't be expected to 'like' all participants equally, but you can take positive steps not to pick on anyone you like less and not to appear to 'warm to' anyone you like more.

- **Avoid taking sides.** When there is a split of opinion within a group – even when you're definitely on one side – try to be seen to be reflecting the opposing arguments and viewpoints fairly and objectively, rather than ganging up with the people whose ideas coincide with your own.

- **No one likes a loser.** If things turn out against you (no coffee, no handouts, no heat, too much noise… the list is endless), don't go on and on about how you tried to arrange it all and it isn't your fault. Accept the adversity on behalf of the whole group, and look for productive ways forward that minimize the inconvenience. Above all, don't publicly blame the person whose 'fault' it is – do this privately later!

- **Don't set yourself apart.** If you are 'apart' – for example, very distinguished in your field – they'll know this already. Avoid name-dropping and other temptations. It's also well worth avoiding unnecessary jargon in your sessions.

- **Don't queue-jump.** We all know how it feels when an 'important person' slips ahead in the queue for lunch. It's better to put up with eating the leftovers from the buffet than to alienate your participants by being seen to be exercising special privileges.

- **Avoid 'top tables'.** This particularly applies to residential training events lasting several days. However much you feel you need to be talking to the client over lunch or dinner, it counts a lot if you are seen to be mixing with your participants. Besides, they tend to be much better company!

44. Addressing conflict in group work

Much has been written about the stages that are quite normal in group work. For example, it is common for teams to progress through stages of 'forming, storming, norming and performing' – not necessarily in one particular order! Groups, however, need not be the same as teams. The following suggestions may help you to minimize the dangers associated with conflict in group work, and to maximize the benefits that can be drawn from people who sometimes disagree:

- **Legitimate disagreement.** It is important to acknowledge that people don't have to agree all of the time, and to open up agreed processes by which areas of disagreement can be explored and resolved (or be accepted as known areas of disagreement).
- **Establish the causes of conflict.** When conflict has broken out in a group, it is easy for the root causes to become subsumed in an escalation of feeling. It can be productive to backtrack to the exact instance that initiated the conflict and to analyse it further.
- **Encourage groups to put the conflict into written words.** Writing up the issues, problems or areas of disagreement on a flipchart or marker-board can help to get them out of people's systems. Conflict feelings are often much stronger when the conflict is still bottled up and has not yet been clearly expressed or acknowledged. When something is 'up on the wall', it often looks less daunting, and a person who felt strongly about it may be more satisfied. The 'on the wall' issues can be returned to later when the group has had more time to think about them.
- **Establish the ownership of the conflict.** Who feels it? Who is being affected by it? Hesitate to probe 'Whose fault is it?', however! Distinguish between individual issues and ones that affect the whole group.
- **Distinguish between people, actions and opinions.** When unpacking the causes of conflict in a group situation, it is useful to focus on actions and principles. Try to resolve any actions that proved to cause conflict. Try to agree principles. If the conflict is caused by different opinions, it can help to accept people's entitlement to their opinions, and leave it open to people to reconsider their opinions if and when they feel ready to do so.
- **Use conflict creatively.** It can be useful to use brainstorming to obtain a wider range of views or a broader range of possible actions that can be considered by the group. Sometimes, the one or two strong views that may have caused conflict in a group look much more reasonable when the full range of possibilities is aired, and areas of agreement are found to be closer than they seemed to be.
- **Capture the learning from conflict.** When conflict has occurred, it can be beneficial to ask everyone to decide constructive things they have learnt about themselves from the conflict, and to agree on principles that the whole group can apply to future activities to minimize the

damage from similar causes of conflict arising again. Try to encourage 'win–win' approaches, rather than 'win–lose' ones.

- **Refuse to allow conflict to destroy group work.** You may wish sometimes to tell groups that achievement of consensus is an aim or a norm, or alternatively you may wish to ask groups to establish only the extent of the consensus they achieve.

- **Consider arbitration processes.** When conflict is absolutely unresolvable, the facilitator may need to set up a 'court of appeal' for desperate situations. The fact that such a process is available often helps groups to sort out their own problems without having to resort to it.

- **Make it OK to escape.** When people know that they can get out of an impossible situation, they don't feel trapped, and in fact are more likely to work their own way out of the conflict. It can be useful to allow people to drop out of a group and move into another one, but only as a last resort. Beware of the possible effects of someone who is seen as a conflict generator entering a group that has so far worked without conflict.

45. Handling difficult questions

A 'difficult' question tends to be one where we don't know the answer, or where there are several ways of approaching the question and we don't know which way is best. Our training events are often judged on the basis of the way we demonstrate our professionalism when faced with such questions:

- **Don't try to pretend you have an answer when you haven't.** We've all dug ourselves into trenches in such situations. It is far better to admit 'I'm not at all sure I can answer this one right now' than to waffle and fudge.

- **Clarify the question.** Help your participants work out exactly what the question means, breaking it down if necessary into separate parts needing separate answers. Write up the agreed version of the question on a flipchart, so everyone can see the words and reflect on the agreed version of the question.

- **Ask for volunteers from your participants.** Often, when there's a difficult question, there will be one or more participants who have more idea than we have about how it could be approached.

- **Give participants some privacy to explore a difficult question.** When such a question is really important, it is worth spending some time where participants in groups can informally brainstorm ways of approaching it. The report-backs from the groups can retain a degree of anonymity about particular ideas that emerge during the group discussions.

- **Turn difficult questions into an ongoing agenda.** Especially at residential training events, it is often worth writing up difficult questions on flipcharts and leaving them on the wall, asking anyone with ideas about how to tackle them to write their ideas on Post-its and stick them on to the respective flipcharts. They can choose to do this anonymously, by sticking the Post-its up during breaks or overnight.

- **Expect that there will be no 'right answer' to a difficult question.** Such questions tend to have a range of alternative answers. Affirm that it's OK *not* to have a ready answer to such a question. Try to collect as many alternative solutions as possible to a problem.

- **Get participants to 'rate' alternative answers.** For each alternative approach, ask 'What's the best thing going about this approach?' and 'What's the biggest danger with this approach?'

- **Offer to find out some answers to difficult questions within a week or two.** For example, offer to consult colleagues in the field concerned, summarize their responses to the questions and circulate the summary to your participants.

- **Welcome difficult questions.** Don't try to divert participants back to the things you intended them to do next. Say words to the effect, 'I'm so glad this came up. It's really important and worth exploring now. Thank you for raising the issue.'

- **Build on your experience.** Next time you run a similar training event, build in the difficult questions as case studies or examples, armed with the thinking that you and previous participants have already done. A training event that tackles difficult questions head on will be seen as much more useful to participants than one that tries to skirt round problematic areas.

46. Working with difficult participants

However enthusiastic you are about your subject, you will sometimes find yourself faced with handling difficult people. There is usually at least one – usually in the back right-hand corner! Interpret their reactions with care. We all have difficult days – whether we overslept, tripped over the cat or got a further electric bill reminder, we can be difficult:

- **Don't have a back right-hand corner in the first place!** When participants are sitting in a circle or a U-shape, it's less likely that anyone can establish the right sort of territory in which to become difficult.

- **Stop, and bring the difficult participant into play.** Say words along the lines, 'I think our colleague here has concerns about what we're doing. Would you like to share them with us all?' Sometimes, people are only difficult when they feel their views are not being considered.

- **Remember aggressive behaviour may indicate insecurities.** When some people are insecure they curl up and go into their shells, but others react in a much more 'open' and aggressive way. Try carefully to find out what might be the cause of their behaviour. They could be apprehensive about a new item or idea you are trying to introduce, or a new way of working. If possible, use a coffee break to try to probe the real cause of any problem.

- **Be firm if necessary.** If you really find you've got a round peg in a square hole, you may consider politely suggesting (during a break, not publicly) that if the training event and its pre-declared objectives don't meet the participant's requirements it may be best to leave, and offer to refund any fee.

- **Try to involve everyone.** Some people may be difficult because they feel left out or marginalized. Frequent small-group activities can dispel anxieties and get most people involved. Busy people have less time to worry.

- **Quieten the overzealous question-asker.** One person who tries to dominate the conversation and asks an incessant series of questions can cause annoyance to others who feel their time is being wasted or that the discussion is going off at a tangent. Watch your audience carefully to pick up the group or individual reactions. When necessary say something along the lines of 'Thank you very much for all these interesting questions. However, we must press on now if we are to finish on time.'

- **Tackle the problem head on.** Say something like 'Would you like to share your problem with the group?' If you feel that openness would not work, ask everyone to jot down one concern or worry they may have. Collect in the questions and issues, and deal with them without naming the originators. Many group members may be pleased that issues have been brought out into the open in this way.

- **Don't disagree with a person – only with ideas or views.** 'I don't think this would work in practice' is a much more sensitive thing to say than 'I think that's a silly idea!' Try to avoid showing favouritism. It is human nature to gravitate towards some people more than to others. However, those who sense that you don't like them are likely to engage in open hostility. Work hard at treating everyone equally.

- **Turn the difficulty into fun.** People don't like their serious objections turned into a joke, so only do this if you really have tried as many constructive tactics as you could think of. Humbling a difficult participant in this way creates a real enemy for the rest of the training event.

- **Take a 'brain break'.** When tempers are getting frayed or discussions becoming heated, little will be achieved. That can be a good time to suggest a walkabout, comfort break or chance to view materials. It provides cooling-off time too.

47. Gender issues

When problems occur in groups because of gender issues, they can be felt more deeply than problems arising from almost any other cause. The following suggestions may help you to avoid some problems of this sort from arising in the first place, or to alert group members themselves to the potential problems so that they can work round them in their own approaches to group work:

- **Think about gender when forming groups.** There are advantages and disadvantages for single-sex groups, depending on the balance of the sexes and other issues, including culturally sensitive ones. In some cultures, females may be much happier, for religious reasons, working in single-sex groups.
- **Try to avoid gender domination of groups.** This can happen because of majority gender composition of groups. If this is inevitable because of the overall gender balance of the whole class, try to manage group composition so that minority participants don't feel isolated.
- **Decide wher single-gender groups might be more appropriate.** For group work on gender-sensitive issues, it can be best to set out to form single-sex groups.
- **Require appropriate behaviour.** For group work to be effective, all participants need to behave in a professional way, with standards that would be expected in an effective working environment. Outlaw sexist or offensive behaviour.
- **Decide when to ring the changes.** Use random group-formation processes to form different kinds of groups for different tasks and activities. For example, form some groups on the basis of month of birthday, others by alphabetical processes, including 'last letter of first name', and so on. This can ensure that groups that develop problems don't continue for too long.
- **Decide when to stick with existing group compositions.** When a set of groups is working well, without any gender-related or other problems, don't just change the group composition without a good reason.
- **Set ground rules for talking and listening.** It can be useful to agree on ground rules that will ensure that all group participants (irrespective of gender) are heard and not talked down by other participants.
- **Avoid setting up excessive competition between male groups and female groups.** When there are gender-specific groups, don't egg a group of one gender on by saying words to the effect, 'Come on, you can do better than them', referring to groups of the other gender.
- **Be sensitive about role assignment.** For example, try to raise awareness about the dangers of tasks being allocated within groups on the basis of gender stereotypes, such as typing or making arrangements being handles by females, and 'heavy' work by males.

- **Alert groups to be sensitive to leadership issues.** It is often the case that, for example, male members of groups may automatically see themselves as stronger contenders to lead the group than their female counterparts, and put themselves forward. When group members are aware that this is an issue, they are more likely to agree on a more democratic process for deciding who will lead an activity, or who will report back the outcomes.

- **Be alert to the pros and cons of putting couples in the same group.** Couples can result in productive partnerships in group work, but can easily become exclusive or dominating if there is only one other person in the group.

- **Avoid sexual preference oppression.** When it is known that certain group participants have different sexual preferences from the majority of the group, there is a tendency for them to be oppressed in one way or another by the rest of the group. It can be delicate to raise this issue in general briefings, and it may be best to respond to it as a facilitator when it is seen to be likely to occur.

- **Keep peer-assessment fair.** When peer-assessment is being used within group work, or between groups, watch out for the tendency for females to underrate and males to overrate.

48. Coping with the unexpected

Your reputation as a trainer will depend not only on your professional expertise, but on your ability to be seen to cope with the unexpected, calmly, professionally and with humour and dignity. The following suggestions may help you to attain this image:

- **Welcome the unexpected.** Life is full of the unexpected. It is only an enemy if we resist it. Look at it this way: a 'competent' trainer works within what is expected; a 'professional' trainer can work within whatever turns up. Aim to be able to cope with anything. (Don't worry that you don't succeed every time – no one can.)

- **Harness the unexpected.** Work out what it really means. Define it. Put it into words that everyone shares the meaning of.

- **Turn the unexpected into 'issues' and 'questions'.** Add these to the questions and issues upon which your training event is based. Sometimes, the things that arise from unexpected developments are more important than the original issues or questions that your training event was meant to address.

- **Seek everyone's views.** When the unexpected turns up, don't feel that you are obliged to have all the answers up your sleeve. It can be the ideal opportunity to say 'I don't really know – what do you think?' to your participants. They will respect you all the more for this.

- **Legitimize the unexpected.** When important matters turn up 'unexpectedly', add these formally to the agenda of your training session. Turn them into additional objectives or intended outcomes.

- **Ask for the unexpected.** Keep asking, 'What *else* may we need to be able to deal with?' When the 'unexpected' comes directly from your training event participants, they already have a sense of ownership of it and are all the more willing to try to work out ways of handling it.

- **Be prepared for the unexpected.** As a training event facilitator, be ready for all the things that *could* happen – overhead projector bulbs blowing, power cuts, a pneumatic drill starting up outside the window, coffee not arriving at all and so on. Always have something else in mind that can limit the damage of the unexpected.

- **Capitalize on the unexpected.** Shamelessly draw learning points from ways that the unexpected has been successfully handled. Participants will remember the way (for example) that you turned the three fire alarms in one morning (due to a fault in the circuit) into a learning exercise. One trainer recently insisted that the fire-bells needed to be at least 20 decibels more audible in a training room to meet occupational health and safety standards.

- **Remember that the unexpected is *shared*.** The unexpected can help bring you closer to your participants. It can help you confirm your role as 'benevolent leader'. It can help them gain respect for your judgement and decisiveness.

- **Always have 'Plan B'!** When it is quite clear that unexpected factors have made your original plan unworkable, let it show that you had in mind all the time an alternative way for the aims of your training session to be achieved.

49. Developing participants' creativity

In many circumstances, people are asked for *one* right answer or correct solution. This leads to linear thinking. Being more creative is a valuable skill and can generate new ideas as well as being fun. The Nobel prize-winning physician Albert Szent-Gyorgyi put it well: 'Discovering consists of looking at the same thing as everyone else and thinking something different':

- **Research participants' creativity.** Ask participants when the last time they came up with a creative idea was. What was it? What motivates them to be creative?

- **Get spoilt for choice.** The best way to get a good idea is to have lots of ideas to choose from. For example, put a paperclip on the overhead projector, and ask participants to think of how many innovative ways they could use a paperclip. Highly successful companies encourage creativity, even though most ideas may be non-runners.

- **Give participants a creativity-centred problem.** For example, ask them how a sheet of newspaper could be placed on the floor so that people standing face to face on it could not touch each other. (No string allowed!) Solution at the bottom of this page.

- **Give participants a situation to improve.** For example, show them a picture of a tin bath with a duck floating on the water it contains. Ask them to think of as many ways of improving the situation to create an ideal bathroom as they can.

- **Mind your language.** When you respond to participants' creative ideas, be aware of the limiting effect that the following phrases could have: 'Good answer', 'That's the correct solution', 'Be practical!' , 'Follow the rules' and 'That's not logical.' Use open language, not 'final' language where possible, for example 'Good. How else could this be done?'

- **Ask 'What if?' questions.** A few questions for starters include:

  What if all 21-year-olds grew to 7 feet over the next 12 months?
  What if all men had babies?
  What if we had no seasons and it snowed all year?
  What if all women over 21 had size 8 feet?
  What if absolutely everyone did not smoke at all?
  What if everyone ate a bowl of All Bran for breakfast every day?

- **Get participants' blood flowing!** For example, when participants have been sitting for a while, put up an alphabet in large letters on an overhead or flipchart, with 'l' and 'r' under each at random:

A	B	C	D	E	F
l	r	r	r	l	l

  Then get everyone to read out the alphabet together, but raising left legs if there's an 'l' and right legs if there's an 'r'!

- **Think in metaphors.** Turn the current problem into a metaphor, for example 'How is motivating your team like climbing a mountain?'

- **Think how great people may have done it.** Ask your participants for the names of great people, leaders or thinkers. Ask them then how they might have solved particular problems, and how *they* might have publicized their successes.

- **Widen horizons.** For example, ask participants what it would be like if the following pairs went for lunch together, and what they would learn from each other: 'bus driver and solicitor' 'librarian and lawyer', 'teacher and astronaut', 'air-traffic controller and politician', 'manager and newspaper editor' and so on.

(Solution to creativity-centred problem above: put the newspaper under the door.)

50. Working one to one

Training events are usually group sessions. However, the things that many participants remember best are those moments when they received your individual attention. The following suggestions may help you to bring individuality to group sessions:

- **Remember that each participant is an individual.** Each has his or her own expectations, views and aims. Try to make time to research these and to respond to them.
- **Don't let plenary discussions degenerate into one-to-one debates.** Use coffee breaks and meal breaks to handle issues where you really need to (or want to) enter into relatively private discussions with individual participants.
- **Extract the issues and matters arising.** Turn individuals' questions and views into things that the whole group can become involved in.
- **Don't take sides in public – avoid making enemies!** Acknowledge issues, questions and problems publicly, and plan to address them with the whole group as your training event proceeds.
- **Choose your times to speak to participants privately.** When your participants are engaged in individual work or small-group work, it is often better to approach particular participants whom you know need specific advice or guidance, rather than doing so in the middle of plenary sessions.
- **Bring everyone in.** When there is an issue or debate where one or two participants have strong views, avoid dialogues. Clarify the contending points of view, and allow the whole group to indicate the prevailing feeling on the issues.
- **Offer to talk to individuals later.** When a problem is identified by a single participant, it can sometimes be better to offer to resolve it outside your training event than to bring it into the limelight.
- **Spare individual participants' feelings.** When you need to disagree with their views, it is better to do so privately than in public. Breaks in training events are sometimes the most important times – and are particularly useful for resolving difficulties or problems.
- **Get close to anyone you really need to talk to.** Don't try to address an individual participant with a problem 'from the front'. Walk right up to the individual, and talk to him or her quite quietly. If you're standing and the person is sitting, you're already at an advantage.
- **Remind everyone that you're just one person – not the management!** Help each individual participant see that your own views are those of an individual, and not automatically 'right' or 'authoritative'.

51. Helping participants to make sense of things

An essential component in successful learning is to 'make sense of' what has been learnt – in other words, to digest it. Here are some suggestions to help your training event participants get to grips with the content of your programmes:

- **Remind participants of the need to 'make their learning their own'.** If they merely regard what they are learning as someone else's ideas, they are unlikely ever really to believe in what they learn.
- **Give participants time.** 'Digesting' some new ideas is not done instantly. People need time to get used to new ideas or new concepts. Plan training event activities that give participants that vital time to get used to new things.
- **Help participants to learn by explaining.** There's often no quicker way to get a grip on something new than to try and explain it to someone else. The act of explaining something necessarily involves getting one's own mind around it.
- **Ask participants to 'put it in your own words'.** This helps them get a sense of ownership of things they are learning – and they will usually remember their own words rather more successfully than our words.
- **Give participants the chance to apply what they've just learnt.** There's nothing better than trying out a new skill or idea, to begin to understand what it really means.
- **Get participants to make summaries.** It's all too easy for us to try to do the summing up, but it's very useful to engage participants in such processes. Let them decide what they think the main learning points are, or the principal ideas to remember. Asking participants to make a mind-map of what they've learnt is a useful ploy.
- **Prepare your own reviews as handouts.** It's useful if you can give your training event participants a digest of the main things from the training event as seen by you. But don't issue such handouts till the end – or better still by post after the training event. Don't undervalue participants' own personal reviews.
- **Help participants identify 'What this means to me is...'** The real understanding comes when we relate what we have learnt to the situations we encounter in our own everyday lives or jobs.
- **Remind participants that understanding can come later than competence.** We can often learn to do things effectively quite some time before we really understand why we are being effective. There is no shame in allowing understanding to happen in the time that it takes to happen.

- **Aim for 'the peace that passeth understanding'.** Sooner or later when we have really understood something, we feel 'easy' with it – and then all the better as trainers to begin to extend our understanding to others.

52. Using role-plays

The benefits of using role-play exercises can be considerable. However, there are risks too, and some trainers are rather afraid of using them. Participants too may have mixed feelings about the prospect of becoming intimately involved in some role-play situations. We hope the following suggestions will help you strike the right balance:

- **Consider the benefits of using role-plays.** You can choose to get participants enacting some of the most difficult aspects of the topic they're addressing – yet in the privacy of a small group and a supportive environment.
- **Remember the dangers of role-playing.** It's possible for participants sometimes to get 'too involved' in the role-play, and personal feelings can become inflamed or hurt. Therefore, it is often wise to be careful in selecting which participants may be asked to take on certain roles.
- **Explain a bit about role-playing.** If everyone knows that they are not playing themselves, but are deliberately adopting a 'stance' in a role-play, they are more likely to be able to do so effectively and without their feelings getting in the way.
- **Keep an eye on activities and role-plays.** Be ready to enter in or even intervene, if you think that something is in danger of getting out of hand, or is going off at a tangent to the intended purpose.
- **Capitalize on printed briefings for roles.** Keep these short, however. For example, in a role-play involving (say) four players, have an A5 card, with the key information on it for each of the participants.
- **Decide whether briefings will be shared or private.** Sometimes a role-play works best when everyone fully knows the roles that other people are playing. At other times, the element of surprise may be needed, and it can be useful for aspects of the respective roles to be kept hidden until the right moment.
- **Consider 'fishbowling' a role-play.** In such cases, you can choose participants (or let them self-select) on the basis of people who are comfortable to give the role-play a try. The chosen participants can then enact the role-play, with others sitting round them, looking in and observing.

- **Think about the possibility of using closed-circuit television, if available.** When you want to have a chosen group run through a role-play exercise, but without everyone watching them directly, you may be able to have the role-play itself occurring in an 'intimate' environment, while being viewed by the rest of the group using CCTV, enabling them to discuss the role-play as it occurs.

- **Debrief role-play activities carefully.** Help participants to separate the feelings they had during the role-play from the learning outcomes that the role-play led to.

- **Always come back to the objectives of a role-play.** Sometimes, you may have decided not to reveal these in detail until the end anyway. It helps a lot if participants can see that there were definite and valuable purposes in getting them involved in role-plays – especially if there were some tense moments during its execution!

53. Ringing the changes

There are many different ways of enhancing the quality of learning in trainee groups. The following suggestions expand on the question-and-answer ideas given elsewhere in this book, and are among the processes that quality reviewers are looking for in their observations of group work:

- **Get individual trainees to prepare and present seminars.** This can include the trainee leading the seminar taking questions from the rest of the group, and maybe also from the tutor involved in the group. The attention of the trainee audience can be significantly increased by getting the trainees receiving the seminar to use processes of peer-assessment, with straightforward and well-expressed criteria that have preferably been formulated by the trainee group.

- **Consider getting pairs or groups of trainees to prepare and present seminars.** This can be less intimidating than solo performances, and can involve the development of useful cooperation and collaboration skills. Again, peer-assessment can help *all* the trainees involved get more from such seminars.

- **Use tutorless groups for appropriate learning activities.** These give trainees the freedom to contribute without the fear of being found lacking, or making mistakes in front of a tutor. For such groups to work well, it is useful to provide the trainees with carefully formulated briefings in print, and to require an appropriate report-back product.

- **Use buzz groups in large-group sessions.** These are particularly useful for generating in an informal way a lot of ideas or opinions, which can then be reported back and explored in greater depth with the large group.

- **Use brainstorming techniques to generate ideas.** This is useful in small groups, and still works well with groups of 20 or more trainees. It is important to formulate strict ground rules for brainstorming, such as 'Give no comment on ideas already given', 'Say "pass" if you've nothing to add when it's your turn' and 'Think creatively and say anything that comes to mind'. After producing as many ideas as possible in a few minutes, the group can start prioritizing and clustering them.

- **Use snowballing or pyramiding to refine ideas.** This can be a way of enhancing learning in quite large groups by getting trainees to work together in a structured way. For example, get trainees in pairs to think of ideas, then combine with another pair to take the ideas further and then combine with another four to prepare a report-back to the whole class.

- **Use crossovers to enhance trainees' communication in groups.** For example, divide a group of 16 into four groups of four. Set the small groups a first-stage task, and then ask one member from each group to move to another group and report the findings. Set the second stage of the task to the revised groups, then ask a different member to move on and report, and continue doing this till everyone has worked with everyone else.

- **Consider using fishbowls in medium-sized groups.** For example, from a group of 20 trainees, 6 could be drawn (or volunteer) to sit in a circle in the middle of the room. The inner circle could then be briefed to discuss a scenario, with everyone else observing, and with an exchange mechanism by which trainees from outside the group wanting to make contributions could replace someone in the group.

- **Use role-plays to help trainees contribute more easily.** Some trainees who are reluctant to contribute to group discussions or debates because of shyness lose most of such inhibition if they are playing someone else. Printed handout sheets giving sufficient details of each role help trainees to adopt the role they are intended to play, and are useful for allowing each trainee to react to the other roles involved as they unfold in the role-play.

- **Self-help groups can enhance trainees' learning.** It can be worthwhile to start such groups up with tutor support, and help the trainees in each group start to generate their own ground rules and targets. Then the groups can be left to operate without further support, other than perhaps a mechanism to bring unresolved problems to a class meeting or to a tutor.

54. Filling five minutes to coffee!

It is always useful to have a collection of 'fillers' up your sleeve. However well we try to plan our time, situations will occur when it is really not worth starting on that new or different topic area. Try not to prolong an activity or topic just for the sake of it:

- **'Design a poster in three minutes indicating what your group has gained from the session.'** This is a good way of still maintaining the topic, and getting groups to collect their thoughts together. It can also be a lot of fun especially if they are to produce large and colourful posters. The two final minutes can be spent viewing the products of other groups.

- **'What have been your most positive learning experiences from the session, and why?'** Allow three minutes to write a few comments on a Post-it or scrap of paper.

- **Buy a puzzle book.** These can give you lots of ideas for little time-fillers. For example: 'A beetle goes through five sets of encyclopaedias A–E that are sitting side by side on a shelf. The beetle starts on page one of Book A, and continues to the last page of Book E. Each book is 2.5 inches thick and each cover 0.1 inch thick. How far does the beetle travel?' Mathematicians in the group are always worst at this sort of activity – so be forewarned! Solution at the end of this section.

- **Twenty best tips for coping with stress.** We all face varying amounts of stress, which we handle with varying degrees of success. What is our best method? Is it digging up all those weeds, treating ourselves to a bag of sweets, 10 minutes on the exercise bike or a fight with a pillow? If participants don't wish to disclose them in public, get them to write their tips down on Post-its and stick them to a wall for everyone to pick up some tips over lunch.

- **Reward your participants for working hard.** We are all so busy leading our own lives, and meeting all those work deadlines, that we sometimes forget to say 'thank you' to those who help us. Brainstorm as many as possible ways of saying 'thank you'. Then vote on the three most useful suggestions. It is amazing how creative your participants may be with this activity, especially when they know lunch is about to be served!

- **'What do you hope to achieve in 12 months' time?'** Give everyone an envelope and a small piece of paper, and ask them this. The answers can include both professional and personal ambitions and hopes. Ask individuals to seal their envelopes, and put them in a secure place or give them to a good friend, to consult again in 12 months. Suggest they put a note in their calendars or diaries to remind them to reopen their envelopes to check how many of their plans have been achieved.

- **'What would you do with a £50 book token?'** Ask your participants to imagine they've been given such a book token to spend on the topic of your training event. What books would they buy, and why? Use this to build your own bibliography!

- **Castaway on a desert island.** You are allowed one novel – or CD – only. What would each of your group members take, and why? Make your own presents list!

- **'The most interesting seminar I have ever attended is... because...'** This exercise is a good way of building up tips for your next seminars or training events. What makes a 'gold star' training event?

- **Criteria for the Best Boss of the Year Award.** What makes a good boss? Ask the group for one characteristic they would like to see in their current boss – or the best characteristic their current line manager displays. Then vote for the three best characteristics.

(Solution to encyclopaedia-eating beetle puzzle above: it depends! If the volumes are the right way up, the beetle travels through 5 × 2.5 inches of book and 8 × 0.1 inch of covers – 13.3 inches altogether. If volumes A and E are upside down, the beetle goes through only one cover of each of these and all of volumes B, C and D – 8.3 inches altogether.)

55. End with a bang, not a whimper

There's nothing worse than when a training event just seems to fizzle out. Or when participants seem to slip out one by one, and only the keen ones remain till the end. Such things are our nightmares made of. Here are some ways to bring your training events to successful conclusions:

- **Keep your eye on the time, so you can end promptly.** This also means not trying to cram in to the last hour all the things you wished you'd said during the whole training event.

- **Avoid long 'general discussion' or 'matters arising' sessions.** It's tempting to round off training programmes with such sessions, but it's best deliberately to keep them quite short.

- **Get everyone to contribute in final plenaries.** Avoid the normal happening of two or three participants having a lot to say, and other people getting fed up of hearing them. Use rounds of short, sharp questions, asking everyone for their answers or show-of-hands votes.

- **Save something for participants to do near the end.** For example, give them each an action planning sheet, a few minutes to make individual plans and then a few minutes to compare their plans with each other.

- **Have something important to give participants at the end.** Save one of your handouts to pass round then – especially one that sums up most of the things that have been covered by your training event.

- **Encourage participants to stay in touch.** Where your participants come from different places or sites, it can be useful to get them all to fill in their phone numbers on to a single sheet, and circulate this sheet to them afterwards along with any other papers arising from the products of their activities during your training event.

- **Gather your own feedback.** Find out what participants' impressions of the training event are. You can always gather more-considered impressions later too. Remember, however, that impressions can change when they come to try to implement the things that your training event was intended to help them become able to do.

- **Remind participants what they've done.** Go back to the aims of the training event, and the expectations of the participants, and help them to see what has been achieved. If necessary, flipchart a list of 'matters outstanding', which could perhaps be addressed by a further event.
- **Remember to thank your participants.** Thank them for their work during the training event, and their cooperation in achieving the aims of the programme.
- **Have a further round of tea, coffee and juice at the end.** This can allow participants who need to get away promptly to leave when the training event finishes, and can also allow those who would like to talk further to you or to each other to do so for as long as they wish.

56. Time management

How much time there is to be managed is open to question! Often trainers have much of their time predetermined by teaching timetables and research commitments. But even if only a quarter or third of your working time is under your control, the following tips may help you to make it more productive:

- **Budget your time.** Your 'budget' is that time in your working day that is not predetermined by your teaching timetable, research commitments and other duties. If your immediate reaction is 'What's left?', read on. To budget effectively, you will need to tackle tasks systematically rather than trying to do everything at once.
- **Keep a list of the work you need to do under a series of headings.** These headings could make up a priority list of: *must do immediately*; *should do soon*; *may be put on the back burner*. Or they could reflect a four-way split of items of work as: *urgent and important*; *urgent but routine*; *important but not urgent*; *routine and not urgent*. This task list is best drawn up on a daily basis, crossing out or carrying forward items as you tackle them.
- **Avoid the temptation to do the routine and not urgent tasks first.** They tempt because they can be simple, distracting or even fun. But keep a note of them; they can be done in the quieter patches. However, there are benefits to be gained from spending no more than half an hour on a non-urgent task before starting on an urgent one.
- **Whichever list you use, remember it is dynamic and will need to be reviewed daily.** Time has a nasty habit of moving things on and what was once not urgent emerges suddenly as something needed yesterday. Remember too that you may be better off by doing three things from your list in part than spending all your time budget on just one of them.
- **Use a wall chart or a 'What am I doing?' grid.** Such devices provide you with a means to plan ahead and schedule your known commitments. They also tell other people about your

current activities. It's useful for your colleagues if you also include a location and a note of how you may be contacted.

- **Keep your paperwork well filed.** It's a temptation just to fill the in, out and pending trays! Do this and you'll inevitably spend ages looking for that vital piece of information or in despair assume that it's been lost (or not received). Use a relatively quiet time to set up, maintain and update your filing system.

- **Is your journey really necessary?** Avoid multiple trips to the photocopier or mail point. Ask yourself, 'Rather than see someone, would it be quicker to phone, e-mail or write?', 'Do I really need to go to such-and-such meeting?' or 'Do I actually need to go to the *whole* of that meeting?'

- **Work out which tasks you can delegate, and do so.** Even with tight staffing levels, there will be clerical and technical support staff. Often such staff are better able than you to do the routine jobs like typing, filing or photocopying. They can be quicker too! Junior colleagues may be pleased to help as a way to help them develop their skills or 'visibility' in your organization.

- **Each day, schedule particular times to make your phone calls and to check your e-mail.** Making and receiving calls and e-mails *ad hoc* across the working day can be time-wasting and distracting from other tasks. Invest in an answerphone or voice-mail system to control but not lose calls. Encourage those you phone, but never seem to find available, to invest in similar technology.

- **Try the 'do it now' technique.** Don't be put off if you can't do the whole task in one bite. Break it up into smaller components that you can and will do straight away.

- **In the end you must decide what kinds of activity have a high pay-off or a low pay-off for you in terms of your time investment.** You may find that, for you, doing your paperwork by e-mail and phoning rather than writing will have high pay-offs. And you might find that attending meetings has a low pay-off, as might also writing jobs-to-do lists!

57. Workload management

Heavier workloads have become a fact of life for most trainers. It seems highly unlikely that this situation will change. The following suggestions may help you manage your workload that little bit more smoothly:

- **Don't waste energy on trying to turn the clock back.** What some people affectionately refer to as 'the good old days' are very unlikely to return. One danger is that we spend so much time talking about how much better things once were that we put even more pressure on the time and energy we have to face today and plan for tomorrow.

- **Prioritize your own workload.** It is useful to go through all the tasks and roles that you undertake, asking yourself which are the *really* important ones and which are the ones that would not have significant effects on your trainees if you were to prune them or abandon them.

- **Manage your time.** When snowed under with work, the danger is that time seems to manage you. It can be worth spending a couple of hours on a time-management training programme. Look for that one good idea that will save you a couple of hours, again and again.

- **Cut your assessment workload.** This does not mean reducing the quality of your assessment. It is widely recognized that over-assessment is bad for trainees, and in former times it was all too easy for such patterns of over-assessment to be established. Now may be the time to think again about how much assessment your trainees really need, and to improve the quality of this but at the same time significantly reduce its volume.

- **Make good use of learning resource materials.** Trainees nowadays learn a great deal more from computer-based and print-based materials than once was the case. The quality of learning resource materials is improving all the time, and such materials are getting steadily better at giving trainees opportunities to learn-by-doing, and to learn from healthy trial and error. Materials are getting much better at providing trainees with feedback on their individual progress and performance. Making the most of such materials can free up valuable face-to-face time with trainees, so you can deal with their questions and problems rather than merely imparting information to them.

- **Make better use of learning centres, when available.** Arranging for your trainees to do relevant parts of their learning in such centres can bring variety to their learning environment, and can relieve you of some of the responsibility for looking after them.

- **Make good use of your administrative and support staff.** It is easy to find yourself doing tasks that they could have done just as well, and often they could have done them more efficiently than you.

- **Make better use of feedback from trainees.** Listen to their concerns, and focus on them, making your own work more useful to them at the same time. They know better than anyone else where their problems lie, so it is worth making sure that your valuable time is spent addressing the right problems.

- **Cut your administrative workload.** Life may seem to be full of meetings and paperwork, but is it all really necessary? A well-chaired one-hour meeting can usually achieve as much as a much longer one.

- **Don't carry your entire workload in your mind.** We can only do one thing at a time, so when doing important work such as teaching and assessing trainees, don't get sidetracked into worrying about the numerous other tasks jostling for your attention.

- **Give yourself a break.** One of the symptoms displayed by people under pressure of work is that they seem to forget that we all need time off, and the world won't grind to a halt if we don't do everything on our 'to do' lists. Having a break and switching your mind away entirely from the pressures will mean you can return to the fray re-energized and strengthened.

58. Stress management

The trainer's job can be extremely stressful as staff are put under increasing pressure to work longer hours, possibly in unfamiliar ways. At the same time, trainees are becoming more diverse and have an ever-widening range of requirements and expectations. These tips cannot eliminate your stress, but may suggest some strategies to help you deal with it:

- **Get better at recognizing the physical signs of stress.** These include raised heart rate, increased sweating, headaches, dizziness, blurred vision, aching neck and shoulders, skin rashes and lowered resistance to infection. When people are aware that such symptoms may be caused by stress, it helps them to look to their approaches to work to see if the causes may arise from stress.

- **Get better at recognizing the behavioural effects of stress.** These include increased anxiety, irritability, increased consumption of tobacco or alcohol, sleep disturbance, lack of concentration and inability to deal calmly and efficiently with everyday tasks and situations.

- **Increase awareness of how the human body reacts to stress.** Essentially this happens in three distinct stages. 'The alarm reaction stage' causes defences to be set up and increased release of adrenalin. 'The resistance stage' is when the body will resist the stressor or adapt to the stress conditions. 'The exhaustion stage' results when attempts by the body to adapt have failed, and the body succumbs to the effects of stress.

- **Don't ignore stress.** There are no prizes for struggling to the point of collapse; indeed, this is the last thing you should be doing. As the symptoms of stress become apparent to you, try to identify the causes of your stress and do something about it.

- **Get over the myths surrounding stress.** Research has shown that stress should not be regarded as being the same as nervous tension, that it is not always a negative response and that some people do indeed survive well and thrive on stress. In a training organization, it is more important to manage stress than to try to eliminate it.

- **Look to the environmental causes of stress.** These include working or living under extremes of temperature, excessive noise, unsuitable lighting, poor ventilation or air quality, poorly laid-out work areas and even the presence of vibration. In your own institution, finding out what people think of such environmental conditions is a good first step towards adjusting them.

- **Look to the social causes of stress.** These can include insufficient social contact at work, sexual harassment, racial discrimination, ageism, inappropriate management approaches, unhealthy levels of competition, and conflict between colleagues. Any or all of these, when present, can be discovered and identified by asking people about them.

- **Look to the organizational causes of stress.** These include inappropriately heavy workloads, ineffective communication, excessive supervision or inadequate supervision, lack of relevant training provision, undue concern about promotion or reward systems, and unsatisfactory role perceptions. Once identified, all of these causes can be remedied.

- **Cultivate the right to feel stress, and to talk about it.** Stress is at its worst when it is bottled up and unresolved. It should be regarded as perfectly natural for people's stress levels to vary in the normal course of their work. When stress is something that can be discussed, it is much more likely that the causes will be addressed.

- **Allow yourself to feel anger.** It isn't surprising that people under stress often feel full of rage, which is often not specifically directed. People often become very frustrated when they feel powerless, so it may be worth taking stock of what is and what is not within your control. Anger, once generated, can be directed in many directions, and the most harmful of these is inwards. All the same, it is unwise as well as unprofessional to vent your rage on others, especially innocent bystanders who are caught in the crossfire. Find ways to let off steam that are not destructive to yourself and others.

- **Write it out of your system.** Some people find it very helpful to write about the issues that stress them and make them angry. This can take the form of a diary in which you record your feelings and analyse the situation, or letters you would like to send to the people who are causing you stress, or other forms of writing to take your mind off the current situation.

- **Have some fun.** Look for ways in which you can de-stress yourself by doing things that make you happy. A little hedonism goes a long way. Think about the things that give you pleasure like cooking, reading for pleasure, going to concerts or having a day of total sloth. Regard these as part of a programme of active stress management rather as a guilt-inducing interference with your work. You deserve some time for yourself and you shouldn't regard it as a luxury.

- **Don't be afraid to go to the doctor.** The worst excesses of stress can be helped by short-term medication and medical intervention of some kind. People are often unwilling to resort to a visit to their GP for matters of stress when they wouldn't hesitate to seek help for a physical ailment. Don't let such feelings get in the way of finding the kind of support you need.

- **Try not to worry about not sleeping.** Sleep disturbance is one of the most common features of stress, and worrying about it makes it worse. Try to ensure that you are warm and comfortable at bedtime, avoid working for at least an hour before you retire and use music or reading to help get you into a relaxed state. If sleep doesn't come, try to use the rest period to recoup some energy and try not to go over and over in your mind what is troubling you. Taking exercise and cutting down on your caffeine intake can help.

- **Use relaxation techniques.** There are innumerable methods that can be used to help you unwind, including deep breathing, massage, aromatherapy and meditation. It might be worth your while to explore the techniques that sound most attractive to you and try to use them to help you cope with stress.

- **Work it out in the gym.** Taking physical exercise at the end of a long, stressful day may feel like the last thing on earth you want to do, but lots of people find it helps them relax. Join a gym, take the dog for long walks, swim, take up golf, play a mean game of squash or just do aerobics at home to help your body to become as tired physically as your mind is mentally. Find out what kind of exercise works best for you and try to use it as a bridge between your working life and your own time. Try not to let your exercise requirement end up feeling like another kind of work you have to do.

- **Get a life outside your work.** Family and friends still deserve your attention, even if work is very busy. We all need to learn to keep a sense of proportion to our lives. Try not to neglect hobbies and interests, even if you sleep through the film or nod off after the sweet course. Let your pets help you to remember how to be a human, too!

- **Take a break.** Often our panics over time management are caused not so much by the amount we have to do as by whether we feel we have sufficient time to do it in. Try to take a real break from time to time, so as to help get the workload into proportion. A little holiday or a whole weekend without work occasionally can make you better able to cope with the onslaught on your return.

- **Overcome powerlessness with action.** When you are stressed out, it is often because you feel totally powerless in the situation. It can be useful to look at the areas you do have some control over and try to do something about them, however minor. This may not change the overall picture very much, but will probably make you feel better.

- **Talk about your problems.** Actually voicing what is stressing you to a colleague, a line manager, the person you are closest to or even your cat can sometimes improve the situation. Bottling it all up through some misplaced sense of fortitude can be dangerous.

- **Try counselling.** Many organizations have someone to whom staff can turn for trained counselling in times of great stress. Otherwise you could look elsewhere through your GP or in the phone book under 'therapeutic practice' or 'alternative medicine' to find someone who can guide and support you through the worst patches. This is often more productive than piling all your stress on to your nearest and dearest, who usually have problems of their own.

- **Try not to personalize a situation into hatred and blame.** It is easy to fall into the trap of seeing all your stress as being caused by an individual or group of people who have it in for you. Of course, it may be the case, but high-stress situations are not usually caused by conspiracy!

- **Avoid compounding the problem.** If things are pretty stressful at work, try to avoid making important life changes at the same time, such as moving to a larger house or starting a family, if these can be deferred for a while.

- **Audit your intake of stimulants.** For those whose culture allows alcohol, a little can be felt to be a wonderful relaxant, but excessive intakes can be problematic. It's natural to drink a lot of beverages containing caffeine when trying to get through a lot of work, but it can interfere with your metabolism and sleep patterns. Eating rich food too late at night and smoking too much can also get in the way of being calm. Moderation may be boring but is a good policy for those under stress.

- **Try to adopt a long-term perspective.** It can be really hard to project into the future and to review current stress as part of a much larger pattern but, if you can do it, it helps. Much of what seems really important now will pale into insignificance in a few weeks, months or years.

- **A problem shared is a problem doubled!** Stressed people meeting in groups can reinforce each other's stress by constantly rehearsing the problems. Encourage the group to agree a moratorium from time to time on chewing over the same old issues. Maybe have a meal out as a group together or go to the races together instead. It won't take away the stress, but it might help you forget about it for a while.

59. Working well with colleagues

Working in a training institution can be really miserable if the people around you aren't supportive and helpful. Try to start by ensuring that the people around you find you a helpful and supportive colleague, and you may be delighted at how the condition can spread:

- **Help out when the going gets tough.** If someone in your team is struggling, it makes a big difference if you are prepared to roll up your sleeves and lend a hand, whether it is in collating marks, stuffing envelopes or preparing for an important event. With luck they will reciprocate when you are having a tough time too.

- **Don't spring surprises on colleagues unnecessarily.** If you know you are going to be away for an extended period, or if you can't fulfil your obligations, try to give as much advance notice as possible. This will enable colleagues who have to fill in gaps for you to build it into their own schedules.

- **Keep to deadlines, especially when they impact on others.** If you are late doing your own marking, for example, or in putting together your section of a report, it will often affect others whose own time management will be thrown out of kilter. Try as far as humanly possible to do what you have said you will within the time available.

- **Keep track of what your colleagues really appreciate in what you do.** Try to do more of these things whenever you can. It can also be worth working out what a 'terrible colleague' might be like, maybe by making a word-picture of a hypothetical case, and avoiding doing the sorts of things that may be brought to mind by such a picture.

- **Find out how colleagues feel.** Don't just wait for them to tell you how they feel, and don't keep informal conversations to work-based topics. Simply asking 'How are you feeling today?' or 'What's on top for you just now?' can be open-ended questions that allow colleagues to share with you things that are important to them at the time, but that would just not have arisen in normal work-oriented discussions.

- **Be considerate when sharing an office.** Often staff workrooms are extremely cramped for space, and colleagues who leave papers all over a shared desk and who hog all available storage space make life difficult for others. Don't leave dirty cups around, clear up your own mess and be thoughtful about noise. If trainees need to be seen privately, try to agree times when fellow tutors can have uninterrupted use of the space.

- **Be punctual for meetings.** Everyone slips sometimes, for very good reasons, but as a rule try to ensure you are always spot on time for meetings, so other people aren't kept waiting for you while you make a last-minute phone call or a cup of tea.

- **Keep colleagues informed about what you are doing.** People need to know what you are up to when this impacts on their work. If, for example, you know you will be filling the office with a lot of bulky portfolios to mark, it might be a good idea to tell colleagues before they fall over the boxes coming into the room. Tell them also when you will have visitors, when you will be away and when you expect to have to see a lot of trainees.

- **Be gracious when rooms are double-booked.** This inevitably happens from time to time and can be the cause of much disagreement. Colleagues with two or more groups of trainees needing to use the same room should tackle the problem together, rather than having a slanging match over who had booked the room first. It makes sense for the group in situ or the larger group to occupy the available room with their tutor, while the other group is asked to wait somewhere like the refectory or quietly in the corridor until another room is found.

- **Leave teaching spaces as you found them (or better).** If you move furniture or use the walls for display, try to leave the room fit for use by others when you leave. Encourage trainees to clear their own litter and leave the space tidy.

60. Keeping up to date

It is all too easy to get caught up in the design and delivery of training events at the expense of building in time for our own professional development:

- **Subscribe to a journal.** Try and subscribe to at least one journal that will help you to keep up to date with developments. If you can, form local or regional groups, so that each group member can subscribe to a different journal, and then circulate it round group members.

- **Search the Internet.** This is exciting technology for those who have access to it. If you're not familiar with how to use the World Wide Web, book yourself on to a training session.

- **Trainers do it with books!** Try to read a new book at least every two months. Look out for book reviews in appropriate journals to help guide your reading. While travelling between jobs, spend half an hour in the nearest bookshop. Don't forget to use your local library too, and any college or university whose library you have easy access to.

- **Start a reflective journal.** One way of keeping up to date is by reflecting on what you do currently. Fairly promptly after each session you run, write down things that went particularly well and things that were not so successful. Jot down questions to yourself about your practice. Also, reflect back, and jot down changes you have made on the basis of experience.

- **View a new video every couple of months.** Build time in your diary to make use of such resources. Find out how to get to see material on video, for example in libraries, or learning resources centres in colleges or companies. Swap your own videos with visiting colleagues.

- **Join a trainers' e-mail network.** Many new networks are starting up on the Internet. If there isn't yet one in your own specialist area, think of starting one yourself. If you don't have Internet facilities, ask your boss when you may expect your organization to get connected. With a computer, a modem and some software, you could set yourself up from home.

- **Talk to colleagues.** It is amazing how much useful information we can all pick up simply by talking to friends and colleagues. Ask them about their latest 'best read' or the most interesting recent article they've seen. Ask them about the best session they've done recently.

- **Travel with a talking book.** These cover a whole host of topics and are available freely from local libraries. They can be a wonderful asset on boring journeys to work, or when stuck in inevitable traffic jams. You can even listen to them when undertaking your stress management programme on the exercise bike or the cross-country ski machine!

- **Rank the 'trainers' top 10 conferences'.** Conferences seem to be advertised around every corner and in every envelope that comes into the in-tray. Ask around, and get to know the conferences that consistently offer good programmes. Use conferences to find people to network with. You don't have to attend conferences to derive at least some benefit from them – for example, follow up reviews of conferences and obtain the proceedings of useful ones if they are published.

- **Gain an additional qualification.** We're never too old to learn! There are so many exciting courses around. Even those that don't lead to a qualification can do wonders to recharge our batteries, and to help us discover new, like-minded people.

Chapter 2

Group-based training

Group learning is about getting people to work together well, in carefully set-up learning environments. The human species has evolved on the basis of group learning. Learning from other people is the most instinctive and natural of all the learning contexts we experience, and starts from birth. Although learning can only be done by the learner, and can't be done 'to' the learner, the roles of other people in accelerating and modifying that learning are vitally important. Other people can enhance the quality of our learning, and can also damage it. But how best can we make use of collaborative learning within our training programmes?

This chapter is about how to facilitate group learning. We explore what we as facilitators can do to help trainees to work together effectively, as well as identifying the things that are most likely to go wrong in group contexts, to find tactics that add up to a strategy for enabling successful group learning to happen.

Group learning has never been as important as it now is. Yet we are still in a world where most teachers, educators and trainers are groomed in instruction rather than facilitation. This collection of practical suggestions is intended as further help in adjusting the balance towards facilitation rather than training.

The chapter starts by offering tips about **how to set groups up**. There are no second chances to get groups off to a good start. The first few minutes of the lifetime of any group can set precedents and establish the atmosphere in ways that are difficult or impossible to reverse. The suggestions in this section are intended as a starting-point from which to select and adapt the ideas that make most sense in the context of your own group learning contexts.

Consideration is then given to learners themselves. Group learning involves two main kinds of processes – learning processes and the processes of working with others. We take a closer look at learning processes, in general as well as in the particular context of collaborative learning. Suggestions are offered about ways of helping participants in groups to **learn-by-doing, learn through feedback** and **learn from their mistakes** too. All of this depends at least to some extent on **participants' levels of motivation** – how strongly they want to learn and how well they have ownership of their need to learn. The section also includes some discussion of **leadership** – and, equally important, **followership** – roles. This section ends with some suggestions on how to motivate group participants (and significant others in the overall picture of their learning), by expressing the **benefits that can arise from successful group learning**.

The chapter ends with ideas for **troubleshooting group learning**. There are things that trainees do – and things we ourselves do (or fail to do) as learning facilitators – that can damage group learning. For each identified trouble-cause, there are some tips on how to reduce it or avoid it.

1. Preparing participants for group work

Participants often feel that they are competing with each other, and need considerable encouragement to relax such feelings and begin to work collaboratively effectively. The following suggestions include a first look at several aspects of group learning, and are expanded upon in later parts of this book:

- **Help participants to understand the benefits of being able to work together in groups.** Explain to participants that there are real skills to be gained from group work tasks, and that the ability they will develop to contribute effectively to teams is important to employers.

- **Think about the different ways of forming groups.** These include forming groups randomly using alphabetical lists, forming groups on the basis of background, interest or ability, and allowing participants to choose their own group compositions. Each method has its own advantages and drawbacks. The best compromise is to rotate group membership and ensure that participants are not 'stuck' in the same group for too long, especially if it doesn't have a successful dynamic.

- **Think about the optimum group size for the group tasks you have in mind for participants.** The most suitable group size will differ according to the nature of the task. Pairs are ideal for some tasks, while for other kinds of group work threes, fours or fives are better. If the group is larger than about six, individuals tend to opt out or feel unable to make useful contributions to the group.

- **Give participants some training in group processes.** It can be useful to use an ice-breaker with the whole class, during which participants work for a short while in groups and are then briefed to analyse exactly what went well and what didn't work in the group episode, and to identify reasons for good and bad processes.

- **Structure participants' early attempts at group work.** It can be helpful to provide quite detailed lists of briefing instructions and ask each group to allocate the tasks among the members. This can be useful towards helping groups to work out their own directions and then to allocate them fairly in future group work.

- **Help participants to understand the reasons why group work can go wrong.** The more participants know about the things that work, and the hazards of interpersonal relationships and group dynamics, the better they can cope with the aspects of human nature that inevitably play their part in any kind of group situation.

- **Ensure that there are suitable places for participants to work in groups.** Arrange that there are places where participants can talk, argue and discuss things, and not just in whispers in an area that is supposed to be kept quiet. It is also useful if the group work venues are such that participants are not being observed or overheard by their trainers, or by any other groups, at least for some of the time they work together.

- **Consider using IT to facilitate group working.** If group members can use computers and the Internet to contact each other, they can continue their group work without face-to-face meetings. In fact, group members could be anywhere in the world and could work together across different time zones!

- **Give participants support and guidance when things go wrong.** It is not enough just to criticize a group where processes have failed; participants need advice on what to do to rectify the situation, and how to handle disagreements or conflicts successfully.

- **Be fair and firm with assessment.** Always ensure that individuals' contributions are fairly measured and assessed. Don't allow participants to think that they will all earn the same mark even if they have not all made equal contributions to the work of the group. Logs of meetings, breakdowns of who agreed to do what, and evidence of the contributions that each member brought to the group can all be prepared by participants, and can all lend themselves to assessment at the end of the group work.

- **Get participants to evaluate the effectiveness of their group work.** Including such an evaluation as an assessed element in each participant's work can cause all the members of a group to reflect on the processes involved in their working together, and deepen their learning about the processes involved in effective team working.

2. Ways of forming groups

There are many different ways in which you can create groups of trainees from a larger class. All have their own advantages and disadvantages, and it is probably best to use a mixture of methods so that trainees experience a healthy variety of group composition, and maximize the benefits of learning from and with each other:

- **Friendship groups.** Allowing trainees to arrange themselves into groups has the advantage that most groups feel a sense of ownership regarding their composition. However, there are often some participants 'left over' in the process, and they can feel alienated through not having been chosen by their peers. Friendship groups may also differ quite widely in ability level, as high-fliers choose to work with like-minded participants.

- **Geographical groups.** Simply putting participants into groups according to clusters as they are already sitting (or standing) in the larger group is one of the easiest and quickest ways of dividing a class into groups. This is likely to include some friendship groups in any case, but minimizes the embarrassment of some participants who might not have been selected in a friendship group. The ability distribution may, however, be skewed, as it is not unusual for the participants nearest the trainer to be rather higher in motivation compared to those in the most remote corner of the room.

- **Alphabetical (family-name) groups.** This is one of several random ways of allocating group membership. It is easy to achieve if you already have an alphabetical class list. However, it can happen that participants often find themselves in the same group, if several trainers use the same process of group selection. Also, when working with multicultural large classes, several participants from the same culture may have the same family name, and some groups may end up dominated by one culture, which may not be what you intended.

- **Other alphabetical groups.** For example, you can form groups on the basis of the last letter of participants' first names. This is likely to make a refreshing change from family-name alphabetical arrangements. Participants also get off to a good start in seeing each other's first names at the outset.

- **Number groups.** When participants are given a number (for example, on a class list), you can easily arrange for different combinations of groups for successive tasks, by selecting a variety of number permutations (including using a random number generator if you have one on your computer). Groups of four could be '1-4; 5-8...' for task 1; '1, 3, 5, 7; 2, 4, 6, 8...' for task 2; '1, 5, 9, 13...' and so on.

- **Class list rotating syndicates.** Suppose you had 24 participants in a class, and on an overhead printed their names down the transparency. You could draw separate columns down the overhead parallel to the names, and write in the letters opposite their names for successive group tasks, for example starting with 'A, A, A, A; B, B, B, B...', then 'A, B, C, D, E, F; A, B, C, D, E, F...' to form two successive, different sets of four-member groups, and then 'A, B, C, D; A, B, C, D...' for a new arrangement of six-member groups and so on.

- **Astrological groups.** When selecting group membership from a large class, it makes a change to organize the selection on the basis of calendar month of birth date. Similarly, 'star signs' could be used – but not all participants know when (for example) Gemini starts and finishes in the year. This method often leads to groups of somewhat different sizes, however, and you may have to engineer some transfers if equal group size is needed. Participants from some religions may also find the method bizarre or inappropriate.

- **Crossovers.** When you wish systematically to share the thinking of one group with that of another, you can ask one person from each group to move to another group. For example, you can ask the person with the earliest birthday in the year to move to the next group clockwise round the room, carrying forward the product or notes from the previous group and introducing the thinking behind that to the next group. The next exchange could be the person with the latest birthday, and so on. When doing this, you need to make sure that not too many participants end up stuck in the same physical position for too long.

- **Coded name labels.** Give out self-adhesive labels for participants to write their names, but with a series of codes already on the labels. A three-digit code of a Greek letter, normal letter and number can lead to the possibility of all participants finding themselves in three completely different groups for successive tasks. Six of each letter and number allows an overall group of 36 participants to split into different sixes three times, for example, with each participant working cumulatively with 17 other participants.

- **Performance-related groups.** Sometimes you may wish to set out to balance the ability range in each group, for example by including one high-flier and one low-flier in each group. The groups could then be constituted on the basis of the last marked assignment or test. Alternatively, it can be worth occasionally setting a task with an all-high-fliers group, an all-low-fliers group and the rest randomly in middle-ranking groups, but this (though appreciated by the high-fliers) can be divisive to overall morale.

- **Skills-based groups.** For some group tasks (especially fairly extended ones), it can be worthwhile to try to arrange that each group has at least one member with identified skills and competences (for example, doing a Web search, using a word-processing package, leading a presentation and so on). A short questionnaire can be issued to the whole class, asking participants to self-rate themselves on a series of skills, and groups can be constituted on the basis of these.

- **Hybrid groups.** You may wish to organize participants by ability or in learning teams, and may at the same time wish to help them avoid feeling that they are isolated from everyone they already know. In this case, you can ask each of them to nominate a partner they would like to work with, and then group the pairs as you feel most appropriate.

3. Group size considerations

Helping participants (and colleagues) to maximize the benefits of collaborative working depends quite significantly on choice of group size. This needs to be appropriate to the tasks involved, as well as to the nature of the individuals constituting the group. Each group size possibility brings its own advantages and disadvantages. The following comments and suggestions on particular group sizes may help you to plan the composition of groups:

- **Pairs.** It is usually relatively easy to group participants in twos – either by choosing the pairs yourself, random methods or friendship pairs. Advantages include a low probability of passenger behaviour, and the relative ease for a pair to arrange meeting schedules. Problems can occur when pairs fall out.

- **Couples.** In a class of participants, there may be some established couples. When they work together on collaborative work, the chances are that they will put a lot more into group work than ordinary pairs, not least because they are likely to spend more time and energy on the tasks involved. The risks include the possibility of the couple becoming destabilized, which can make further collaborative work much more difficult for them.

- **Threes.** Trios represent a very popular group size. The likelihood of passenger behaviours is quite low, and trios will often work well together, sharing out tasks appropriately. It is easier for trios to arrange meeting schedules than for larger groups. The most likely problem is for two of the participants to work together better than with the third, who can gradually (or suddenly) become, or feel, marginalized.

- **Fours.** This is still quite small as a group size. Passenger behaviour is possible, but less likely than in larger groups. When subdividing group tasks, it can be useful to split into pairs for some activities and single individuals for others. There are three different ways that a quartet can subdivide into pairs, adding variety to successive task distribution possibilities.

- **Fives.** The possibility of passenger behaviour begins to increase significantly now, and it becomes more important for the group to have a leader for each stage of its work. However, because of the odd number, there is usually the possibility of a casting vote when making decisions, rather than the group being stuck equally divided regarding a choice of action. There are many ways that a group of five can subdivide into twos and threes, allowing variety in the division of tasks among its members.

- **Sixes.** The possibility of passenger behaviour is yet more significant, and group leadership is more necessary. The group can, however, subdivide into threes or twos, in many different ways. It is now much more difficult to ensure equivalence of tasks for group members.

- **More than six.** Such groups are less likely to be suitable for group or team tasks, but can still be useful for discussion and debate, before splitting into smaller groups for action. Passengers may be able to avoid making real contributions to the work of the group, and can find themselves outcasts because of this.

- **Even larger groups.** When it is necessary to set up working groups that are much larger than six, the role of the leader needs to change considerably. A skilled facilitator is needed to get a large group collaborating well. It can be advantageous for the facilitator to become somewhat neutral, and to concentrate on achieving consensus rather than attempting to set the direction of the group.

- **Playing to strengths.** A group can reach targets faster and more efficiently by choosing to use the identified strengths of each of its members, when subdividing tasks and roles. The learning pay-off, however, is less than when playing to weaknesses (see below). When the overall product of the group is being assessed, groups tend to play to strengths.

- **Playing to weaknesses.** A group that chooses to play to identified weaknesses is one of the most effective ways to develop skills and attitudes of its members. The members of the group with identified strengths can set out to help colleagues develop themselves in these attributes, bringing increased learning pay-off to the work of the group. The work of the group is of course slower, and the product of the group may be less impressive than were it to play to strengths. When the group processes (rather than the overall product of the group work) contribute substantially to assessment, a group may choose to play to weaknesses, so that the processes are higher on its agenda, and better evidenced in its record of work.

4. Getting groups started

Once group work has gathered momentum, it is likely to be successful. The greatest challenge is sometimes to get that momentum going. The first few minutes can be crucial, and you will need all of your facilitation skills to minimize the risk of groups drifting aimlessly in these minutes. Take your pick from the following suggestions about getting group work going right from the start of a task:

- **Foster ownership of the task.** Wherever possible, try to arrange that the members of the whole group have thought of the issues to be addressed by small-group work. When possible, allow members to choose which group task they wish to engage in. When participants have chosen to do a task, they are more likely to attempt it wholeheartedly.
- **Start with a short group ice-breaker.** Before getting groups under way with the main task, it can be useful to give them a short, 'fun' ice-breaker so that each group's members get to know each other, relax and become confident to work with each other. See the next section for some ideas about ice-breakers.
- **Keep the beginning of the task short and simple.** To Einstein is attributed 'Everything should be made as simple as possible, but no simpler.' Make sure that the first stage of each group task is something that does not cause argument, and does not take any time to interpret. Once a group is under way, it is possible to make tasks much more challenging.
- **Don't rely only on oral briefings.** Oral briefings are useful, as they can add the emphasis of tone of voice, facial expression and body language. However, when only oral briefings are given for group learning tasks, it is often found that after a few minutes different groups are attempting quite different things.
- **Use printed briefings.** It is useful to put the overall briefing up on an overhead transparency or PowerPoint slide, but if then groups move away into different syndicate rooms, they can lose sight (and mind) of the exact briefing. It is worth having slips of paper containing exactly the same words as in the original briefing, which groups can take away with them.
- **Visit the groups in turn.** It can make a big difference to progress if you spend a couple of minutes just listening to what is happening in a group, chipping in gently with one or two useful suggestions, and then moving on. During such visits, you can also remind groups of the deadline for the next report-back stage.
- **Clarify the task when asked.** Sometimes, groups will ask you whether you mean one thing or another by the words in the briefing. It is often productive if you are able to reply, 'Either of these would be an interesting way of interpreting the task; you choose which interpretation you would prefer to address.' This legitimizes the group's discovery of ambiguity, and can increase the efforts they put into working out their chosen interpretation.

- **Have an early, brief report-back from groups on the first stage of their task.** This can help to set expectations that everyone will be required to be ready for later report-back stages at the times scheduled in the task briefing. Any group that finds itself unprepared for the initial report-back is likely to try to make sure that this position does not repeat itself.

- **Break down extended tasks into manageable elements.** Often, if the whole task is presented to groups as a single briefing, group members will get bogged down by the most difficult part of the overall task. This element might turn out to be much more straightforward if they have already done the earlier parts of the whole task.

- **Try to control the amount of time that groups spend on successive stages of each task.** It can be useful to introduce a sense of closure of each stage in turn, by getting groups to write down decisions or conclusions before moving on to the next stage in the overall task.

5. Ice-breakers: some ideas

There are countless descriptions of ice-breaking activities in books and articles on training. An ice-breaker is most needed when members of a group don't already know each other, and when the group is going to be together for some hours or days. Most ice-breakers have the main purpose of helping individuals get to know each other a little better. Here are some ideas to set you thinking about what the most appropriate ice-breakers could be for your own groups. Some ice-breakers can be very quick, acting as a curtain-raiser for the next activity. Others can be extended into larger-scale activities at the start of a major group project. Don't try to rush these:

- **Triumphs, traumas and trivia.** Ask everyone to think of one recent triumph in any area of their lives (which they are willing to share), ask them to think of a trauma (problem, disaster and so on) and ask them for something trivial – anything that may be interesting or funny. Then ask everyone in turn to share a sentence or so about each. Be aware that this activity often brings out a lot of deep feelings, so keep this for groups whose members need to know each other well, or already do so.

- **What's on top?** This can be a quick way of finding out where the members of a group are starting from. Ask participants to prepare a short statement (one sentence) about what is, for them, the most important thing on their mind at the time. This helps them to clear the ground, perhaps if they are (for example) worrying about a sick child, or a driving test, and enables them then to park such issues on one side, before getting down to the tasks to follow.

- **What's your name?** Ask everyone in turn to say their (preferred) name, why they were called this name and what they feel about it. This not only helps group members to learn each other's names, but also lets then learn a little about each other's backgrounds, views and so on. Bear in mind that some people don't actually like their names much, so make aliases acceptable.

- **Pack your suitcase.** Ask individuals to list 10 items that they would metaphorically pack into a suitcase if they were in a disaster scenario. Emphasize that these items wouldn't literally have to fit into a suitcase, and could include pets, but shouldn't include people. Ask them to mill around a large room, finding a couple of others who share at least two items from their list. This enables them to get into groups of three or four, with plenty to talk about, before you get them started on the actual group work.

- **What I like, and what I hate.** Ask everyone to identify something that they really like, and something they really loathe. Ask them then to introduce themselves to the rest of the group, naming each thing. This helps participants to remember each other's names, as well as to break down some of the barriers between them.

- **What do you really want?** Ask everyone to jot down what they particularly want from the session about to start, and to read it out in turn (or stick Post-its on a flipchart, and explain them). This can help group members (and facilitators) to find out where a group is starting from.

- **What do you already know about the topic?** Ask everyone to jot down, on a Post-it, the single most important thing that they already know about the topic that the group is about to explore. Give them a minute or so each to read out their ideas, or make an exhibition of them on a flipchart. This helps to establish ownership of useful ideas within the group, and can help facilitators to avoid telling participants things that they already know.

- **Draw a face.** Ask everyone to draw on a scrap of paper (or a Post-it) a cartoon 'face' showing how they feel at the time (or about the topic they're going to explore together). You may be surprised at how many 'smiley faces' and alternatives can be drawn.

- **Provide a picture, with small cartoon figures undertaking a range of activities.** Then ask participants to say which activity feels closest to the way they feel at the moment (for example, digging a hole for themselves, sitting at the top of a tree, on the outside looking in and so on). Use this as a basis for getting to know each other through small-group discussion.

- **Discover hidden depths.** Ask participants in pairs to tell each other 'one thing not many people know about me' that they are prepared to share with the group. Then ask participants to tell the group about their partner's 'hidden secret', such as ballroom dancing, famous friends, ability to build dry-stone walls or whatever. This is a particularly good exercise when introducing new members to a group who already know each other, or when a new leader joins a well-established group.

- **Make a junk sculpture.** Give groups of four or five participants materials such as newspaper, disposable cups, string, Sellotape, plastic straws and so on. Ask them to design and produce either the highest possible tower, a bridge between two chairs that would carry a toy car, or some other form of visible output. Ask them to think, while on task, about the group processes involved (who led, who actually did the work, who had little to contribute and so on). Ask them to unpack these thoughts and share in plenary their summarized conclusions about the group processes.

- **Develop verbal skills.** Ask participants in pairs to sit back to back. Give one of each pair a simple line drawing comprising squares, triangles, rectangles and circles. Without letting their partners see the original, ask those holding the drawings to describe what is on the page, using verbal instructions only, so that their partners can try to reproduce the original on a fresh sheet of paper. After a fixed time, let them compare the originals with the copies, and ask them to discuss what the task showed them about verbal communication. A similar task can also be designed, using plastic construction bricks.

- **Make a tableau.** Ask groups of about seven or eight participants to decide on a theme for their tableau (for example, the homecoming, the machine age, playtime) and ask them to compose a tableau using themselves as key elements. Ask each group in turn to 'present their tableau' to other groups, and then to discuss how they went about the task. Polaroid or digital photos of the tableaux can add to the fun, but do not use this activity if you feel that group members are likely to be sensitive about being touched by others.

- **Organize a treasure hunt.** Give each group a map of the training centre or campus, and a set of tasks to complete across the location. For example, task elements can include collecting information from a display area, checking out a reference item via the Internet, collecting prices for specific items from the catering outlet, drawing a room plan of a difficult-to-locate study area, and so on. Different groups should undertake the tasks in a different order, so that individual locations (and people) are not mobbed by hosts arriving at the same time. Give a time limit for the treasure hunt, and award prizes for all who complete on time. This activity helps participants to get to know each other and their learning environment at the same time.

- **Which of these are 'you'?** Give everyone a handout sheet containing (say) 20 statements about the topic to be explored. Ask participants to pick out the three that are most applicable to them. Then ask everyone in turn to disclose their top choice, asking the rest to show whether it was among their own choices.

- **Interview your neighbour.** Ask participants in pairs to interview each other for (say) three minutes, making notes of key points that they may wish to report back in summary of the interview. Then do a round asking everyone to introduce their neighbour to the rest of the group.

6. Helping participants to think about their learning

Becoming better at learning is one of the most important aims for anyone participating in education or training programmes. To help participants to be effective at learning in group situations, it is useful to help them to reappraise, if necessary, their thinking about how they learn best, so that they can take control of their learning processes consciously and develop them systematically. The following suggestions may help you to alert participants to how they learn well:

- **Remind participants how long they've been learning to learn.** Ask them to reflect on just how much they actually learnt during the first two or three years of life. Remind them that most of this learning they did more or less under their own steam, without any conscious thought about teaching, training or even learning. Remind them that they still own the brain that did all of this, and can still use it to learn vast amounts of new knowledge, skills and competences.

- **Ask participants about their learning in school and college.** They will have learnt large amounts of information, and will have forgotten most of this. Also, however, they will have learnt a great deal about how to take in knowledge and information, and will still have this skill.

- **Remind participants that much of their real learning will have occurred in group situations.** While they will remember setting out systematically to learn some things on their own, the majority of their learning will have happened with other people around them.

- **Remind participants that they never stop learning to learn.** Ask participants to think about some of the things that they have learnt only recently. Ask them *how* they learnt it. Ask them what they found out about themselves while learning it. Ask them who else was involved in one way or another during this learning.

- **Provide programmes for participants to learn about learning.** Training programmes can help participants to tune in to the power of their own minds. A good learning facilitator can help participants to gain control of the processes by which they learn most efficiently, and how best they can use other people to help them to learn well. Many people find it useful to explore how their minds work in the company of other people, and learn from each other's experiences.

- **Provide resources to help participants to learn about their own learning.** Not everyone is comfortable attending a training programme about learning to learn. Some participants fear that inadequacies or deficiencies may be exposed. Computer-based or print-based packages that help participants explore their own learning in the comfort of privacy may be more attractive to such participants. Such packages can also help participants to reflect on the differences between learning alone and learning with others.

- **Get participants asking themselves, 'What did I learn about myself when I learnt this?'** Learning to learn is closely connected with understanding one's own mind, and one's own preferences and choices. Suggest that people learn even more about themselves when they reflect on group interactions.

- **Get participants asking, 'What really worked when I learnt this?'** The chances are that the factors that made one element of learning successful will be transferable to their next element of learning. There are long words for this, such as 'metacognitive processing', but it's simply about helping participants to be looking inwards at what works for them when they learn, and what doesn't. In particular, it is useful to get people thinking about what works best for them in group situations, so that they can help to make learning groups more productive.

- **Get participants teasing out what slows their learning down.** The more we all know about how the brakes work, the better we can use them when we need them. In the context of group learning, it is helpful for all group members to be aware of the things that can interfere with effective collaborative learning, so that they can minimize such effects.

- **Legitimize learning-to-learn in the appraisal cycle.** If your organization uses regular appraisal or review interviews, include the agenda of what participants have learnt about their own learning since the last interview, and ask them to comment on how much of this learning was in group contexts.

- **Get individuals to articulate 'learning-to-learn' targets.** Target setting should not just be about gaining further knowledge, competences or skills, but should include setting out goals relating to the further development of a learning toolkit of approaches and methods. When individuals have defined their targets already, it is much quicker for a group to start off by finding out how many of these targets are congruent.

7. Group learning means learning-by-doing

'One must learn by doing the thing; though you think you know it, you have no certainty until you try' (Sophocles, 495–406 BC). A lot has been said (and written) about how human beings learn most effectively. Psychology is still a very young science! Some of the theories and models are more easily related to practice than others. It is worth asking participants about to learn in group contexts how they became good at something, comparing their answers with each other's and with the responses given below, and then following up the implications of participants' answers to these questions. This will help you to find out more about how to help participants to learn effectively together:

- **Think of something that you know you do well.** How did you become good at this? Most participants reply with words such as 'lots of practice', 'I learnt this by doing it' and 'I became good at this through trial and error.' Seeing the common ground in their answers to these questions can help participants to see how they can learn well collaboratively.

- **Avoid pigeon-holing participants into 'learning styles'.** While there is much to be gained in alerting people to their preferred ways of learning, there is a serious danger that they end up feeling that they are trapped in the styles that they seem to have adopted for themselves. Human beings are very versatile animals, and can change their approaches to learning much more easily than is sometimes suggested.

- **Cater for learning-by-doing by groups.** This is sometimes called 'experiential learning'. If you intend participants to become skilled, competent or knowledgeable about something, by far the fastest and most efficient way is to get them having a go, together, at whatever is involved. The task briefings for group learning are vitally important.

- **Reading is not necessarily doing.** Don't assume that if you provide participants with information (print-based or electronic) that they will automatically be able to learn from it, just by reading it. While reading may be a key step, it is essential that they do things to apply and try out what they read, every bit of the way along the learning curve, not just at the end of it.

- **Listening to experts is little to do with doing.** Lectures and training programmes often involve too much of trainees listening to experts. Knowledge and skills do not enter participants' minds through their ears. A small amount of listening needs to be followed quickly by an episode of learning-by-doing.

- **Listening to each other has a lot to do with effective group learning.** We all try to deal sensitively with situations involving people who are 'hard of hearing', but it takes much greater skill to deal with those who are 'hard of listening'. Alert group members to this issue.

- **Make it possible for participants to practise sufficiently.** Repetition counts a lot in learning-by-doing. Repetition helps participants to build up speed, and this helps them to develop confidence. When people have practised something several times, they become more competent and proficient at doing it, and have to think less about how to go about it successfully. Group learning is an ideal context for practice.

- **Make it OK to get things wrong at first.** Learning from one's mistakes is a healthy, natural and productive way of learning. The art of helping people to learn from their mistakes lies in setting the scene for them to make mistakes in a comfortable, blame-free environment. Design safe practice opportunities for learning, and try to ensure that learning groups avoid a blame culture.

- **Choose learning resources that keep learning active.** Interactive open or flexible learning packages can give participants the learning-by-doing practice that they need, whereas textbooks or manuals may merely provide them with the information that they need. Learning is about *using* and *applying* information, not just storing it up in one's memory. Resource-based group learning needs to be about working collaboratively with resources, not just allocating individual tasks to group members.

- **Retain some degree of the comfort of privacy in which to make mistakes.** Where people can have a go at something under conditions where no one else sees them get it wrong, they are better able to learn comfortably from mistakes. Learning resources that have self-assessment tasks and exercises make good use of this principle, and allow participants to find out about their own mistakes in the comfort of privacy, and to avoid making them when other people would notice them.

- **Think about the differences between training and teaching.** A good trainer gets trainees learning-by-doing, and facilitates their learning. Teachers tend to try to 'deliver' information, experience and wisdom, but there's not too much chance of it being received successfully. Turn your teachers into good trainers.

8. Group learning means learning through feedback

Learning is a natural human process. Human beings are creatures with feelings. Most human beings are social animals, and have feelings about each other as well as about anything they are learning. It is worth exploring how feelings affect the quality of learning. The following suggestions can help you to tease out the importance of the role of feedback in helping people who are learning together to develop positive feelings about their progress:

- **Legitimize feelings.** In some cultures, people tend to hide from their feelings, or to try not to let their feelings show. In group learning contexts, failing to confront and to work with human feelings can set up unnecessary barriers and defences, and can undermine the potential of the group. Make it all right to have 'feelings'. Often we have feelings about things that we have not yet rationalized, but the feelings are every bit as real as our logical thoughts. Encourage participants to share their feelings, and to make their feelings known. 'How do you feel about this?' is a very useful discussion starter.

- **Ask participants to identify something they *feel* good about.** This can be a positive attribute in their own make-up, or an aspect of their personality that they have a sense of pride in. It can also be something that they have learnt that they feel pride in. Don't embarrass them by asking them what it is, but instead then ask them the next question...

- **Ask them what's the evidence they have to support their positive feelings.** Most people are likely to reply along the following lines: 'other people's reactions', 'feedback from other people' or 'seeing the results'. Point out the importance of feedback from other participants in helping to develop positive feelings, and the consequent importance of feedback in successful group learning.

- **Get participants in pairs to think of a compliment about each other.** Then get them to say it to each other. They are quite likely to laugh. Ask them why they did so. They are likely to use words such as, 'I was embarrassed.' Point out that they have just done something that is likely to be directly contrary to their responses to the question in the preceding tip, and (in admittedly a pleasant way) that they nave in effect rejected some positive feedback and devalued the potential benefit to them of the feedback.

- **Suggest that participants try giving each other a compliment, this time thanking each other for the feedback.** Help them to see that by accepting the feedback rather than shrugging it off as unimportant, they have opened the door to further positive feedback and have used the feedback to improve their feelings about whatever might have been involved. Explain how the process of helping participants to accept positive feedback can contribute strongly to effective group learning.
- **Ask participants to think of some critical feedback about each other.** Then, if you dare, ask them to articulate this feedback and to thank each other for it. Point out how this is the other side of the picture, and that critical feedback can also be very valuable in group learning, but only if it is accepted graciously, and then analysed and considered. Also point out the dangers of shrugging off useful feedback by adopting a defensive stance and effectively closing the door to any further critical feedback being offered.
- **Ask participants to think of ways that they can deliberately seek out feedback from each other.** Remind them that it may be up to them as individuals to open the doors for both positive and critical feedback, and that the more feedback they solicit, the greater they can make rational and constructive use of it. Draw out the connections between a group climate or culture of free exchange of feedback, and cumulative effective learning.
- **Ask participants to reflect upon the various processes through which they can obtain feedback.** Help them to explore their own preferences for face-to-face feedback, written feedback, first-hand feedback and second-hand feedback.
- **Get participants thinking about how they can keep track of the feedback they receive, and their follow-up actions.** Help them to realize that feedback is only really useful if they turn it into action and development. Suggest ways of group members keeping a record of both positive and critical feedback, and linking this to action planning and further evaluation of their actions.
- **Help participants to work out how they can keep track of the effects of feedback that they give to others.** It can be valuable to follow up positive feedback that they have given, to make sure that the recipients have really allowed themselves to grow from it and take it fully on board.
- **Remind participants how much we all learn from other people's comments.** Ask them to think of something about themselves they feel good about, and then to jot down a few words about how they know they *feel* good about this. Their answers will often involve 'other people's comments or reactions' – in other words, feedback.

- **Give 'expert-witness' feedback when appropriate.** As you are the facilitator of a training event, participants will wish to have your views on important issues. But be careful that they don't regard you as an authority on everything!

- **Gather feedback yourself from participants.** Lead by example – show participants how you can be receptive to their feedback and accept it, whether positive or negative.

- **Persuade participants actively to seek feedback.** Help them to become better at asking leading questions so that other people will give them reactions and comments about their performance or achievements.

- **Help participants to use non-verbal feedback.** Alert them to the value of facial expressions and body language as means of gathering feedback. Also, don't forget to use these sources of feedback yourself as you facilitate their learning.

- **Build feedback sessions into your training events.** These can be sessions where participants not only tell you how they think the sessions are going but, more importantly, tell you how they are feeling about the training event, the topics and themselves.

9. Make the most of learning from mistakes

'An expert is a man who has made all the mistakes, which can be made, in a very narrow field' (Niels Bohr, physicist, 1885–1962). Learning from trial and error is a perfectly valid way to learn. Learning from mistakes is how most people learn many important things. Obviously, it is important to protect participants from any serious consequences of learning from their mistakes, but this is usually quite feasible to arrange. The following suggestions may help you to turn 'mistakes' into a valuable pathway towards successful group learning:

- **Ask participants to think of something that they are *not* good at.** Ask them to explore *why* they think that they have not become good at whatever it is. Ask them to work out what might have gone wrong in their learning for such an element of their life. Allow group members then to see how much they are likely to have in common regarding learning from things that went wrong.

- **Remind participants that problems are bonding opportunities.** When members of a group have a problem to solve, it can bring them closer together than if things had worked out without there ever having been any problems.

- **Help participants to sort out any 'self-blame' aspects.** People are very likely to take the blame on to themselves. They are quite likely to link their lack of success to personal deficiencies in their approaches to learning. Ask them to go a little further and work out whether what went wrong can be tracked down to their *actions* (or the lack of particular actions) rather than to their personalities or natures. It usually can!

- **Ask participants to think further about someone else being to blame.** Ask them to move beyond blaming particular people, and to look instead at the actions that these people took (or did not take). Help them to see how much better it is to concentrate on analysing actions than to think negatively about personalities, and to distance their thoughts about what people *are* from their analysis of what people *do*. Remind them that it is much easier to cause changes in what people *do* than in what people *are*. Confronting the concept of blame in this way can help groups to set out to avoid a blame culture.

- **Help to talk participants away from the concept of blame.** While it can be useful to pin down the causes of things that go wrong to *actions* or to lack of actions, it is best to distance these actions from the people who were involved.

- **Get participants to think about the real value of learning from things that went wrong.** Ask them to work out whether their learning from mistakes may have turned out to be deeper and more enduring than their learning from successes. Prompt participants to view things that go wrong as potentially valuable learning experiences. Suggest that this can be a key value in group learning, and can help *all* experiences to deliver their maximum benefit to everyone concerned.

- **Exploit the power of games and simulations.** These can provide safe circumstances for learning collaboratively important skills through trial and error. It is worth designing particular simulations to provide participants with the opportunity to practise their reactions to difficult real-life circumstances, so that when they meet them for real, they are better able to tackle them confidently.

- **Play with negative brainstorming.** Anticipate things that could go wrong in a learning group, and get participants to brainstorm as many ways as they can think of for things to go wrong more badly and more quickly. Often, doing the reverse may help to prevent things from going wrong in the first place, and the advance thinking may be useful when something is noticed that could lead to a problem.

- **Capture things that actually go wrong.** Turn these into case studies with which to train other people, so that the lessons learnt from unfortunate group happenings are translated more widely into the experience base available to learning groups.

- **Advocate the value of unconditional positive regard for people.** Even when it may be necessary in learning groups for members to be critical of each other's actions, it remains possible (and highly desirable) to value and approve of the people themselves. Use examples in your own experience about how well people respond to feeling valued, and how this can make fast and dramatic changes to their actions.

10. Helping participants to develop their motivation

One indicator of a healthy learning group is a general ethos where participants *want* to learn. This is sometimes called 'intrinsic motivation', but the straightforward word 'want' is more powerful. Incentives such as money or promotion can help participants to want to learn, but this is really 'extrinsic motivation', and it is even better if the want to learn comes from inside people. The following suggestions may help you to fuel group members' want to learn:

- **Get participants thinking about 'What's in it for me to make me learn this collaboratively?'** Group learning requires the investment of time and energy, and it would be unreasonable to expect participants to put their hearts into it unless they can see some reason to make it worth their while.
- **Ask participants who are already learning successfully collaboratively why it works for them.** You may be surprised by the rich diversity of motivations that fire different people. The more you find out about what keeps successfully motivated people learning in groups, the more you can spread some of their motivators to other people.
- **Get participants to upgrade their reasons for learning in groups.** Sometimes, participants are learning out of a vague sense that they should be doing so, or because the groups have been set up for them. Help them to find more tangible reasons for striving to learn well collaboratively, so that when the learning becomes more difficult, they have something stronger to keep them going.
- **Establish personal ownership for wanting to learn.** Different reasons for learning fire different people. It is best when everyone in a learning group feels a sense of ownership over their own rationale for learning in the group. Sometimes participants may have quite unique or even strange reasons for learning, but so long as their reasons work for them, this is fine.
- **Get participants to work out their own intended learning outcomes for group learning.** Help them to be specific and realistic. Help them to set sensible timescales for each learning outcome. Help them to structure their planned learning into manageable steps.
- **Suggest to participants that they make their intentions public.** Telling other participants about our planned learning outcomes can help us to achieve them – we prefer not to be found to have failed to live up to our plans. It can be particularly useful to let other members of a learning group in on planned personal targets and deadlines – they can then offer a significant driving force.
- **Channel group members' motivation into learning-by-doing.** If participants want to make sure that their learning is active, they are much less likely to fall into learning limbo, and will be watching the learning pay-off that they are deriving from each part of their learning processes.

- **Help group members to want to learn from feedback.** Feedback is a vital process for successful learning, and it is worth getting participants to develop a thirst for feedback, rather than just being content with using it when it happens to be received. Participants who are seeking out feedback are able to learn much more quickly, by adjusting their approach continuously rather than occasionally.

- **Encourage participants to want to digest what they learn.** Making sense of complex ideas does not always happen easily, but when participants are *trying*, together, to make sense of them it is more likely to happen. Remind participants, however, that some things take their own time to digest, and that it is often possible to be perfectly competent at doing something without yet being able to understand it.

- **Get participants in learning groups to look back at their successful learning.** Help them to celebrate their successes. Help them to explore *how* their learning was successful, and to capture what they have learnt about their own approaches, so that they can harness this to make their next episode of group learning even more successful.

11. Needing to learn can be enough

There are times when, with the best will in the world, it is hard to want to learn a particular thing. Then, some other kind of motivation may be needed. The following suggestions may help you to help participants discover alternative driving forces for their group learning:

- **Ask participants about what kept them going in the past.** Ask them to think of something they did not really want to learn, but kept on and did in fact learn successfully. Ask them, 'What kept you at it?' Many of the same driving forces may continue to be available for future learning. The remainder of this set of tips is based on some of the most common driving forces that can keep group members investing in their collaborative learning.

- **Necessity is the mother of much learning.** When participants can see *why* it would be useful for them to learn something, it can help them to invest the time and energy that it will take. Try to get group members thinking for themselves about how the learning in question will serve them well. When they have ownership of their need to learn something, they are much more likely to try to learn it.

- **Get group members to look to beyond their learning.** Learning can often provide a passport to opportunities that would otherwise be unavailable to them. Even when there may be no immediate intention to go for the opportunities, it is attractive to have the option.

- **Strong, positive human support fuels learning.** When participants have a lot of encouragement, they don't usually want to let down their sponsors or backers. Ideally, this strong support can come not only from fellow members of a learning group, but also from other people beyond the group.

- **Participants like to be praised and celebrated.** Many a participant has kept going, when the going got tough, by thinking ahead to the moment of glory, when success would be celebrated, perhaps with them being presented with an award or a degree. Remind group members of the rewards, especially when they are tackling difficult learning.

12. Harnessing participants' motivation

When people really want to learn something, it should not surprise us how successful they are in their learning. The more you can create or amplify your participants' want to learn, the more productive will be your training events:

- **Make your advance publicity attractive.** If the intended training outcomes look relevant and clear, and if the planned training event processes look well organized and contain variety, your participants should arrive with a healthy 'want' to learn.
- **Be likeable!** First impressions count a lot. If your participants like you, they will be much more likely to want to learn from you. Smiles go a long way. Also, don't create tension by showing any frustration you feel – for example, when a participant arrives late.
- **Find out what participants already want.** I've included a set of tips on identifying and harnessing participants' expectations elsewhere. When you know what they want, give them as much as you can of it – as well as other things you know they need!
- **Remember to address the question, 'Why?'** When participants are trying to master something new, they need to have good reasons for making an effort.
- **Work out 'What's in it for you is…'** Sometimes, a training programme is naturally geared to the needs of the company or organization; however, it always helps to identify benefits of becoming trained that relate to your individual participants. One way of approaching this is to ask them outright 'What's in it for you?' and to help them add each other's answers to their own.
- **Value participants' existing skills and knowledge.** Where possible, avoid telling them things they already know. Give *them* the credit for contributing ideas and information. When participants feel valued, they want to learn more.
- **Make it *their* training event, not yours.** Use their words on flipcharted summaries of discussions. Stick up the products of *their* group work for all to see.

- **Give participants choices.** For example, let them choose whether to do a task individually or in small groups – be prepared to let some work individually while others choose to work collaboratively. When possible, give a short menu of tasks that individuals and groups can choose from.
- **Be prepared to negotiate.** For example, in a residential course, an unplanned 'swimming or siesta' afternoon may be repaid amply by participants' increased productivity later in the course.
- **Be enthusiastic – but not threateningly so.** Enthusiasm is infectious, and can amplify the want to learn – as long as participants don't feel intimidated by your zeal.

13. Post-it exercise on how participants learn

The following sequence of activities can be very useful for alerting participants to the principal processes underpinning effective learning. It helps them to have ownership of these processes, and to make use of them consciously in their learning.

- **Issue four Post-its to everyone, and brief them as follows:** 'I'll be asking you four questions about your own learning. Each question is in two parts. Just think about the first part, and then write your answer to the second part on a Post-it. Just write a few words for this, in large letters, so it can be read easily when placed on view.' If you can, use Post-its of four different colours. This can help the resulting exhibition to be more attractive, and can draw out the trends more successfully.
- **How do you learn well?** 'Think of something you do well – something you're good at. It could be academic, professional, or a hobby or sport. Write on a Post-it a few words about *how* you came to do this successfully.'
- **Make exhibition one.** Ask participants to stick their Post-its on a flipchart (or wall, or door). Let them see for themselves the most common factors. Expect to draw out from these: practice, learning-by-doing, learning through trial and error.
- **What makes you feel good?** 'Think of something you like about yourself – something that gives you a sense of pride. Write a few words on the next Post-it about *why* you feel good about this – what's your evidence? What's the basis of this positive feeling?'
- **Make exhibition two.** Allow the group to see for themselves the most common factors, which are very likely to revolve around feedback, other people's comments or reactions, praise and seeing tangible results.

- **What stops you learning?** 'Think of something you're *not* good at. Write a few words on the next Post-it about what went wrong in learning this, and who (if anyone) was to blame.'

- **Make exhibition three.** All sorts of factors are likely to come up in this, but draw out examples of 'didn't want to learn it in the first place', 'breakdown in communication', 'didn't understand it' and 'poor teaching'.

- **What keeps your learning going?** 'Think of something you're good at, but didn't want to learn at the time. Write down on your final Post-it a few words about what kept you at it.'

- **Make exhibition four.** Many different factors are likely to arise here, but expect to be able to find motivators like 'needed it for what I wanted to do next', 'strong positive support from someone' and 'didn't want to let someone down'.

- **Sum up the five main factors underpinning successful learning.** From the combined Post-it collections, you should be able to draw out overriding confirmation for the following five factors:

  learning-by-doing including practice, repetition and learning from mistakes;
  learning from feedback – other people's reactions;
  wanting to learn – intrinsic motivation;
  needing to learn – extrinsic motivation;
  making sense of what has been learnt, 'digesting' it, increasing understanding of it.

14. Behaviours of a good leader

Much has been written about the qualities and attributes associated with effective leadership. It all, however, boils down to what leaders actually *do*. The following list of 'good leader behaviours' (not presented in any significant order here) can be used as a starting-point for groups working out who will lead and how. The list may also help you to reflect on how you exercise leadership in your training role:

- **A good leader:**

  doesn't confuse leadership with control, and invites participation from all group members;
  earns the respect of other group members;
  notices when someone feels an outsider, and tactfully draws that person in;
  shows no favouritism to individual group members, and treats them as having equal potential;

- gets to know the strengths and weaknesses of group members, and apportions workload accordingly;
- keeps an eye on group dynamics, and defuses conflict before it gets out of hand;
- is always there, particularly at the start of group meetings;
- knows when to keep quiet and let others take the initiative;
- makes space for lateral thinking and off-the-wall ideas that may seem weird at first, but may enrich later thinking;
- allows group members to have ownership of their own best ideas;
- has the tact to guide choices without leaving those whose ideas were rejected feeling let down;
- finds something of value to commend even in the least able group member, and is unstinting in praise for those who contribute a great deal;
- is sensitive to issues of gender, race and age, and makes sure that no one feels disadvantaged or excluded because of such factors;
- doesn't leap automatically to what seems the most obvious solution, but allows diverse views to be expressed and considered;
- has an active brief to ensure equivalence of contribution for group members, so that everyone feels they are being treated fairly;
- undertakes effective project planning, with built-in milestones and checkpoints, to ensure that the group's task is achieved;
- keeps referring back to the task brief, to ensure that work is productive and on target;
- sets SMART goals for the group, which are specific, measurable, achievable, realistic and time-specific;
- has an ever-watchful eye for the evidence that will show the group has achieved its intended objectives;
- manages group resources (including any project budget) carefully to ensure that targets are achieved;
- has contingency plans for when things go wrong;
- admits his or her own mistakes, and shares responsibility when these cause the group's work to go off target;
- doesn't automatically blame others when things go wrong (unless it is genuinely caused by destructive or lazy behaviour of others);
- knows how to delegate effectively, without making group members feel that they have been dumped on;
- puts as much energy into making sure that group process works, as into contributing towards generating the ultimate product;
- knows when to seek outside help, and when the group can continue autonomously;
- is methodical about ensuring that good records are kept of group meetings and delegated activities;
- ensures at the end of each group session that other participants are clear about when and where the next session will take place;
- clarifies for the group members exactly what each individual is expected to do prior to the next meeting;

makes sure that when the group process ends there is a sense of closure, with a final 'washing-up' meeting and, if appropriate, some kind of celebration.

15. Group learning includes following

Leadership is often discussed in the contexts of training and group work, but it can be argued that 'followership' is just as important. Group learning is an ideal context to help all kinds of people to develop and practise leadership skills, but there will always need to be more followers than leaders. We all know the problems that occur when too many people try to lead a group. The suggestions below may help you to ensure that your leaders have skilled followers. They may also help to optimize the learning that can be achieved through well-thought-out following:

- **Brief groups about the importance of followership.** It can be important to legitimize followership as a vital factor to underpin the success of group work.

- **Explain that followership should not be regarded as weakness.** When leadership is rotating between group members, they should regard their work when *not* leading as every bit as important as when they are directing the actions of the group.

- **Accept that followership requires well-developed skills and attributes.** For example, patience may be needed. When it takes a little time for the purpose or wisdom of a leadership decision to become apparent, it is sometimes harder to wait for this to happen than to jump in and try to steer the group or argue with the decision.

- **More followers than leaders are needed.** It is virtually impossible to have a successful group where all members are adopting leading stances at the same time. Though the credit for successful group work is often attributed to the leader, it is often the followers who actually own the success. It is more than good sense to acknowledge this right from the start of any group work situation.

- **Followership is a valuable, transferable key skill.** In all walks of life, people need to be followers at least for some of the time. It can be useful to employ group work situations to help people to develop skills that will make them good followers in other contexts of their lives and careers.

- **Good followership is not the same as being 'easily led'.** Being 'easily led' usually is taken to imply that people are led into doing things against their better judgement. Good followership is closer to being easily led when the direction of the task in hand coincides quite closely to individuals' own judgement.

- **Followership should not be blind obedience.** Encourage group members to think about how they are following, why they are following, for how long they are going to be content with following and what they are learning through following.
- **Suggest that group members experiment with a 'followership log'.** This could be private notes to themselves of their experiences of being led, but it is more important to make notes on their feelings as followers than to write down criticisms of the actions of the leaders. Whether the logs are treated as private or shared notes can be decided later by everyone involved in a group.
- **Legitimize followership notes as authentic evidence of the operation of a group.** Such notes can tell their own stories regarding the relative contributions of members of the group, and the group processes that worked well and those that worked badly. When it is known that followership records will count towards the evidence of achievement of a group, leadership itself is often done more sensitively and effectively.
- **Followership is vital training for leadership.** People who have been active, reflective followers can bring their experience of followership to bear on their future leadership activities. Having consciously reflected on the experience of following informs leadership approaches and makes people's own leadership easier for others to follow.
- **Good followership is partly about refraining from nit-picking.** When people have too strong a desire to promote their individuality, it often manifests itself in the form of expending energy in trying to achieve unimportant minor adjustments to the main processes going on in group work. Good followership involves adopting restraint about minor quibbles and saving interventions for those occasions where it is important not to follow without question.

16. Benefits of group learning

There are countless benefits associated with successful group learning. One way of identifying benefits is to address the question, 'What's in it for me?' There are several different target audiences for these benefits, including:

- trainees (and prospective trainees) themselves;
- trainers and learning facilitators;
- employers (or future employers) of trainees;
- training organizations and institutions.

The following benefits messages may give you a starting-point to 'sell' the concept of group learning to each of these respective target audiences. Each benefits message is intended to explain, to the people needing convincing about group learning, what's in it for them. The messages therefore are written directly to participants, trainers, employers and organizational managers, in the language that they are most likely to warm to.

17. Benefits for trainees themselves

■ **Group learning means that you:**

- **Have a more enjoyable, sociable learning experience.** You will already know that learning on your own can become tedious, and that other people can become distractions from your learning. With group learning, other people actually help your learning to be more successful.
- **Make new friends.** It's useful to have at least some of your friends from among the people studying alongside you. You never know when you may need their help, such as if you're ill and have to miss a session. Many participants find studying with friends so useful that they set up their own learning syndicates, and practice group learning by themselves, to their mutual advantage.
- **Get much more feedback on how your learning is going.** Working with fellow learners helps you to see where you stand. You can tell more easily whether you're ahead of the game, or lagging behind, in which case you can do something about it. Feedback from trainers is still valuable, of course, but you get a lot more feedback when you're working with people, rather than after you've done something and submitted it for assessment.
- **Receive better explanations of things you don't understand.** When fellow learners explain something to you, they are likely to be able to explain it better than someone who has understood it for a long time. Fellow learners will still remember exactly how the light dawned for them, and can help the light to dawn for you too.
- **Learn a lot by explaining things to fellow learners.** When you explain something to a fellow learner who doesn't yet understand it, it's actually you that gets most out of it. Putting something into words to help someone else understand it forces you to get a much better grip on it yourself, and your own learning becomes much deeper and more permanent.
- **Pick up useful skills that employers value.** Group learning is the ideal way to practise your oral communication skills, as well as develop your ability to work in teams. You can practise leadership roles, and (even more important sometimes) get better at letting other people lead the group as well.
- **Gather evidence for your CV.** Ideally, your CV should present a picture not just of a successful learner, but a well-rounded person who is more than able to get on with other people in a variety of different circumstances. Records of what you have achieved through group learning help to portray you as a successful person, not just a successful learner.

18. Benefits for trainers and learning facilitators

Group learning means that you:

- **Have some of the pressure taken away from you.** When learners do at least some of their studying collaboratively, it gives you time to plan what you are going to do next with them, or simply to take a break from leading the group.
- **Have participants who aren't so dependent upon you.** This means that when some of them are having problems getting to grips with an idea or topic, it isn't entirely up to you to help them to sort it out.
- **Have participants who are more likely to be successful.** When group learning is working well, it tends to help both the weaker participants and the stronger ones, and all of this means that your own standing as a successful facilitator is increased.
- **Spend much less time explaining the same things to different participants.** The things you're most often called upon to explain are likely to be ones that participants in groups can explain to each other. This helps them deepen their learning, more than if they were simply to have you, an expert, explain it to them.
- **Can devote your energies to the most important problems.** The things that a group of participants can't sort out for themselves are likely to be the ones where they really need your expertise. This means less time for you explaining routine or straightforward things to individuals.
- **Can learn more from your participants.** Individuals may be too shy or embarrassed to discuss matters arising from their learning easily with you, but in learning groups they can be much more open with each other. You'll often find on eavesdropping a group discussion that you're alerted to things that would not have come to light if learners were working on their own.
- **Can make your sessions with participants more interesting.** For example, getting different groups of participants to look at different sides of a story or scenario can make it more interesting for everyone when small groups come back to share their decisions or findings. Also, you'll have more opportunity to offer participants some choice about which aspects of a problem or issue their group will explore.
- **Find out more about your participants.** Watching participants working together always tells you important things about their individual personalities. This will often help you to understand them better as individuals, and to adjust your own approach to them. Sometimes, this additional information will be important, such as when you're asked to write a reference for a learner.
- **Find out more about your colleagues.** Discussing group learning is often easier than discussing lecturing or training, as group learning is in itself less of a private activity. This means that you may find colleagues more forthcoming about exchanging with you their experiences of working with groups than about other aspects of their work.

- **Can save a lot of time and energy when assessing.** For example, involving groups of participants in peer-assessing each other's work can deepen their own learning as well as save you time. It can be much quicker to moderate a batch of work that has already been peer-assessed than to assess it yourself from scratch.

19. Benefits for employers (or future employers) of trainees

■ **Group learning means that you:**

- **Are likely to have your staff trained in useful transferable skills.** People who have done a lot of group learning are likely to develop communication skills, interpersonal skills and confidence, all of which are valuable attributes in employees.
- **Are likely to be able to make better appointment decisions.** Group learning helps people to come across more naturally at interview, and this helps you to select the most suitable candidates.
- **Gain employees who will continue to work collaboratively.** Most jobs require at least some degree of team playing, and some jobs vitally depend on it. Experience in group learning means that your employees are not having to learn their team-playing skills from scratch.
- **Gain staff who are less dependent on supervision.** Good experience of group learning helps to develop participants' autonomy and self-reliance. This can make the task of supervising them or managing them a lot easier (unless, of course, you're really searching for people who will simply do what they're told to do).
- **Get staff who know themselves better.** One of the most significant benefits of group learning is that people find out a lot about their own behaviours and attitudes The better people know themselves, the better you can find out how to make good use of their talents.
- **Get staff who are better at problem solving and decision making.** Group learning is an ideal training ground for these skills, as participants can experiment with different approaches and learn from each other's solutions.

20. Benefits for training organizations and institutions

It is, of course, impossible to express benefits directly *to* an institution or organization, so this time the benefits are addressed to senior managers:

- **Group learning means that your organization:**

  Will be all the more successful because people work well together. Group learning helps people to be good collaborators rather than competitors. It's fine for *groups* to compete in a healthy way, but not so good for individuals to be watching their own backs all the time.
  (If you're a learning institution) will be less dependent on the expertise of your teachers or trainers. Group learning means that people can learn a lot from each other, and not so much depends on direct teaching or training.
  Will perform better when subjected to external scrutiny. Any external reviewer of teaching quality is likely to be more impressed by successful collaborative activities between participants than simply by watching straight teaching taking place. Such people are usually briefed to look for successful interaction as a basis for learning.
  Will turn out learners who are more employable. The reputation of any learning organization depends on the people who come from it. If your organization gets known as a source of people who can work well collaboratively as well as individually, your participants will be more sought after and, in turn, this can attract more prestige for the organization itself.

21. Group member behaviours that damage group work

The following section looks at a range of participant behaviours that can damage or even destroy group work. These are based on the experience of many facilitators. For each of these behaviours, some tactics are offered below as to how facilitators can reduce the effects on group work. If your groups are using computer communications for their work, some of these behaviours can still arise; you may need to monitor the communications to look out for problems.

Group members being late

Sometimes lateness is unavoidable, but even then it is seen as time-wasting for the group members who have managed to be punctual. Here are some approaches, from which facilitators can select, to reduce the problem:

- **Lead the group towards including an appropriate ground rule on punctuality.** If the group members feel a sense of ownership of such a ground rule, they are more likely to honour it.

- **Point out that punctuality is related to courtesy.** Remind group members that when one of them is late, it is an act of discourtesy to all the other participants who have been kept waiting, including the group facilitator if present.

- **Lead by example – don't be late yourself!** If the facilitator is late, it is not surprising that group members can fall into bad habits. Your own actions are seen as a reflection of how *you* value group learning.

- **Make the beginning of group sessions well worth being there for.** If group members realize that they are likely to miss something quite important in the early minutes of a group session, they are likely to try harder to be punctual.

- **Give out something useful at the start of the session.** For example, issue a handout setting the scene for the session, or return marked assignments straight away as the session starts.

- **Avoid queuing.** If the place where a group meeting is due to be held is frequently still occupied at the starting time for the group session, it can be worth rescheduling the group for 5 or 10 minutes later, so that a prompt, punctual start can be made then, without those who arrive early having to hang around.

Group members not turning up at all

This is one of the most common complaints made by facilitators. Participant non-attendance can have a serious effect on group work, and a variety of approaches (and incentives) can be used to address the problem, including those listed below:

- **Ensure that it really is worth turning up.** If group members are not getting a lot out of group sessions, they naturally value them less, and this can lead to the sessions being lower priority than they could have been.

- **Keep records of attendance.** Simply making notes of who's there and who's not gives the message that you're really expecting participants to turn up and join in. If keeping records isn't enough, see below...

- **Assess attendance.** For example, state that 10 per cent of the coursework element of a programme of study will be based solely on attendance. This is one way of making quite dramatic improvements in attendance at small-group sessions. However, the downside of this way of inducing participants to attend is that some group members may be there in body but not in spirit, and can undermine the success of the group work.

- **Issue something during each session.** Participants don't like to miss handouts, task briefings or the return of assessed work. It is important to make missed paperwork available to participants who could not have avoided missing a session, but don't be too ready to do so for those who have no real reason for absence.

- **Cover some syllabus elements only in small-group sessions.** When participants know that these elements will be assessed alongside those covered in lectures and so on, their willingness to attend the small-group sessions increases.

- **Don't cancel small-group sessions.** Participants are quick to pick up the message that something that has been cancelled could not have been too important in the first place. This attitude then spreads to other people's small-group sessions.

Group members not preparing

Group members can get far more out of small-group sessions if they have done at least some preparation for them. However, many teachers and facilitators complain that participants still arrive without having thought in advance about what the session will be covering. It is difficult to make *every* group member come prepared, and overzealous attempts to do this are likely to cause unprepared participants to decide not to come at all. The following suggestions may help you to strike a workable balance between getting well-prepared participants and frightening off the unprepared:

- **Help participants to structure their preparation.** For example, issuing an interactive handout for them to complete and bring to the forthcoming session is better than just asking them to 'Read Chapter 3 of Smith and Jones.' You could ask them to 'Research your own answers to the following seven questions using Chapter 3' instead, and leave spaces beneath each question for them to make notes as they read.

- **Don't fail to build on their preparations.** If group members go to the trouble of preparing for a session and then nothing is done with the work they have done, they are discouraged from preparing for the next session.

- **Try starting each session with a quick quiz.** Ask everyone one or two short, specific questions, and perhaps ask respondents themselves to nominate the recipient of your next question. This is a way of building on the preparation work that participants have done, and making sure that everyone is included, rather than just those who are most forthcoming when you ask questions.

- **Consider asking them to hand in their preparations sometimes.** This does not necessarily mean that you have to assess them, but you could sift through them while group members are busy with an activity, to gather a quick impression of who was taking preparation seriously. The fact that you do this occasionally will lead to participants wishing to avoid being found lacking again, and so to better levels of preparation.

- **Get them to peer-assess their preparations sometimes.** This has the advantage that they can find out how their own learning is going, compared to other participants'. It also helps them learn from feedback from each other, and the act of giving a fellow participant feedback is just as useful as receiving feedback.

Chatting inappropriately

Small-group sessions are indeed occasions when you want participants to talk to each other, and to learn by explaining things to each other. The dangers of inappropriate chatter can be reduced; the following suggestions may spark off your own ideas about how best to attempt this:

- **Don't assume all chatter is actually inappropriate.** Quite often, if you explore further *why* some group members are chatting, you will unearth good reasons, such as someone explaining something to someone who doesn't yet understand it, or helping someone who missed something to catch up.

- **Go closer to the participants who are chatting.** If the chatter is indeed inappropriate, they will usually stop. If it is something of value, you may wish to join in and help.

Departing early

Relatively few participants risk the embarrassment of leaving formal learning situations, such as presentations, before the end. With small-group work, there is a tendency for premature departure, or for participants to drop out at a natural break in the session, and fail to return for the continuation of the session. The following suggestions may help to minimize such behaviours:

- **Keep groups busy.** One of the most common causes of participants slipping away early from group sessions is that they think there is nothing important still to do. It may be better to give groups too much to do in a given time slot than too little, as long as you also ensure that there is time for 'unfinished business' in future meetings.

- **Be careful with breaks.** If your session is long enough to warrant a refreshment or comfort break, negotiate a firm restart time. Write this on a flipchart, overhead slide or whiteboard, so that everyone sees it as well as hears it. It can be more memorable to use 'odd' reconvening times, such as '10.43, please' rather than 'quarter to eleven, please'.

- **Make the last stages of group sessions particularly valuable to participants.** For example, help participants to summarize what they've been doing. Make debriefings as important as briefings. Sometimes give out a really useful handout right at the end.

Not doing their jobs

A lot of time can be wasted when group members go off on tangents to their intended tasks, or procrastinate about starting the next stage of their work. Work avoidance is human nature at least for some of the time for some people! The following approaches may help you to keep your group members on task:

- **Have clear task briefings in the first place.** It is usually better to have these in print, and for every participant to have a copy. Oral briefings are quickly forgotten, and are much more likely to lead to deviation from the intended tasks.

- **Make the first part of a group task relatively short and straightforward.** This can cause a group to gain momentum more quickly, and this can help to ensure that later, more complex tasks are started without undue procrastination.

- **Specify the learning outcomes clearly.** When participants know what they should be getting out of a particular activity, their engagement is enhanced.

- **Set structured tasks, with staged deadlines.** Most effort is expended as the deadline approaches, especially if participants will be seen to have slipped if their task is not completed by a deadline. Act as timekeeper if you are facilitating group work: gentle reminders such as 'six minutes to go, please' can cause a lot of work to be done.

Being disruptive

Group work is often damaged by one or more participants whose behaviour slows down or diverts the work of others. Disruption is more of a problem in small-group contexts than in formal lectures, for example, as it takes less courage to be disruptive in informal settings. Sometimes there is no easy solution for disruptive behaviour, but the following suggestions may help you to solve some such occurrences:

- **Check that it really is disruption.** If you're a passing spectator to different groups, you may happen to arrive at one particular group just at the moment when one of its members is expressing a strong feeling or arguing a point relatively forcefully. This may be fine with the other members of the group, and it gives the wrong message if the facilitator assumes the worst.

- **Find out why a person is being disruptive.** Sometimes there are identifiable reasons for such behaviour, for example when a group as a whole has become dysfunctional or when the task briefing is being interpreted in different ways by group members.

- **Watch for the same group member being disruptive repeatedly.** It is then usually worth talking to the person concerned, to find out why this is happening. If this does not improve the situation, it may be necessary to reconstitute the membership of groups for successive tasks, so that the disruptive element is fairly distributed across a wider range of participants, rather than a particular group becoming disadvantaged by recurring disruption.

Dominators

These can be among the most serious enemies of effective group learning. They need to be handled with considerable sensitivity, as their 'taking over' the work of a group may be well intentioned:

- **Get the group to reflect on how it is functioning.** For example, once in a while give them a relatively small task to do as a group, even an exercise that is primarily for light relief. Then when they have completed it, ask them to *think* through their answers to questions such as the following:

  - How well do you think you did that as a group?
  - Did someone take the lead and, if so, how did this come about?
  - Who said most?
  - Whose ideas are most strongly present in the solution to the task?
  - Did you always agree with the ideas being adopted by the group?
  - Was there anything you *thought* but didn't actually say?

  This can cause the group to reflect on any elements of domination that may have occurred, and can reduce the tendency for domination in future group activities.

- **Lead a discussion on the benefits and drawbacks of assertiveness.** Then ask group members to put into practice what they have learnt about assertiveness. This can lead to participants watching out for each other's assertive behaviours, and reduce the chance of a particular group member dominating for too long.

- **Confront the dominator privately.** For example, have a quiet word in a break or before the next group session. Explain that while you are pleased that the dominant group member has a lot to contribute, you would like other participants to have more opportunity to think for themselves.

- **Intervene in the work of the group.** Sometimes it is helpful to argue politely with a person who seems to be dominating, to alert other group members to the fact that they are perhaps being led off target by this person. Be careful, however, not to put down the dominator too much – there's little worse for group dynamics than a sullen ex-dominator!

Not listening to other group members' contributions

This can undermine the productivity and ethos of groups of all kinds, from participant group work to high-powered committees. There is no simple solution to the problem, but you can choose which of the following tactics could at least help with the problem:

- **Address the issue in a general briefing.** For example, present the saying, 'We all know how to try to help someone who is hard of hearing, but it's much harder to help someone who is hard of listening.'

- **Use an exercise.** For example, include a group task where at some stage everyone is asked to jot down or report back on the gist of what each other group member said about an issue. This can sometimes alert non-listeners to their problem.

- **Include an element of peer-assessment of contribution.** Clarify that listening well to others' views counts as an important element of contribution. When group members know that their contribution (including effective listening) is to be evaluated at some stage, they are likely to try (perhaps subconsciously) to make sure that they are aware of their own contribution to the group.

Know-all behaviour

This can lead to an extreme form of dominating behaviour. Some of the tactics suggested for domination continue to apply, but you might wish (or need) to go a little further. Consider these additional possibilities:

- **Let the group sort this out for themselves.** Sooner or later, most groups will turn on a know-all – usually at the first suitable occasion when the know-all proves to be wrong! However, the group dynamic can be seriously damaged if things go this far, and the know-all may not recover from the setback and may undermine further work of the group.

- **Have a quiet word with the know-all.** Point out, perhaps, that such behaviour can be interpreted as not just over-assertive, but also quite aggressive, by others. Sometimes it is enough that you have noticed the behaviour, and the person concerned will move quite comfortably into a less aggressive stance in the group.

- **Don't reward the know-all.** Even when this person is right, be careful to give credit to the group as a whole. This can help to remind a know-all that it is the product of the group you are interested in, not that of individual members.

22. Group facilitator behaviours that can damage group work

There are many ways in which group learning facilitators can damage group work. Sometimes facilitators know about the things they do that undermine the success of group work, but more often they simply are not aware that things could be improved. When facilitators know they have a bad habit, it is tempting simply to advise 'Stop doing it!' but this could lead to the reply 'Yes, but how?' The following list of facilitator 'faults' is rather longer than the participants' damaging behaviours already discussed, but it can be argued that facilitators are able to address their own shortcomings even more directly than they can help participants to address theirs. As before, each situation is annotated with some suggested tactics for eliminating or reducing the various kinds of damage that can occur.

Ignoring non-participants

It is tempting to ignore non-participants, hoping either that they will find their own way towards active participation, or that other group members will coax them out of inactivity. Alternatively, facilitators sometimes take the understandable view that 'if they don't join in, they won't get as much out of the group work, and that's really up to them to decide'. However, there are some straightforward steps from which facilitators may select, to make positive interventions to address the problem of non-participation as and when they see it:

- **Remind the whole group of the benefits of equal participation.** This is less embarrassing to the non-participants themselves, and can be sufficient to spur them into a greater degree of involvement.

- **Clarify the group learning briefing.** Place greater emphasis on the processes to be engaged in by the group, and less on the product that the group as a whole is to deliver.

- **Consider making the assessment of contribution to the work of the group more explicit.** When non-participants know that participation counts, they are more likely to join in.

- **Confront a non-participant directly.** This is best done tactfully, of course. The simple fact that the lack of participation was noticed is often enough to ensure that the situation does not arise again.

- **Try to find out if there is a good reason for non-participation.** There often is. Sometimes, for example, a non-participant may find it difficult to work with one or more particular people in a group situation, because of pre-existing disagreements between them. It may then be necessary to consider reconstituting the groups or to see whether a little 'group therapy' will sort out the problem.

- **Explore whether non-participation could be a cry for help.** The act of not joining in the work of a group can be a manifestation of something that is going badly for non-participants, possibly in an entirely different area of their learning or their lives in general.

- **Check, with care, whether the problem is with the work rather than the group.** Non-participation can sometimes arise because of the nature of the task, rather than being anything to do with the composition or behaviour of the group. For example, if the group learning task involves something to do with researching the consumption of alcoholic beverages, it is not impossible that someone whose religion forbids alcohol will resort to non-participation.

- **Check whether non-participation could be a reaction against the facilitator.** If someone does not like the way that *you* are organizing some group learning, that person's reaction could be not to join in.

Allowing domineering people

Domination has already been discussed under the bad habits that group members can engage in, and several tactics have already been suggested there. However, if you *allow* domination, it can be seen as your fault too. The following tactics may include remedies for situations where you notice group learning being undermined by domineering people:

- **Have a quiet word with the domineering person.** This is often enough to solve the problem. Having been seen to be too domineering is usually enough to make a domineering person stop and think.
- **Get the whole group to do a process review.** For example, give them a relatively straightforward collaborative task to do; then ask them all to review who contributed most, why this happened, whether this was fair and whether this is what they want to happen with the next (more important) group learning task.
- **Watch out for why participants dominate.** Sometimes, it's because they are more confident, and it's important not to damage this confidence. It can be better to acknowledge group members' confidence and experience, and gently suggest to them that they need to help others to develop the same, by being able to participate fully in the actions of the group.

Lack of preparation

We've already explored some of the tactics that can be used to solve the problem of lack of preparation by group members. This time, the issue is lack of preparation by the facilitator. The short answer is, of course, 'prepare'. However, the results of this preparation need to be visible to group members. The following approaches can help to ensure that group members can see that you are taking group work as seriously as you want them to do:

- **Make it obvious that you have prepared specially for the group session.** There are many ways of allowing your preparations to be visible, including:
  - coming armed with a handout relating to the particular occasion, rather than just any old handout;
  - having researched something that has just happened, ready to present to the group as material for them to work on;
  - arriving punctually or early, to avoid the impression you were delayed by getting your own act together ready for the session;
  - making sure that you have indeed done anything you promised to do at the last meeting of the group.
- **Keep records of group sessions, and have them with you.** You would not arrive to give a lecture or presentation without having your notes and resources with you, and doing the same for group sessions gives the message that you take such sessions just as seriously as larger-scale parts of your work.

Being too didactic or controlling

This is one of the most significant of the facilitator behaviours that can damage group learning, and experienced facilitators can be the most vulnerable! The quality of group learning is greatly enhanced when participants themselves have considerable control of the pace and direction of their own learning. The following suggestions may alert you to any danger you could be in:

- **Don't try to hurry group learning too much.** It is particularly tempting, when *you* know very well how to get the group to where it needs to be, to intervene and point out all the short cuts, tips and wrinkles. It is much better, however, for participants to find their own way to their goals, even when it takes somewhat longer to get there.

- **Hide your knowledge and wisdom sometimes.** In other words, allow group members to discover things for themselves, so that they have a strong sense of ownership of the result of their actions. As mentioned previously, this may be slower, but leads to better learning. Don't, however, make it show that you are withholding help or advice. When you feel that you may be giving this impression, it is worth declaring your rationale and explaining that it will be much better for your participants to think it out for themselves before you bring your own experience to their aid.

- **Allow participants to learn from mistakes.** Tempting as it is to try to stop participants from going along every blind alley, the learning pay-off from some blind alleys can be high. Help them *back* from the brick wall at the end of the blind alley, rather than trying to stop them finding out for themselves that there is a brick wall there.

- **Plan processes rather than outcomes.** It is well worth spending time organizing the ways that participants can work towards their goals, rather than mapping out in too much detail the things they are likely to experience on the way. The achievement of the group learning outcomes will be much more enduring when the group has ownership of the learning journey towards them.

- **Ask your participants.** Many of the things that can go wrong in training could have been avoided if feedback had been sought on the way. The best way of getting feedback is to ask for it, not just to wait for it. To get feedback on important things (such as whether or not you are being too didactic or controlling) there's no faster way than asking for exactly that.

- **Learn from selected colleagues.** Feedback from other group learning facilitators is always useful. However, it is worth going out of your way to seek feedback from colleagues who have a particular gift for making group learning productive, and being duly selective in the tactics you add to your own collection.

Poor interpersonal skills

This is a really difficult one! It is true, nevertheless, that some group learning situations are damaged by the lack of interpersonal skills of the facilitator. It's not very helpful to advise, 'Go and improve them'! The following list of suggestions may help, if you suspect that this problem could be yours:

- **Find out anyway.** If you imagine that interpersonal skills could be getting in the way of the success of group learning situations you are involved in, ask participants about it. The real problem is often far less daunting than the imagined one.

- **Work out the extent of the problem for yourself.** For example, get into the habit of taking a tape recorder into your group sessions, and playing extracts of the recordings back to yourself from time to time. Don't be secretive about the tape recorder – you need, technically, to have the permission of everyone else present to record their voices. Explain (for example) that you are researching the way your groups are functioning, and emphasize that you're not assessing group members' contributions. If you find tape recordings really useful, it could be worth your while to go further and have a camcorder in your sessions from time to time. Even the most experienced group learning facilitators continue to learn a great deal about their interpersonal skills by seeing themselves in action every now and then.

- **Use group processes that are less dependent on your interpersonal skills.** For example, if you're not too comfortable giving a presentation to a group, prepare a handout instead. Allow participants to explore the handout for themselves, and then initiate a group discussion of the matters arising.

- **Remind yourself that good interpersonal skills aren't everything.** You could, for example, be a leading expert in a field of study, and just not happen to be very skilled at helping groups of participants to explore it. Don't undervalue the strengths that you bring to group learning. Keep looking out for ways you can put your strengths to even more use, rather than worrying about particular weaknesses.

Lack of cultural sensitivity

This is a serious group-damaging behaviour. In fact, lack of cultural sensitivity can be more dangerous in small-group situations than in large-group ones. It is also one of the hardest areas to find out about. Few participants are brave enough to challenge a group learning facilitator with this crime! It is useful for even the most skilled group learning facilitators to undertake a regular self-audit on this issue. The following tactics can help:

- **Read about it.** There is no shortage of published material on equal opportunities, cultural issues and so on. Sometimes when reading this literature, one can be surprised by the thought, 'But sometimes I do this too!'

- **Watch other group learning facilitators, with this agenda in mind.** See what they do to avoid the pitfalls, and also notice when they fall into them. Work out alternative approaches that could have circumvented such problems.

- **Don't make assumptions.** It is particularly dangerous to bring to your role of learning facilitator any preconceptions about the different members of your groups, such as those based on gender, age, ethnic group, perceived social status and any other area where assumptions may be unwise and unfounded. Treating people with equal respect is an important part of acknowledging and responding to individual difference.

- **Talk to group members individually.** When you are working with a mixed group, for example, it is in your informal, individual conversations with its members that you are most likely to be alerted to anything that could be offending individuals' cultural or personal perspectives.

- **Ask directly sometimes.** It is important to pick your times wisely, and to select participants who you believe will be willing to be frank with you if necessary. Rather than asking *too* directly (for example, 'What do I do that could be culturally insensitive?'), it can be useful to lead in more gently (for example, 'What sorts of learning experiences do you find can be damaged by people who are not sensitive enough culturally?', 'How does this happen usually?' and so on).

Favouring clones!

This happens more often than most people imagine. It is noticed straight away by everyone *else* in the group! It can go entirely unnoticed by the perpetrator. It is, of course, perfectly human to have 'warmer' or 'more empathetic' feelings and attitudes towards someone who is more like yourself than other people, or who shares significant attitudes, values and even 'looks'. In particular, teachers of any sort can be flattered and encouraged when they recognize a 'disciple' among a group of people. If you think you could be in danger of indulging in this particular behaviour, think about which of the following approaches might be most helpful to you:

- **Go clone detecting!** From time to time, think around the types of people who make up learning groups you work with, and test out whether any of them are more like you are (and particularly more like you *were*) than the others. Then watch out for any signs that you could be treating them differently (even if only slightly).

- **Don't overcompensate.** It is just as dangerous to be too *hard* on clones as to favour them. Those concerned may have no idea at all why you are being harder on them than on other people. The people you might (consciously or subconsciously) regard as clones may have no inkling that they are in this special position! Subconsciously, you could be putting them under the same sort of pressures as you put yourself under long ago, and exacting of them the standards you applied to yourself.

Talking too much

This is one of the most common of all group learning facilitator bad habits. However, it is just about the easiest to do something about. The following suggestions should contain all you need to rectify this problem, if you have it:

- **Remind yourself that most learning happens by doing, rather than listening.** Concentrate on what your participants themselves do during group sessions, rather than on what you do.

- **Don't allow yourself to be tempted into filling every silence.** In any group process, short episodes of silence are necessary components, space for thinking. When you happen to be expert enough to step in with your thoughts, before other people have had time to put theirs together, it is all too easy to be the one to break the silence. What seems to you like a long silence seems much shorter to people who are busily thinking. Let them think, and then help them to put their thoughts into words. When they have ownership of putting together ideas and concepts, their learning is much deeper and more enduring.

- **Only say *some* of the things you think.** Being the expert in the group (you probably are!), you're likely to know more than anyone else about the topic being addressed. You don't have to reveal all of your knowledge, just some of it. Don't fall into the trap of feeling you have to defend your expertise, or that you need to justify your position.

- **Don't let *them* let *you* talk too much!** It's easier for group members to sit and listen to you than to get on with their own thinking. Sometimes, they can encourage you to fill all of the time, and opt for an easy life.

- **Present some of your thoughts (particularly longer ones) in print.** Use handouts to input information to the group, but not at the expense of getting group members to think for themselves. You can convey far more information in five minutes through a handout than you could in five minutes' worth of talking. People can read much faster than you can speak, and in any case they can read a handout again and again. They can't replay you speaking (unless they're recording it – and, even then, would they *really* replay it all again?).

Intimidating participants

Not surprisingly, this can damage group learning. It does, however, often come as a surprise to group learning facilitators that they can be seen as intimidating. The following suggestions may alert you to some of the circumstances where this can happen, despite your good intentions:

- **Wear your expertise and wisdom lightly.** You may have more than you think. To participants who are new to a subject, your expertise may seem quite formidable.

- **Be aware of your other roles.** For example, you may be assessing the work of group members, now or later. This in its own right can cause a certain degree of intimidation, especially if group members imagine that you're assessing their every word – or that every second of silence while they're thinking how to respond to one of your questions is being added up.

Putting participants down

Few group facilitators would deliberately set out to put participants down. Yet many participants feel that this is exactly what sometimes happens to them in learning groups. The following suggestions may alert you to ways that your participants could feel put down:

- **Take care not to 'dump on ideas'.** This is how participants sometimes perceive the actions of facilitators. You may know, from your experience, that a particular idea will not lead the group to a successful outcome, but it is important not to make the person who thought of the idea feel that it is being ridiculed or dismissed lightly.

- **Watch your language, particularly that concerned with assessment or judgement.** For example, the word 'satisfactory' is hardly ever pleasing to people whose work or ideas are labelled with the word. Nor is 'adequate'. Obviously, 'poor' and 'weak' are negative, damaging words. Such words are sometimes described as 'final language', and there is no way of recovering from the harm they can do to participants' feelings and motivation. 'Fair' is almost as bad. 'Excellent' is also final language, but in a much less damaging way. Many of these judgement words are most dangerous when written rather than spoken. For example, you could say 'very satisfactory' in an entirely positive tone whereas, when written, the reader's interpretation could be 'far less than good'.

- **Remember that *your* words may be taken more seriously than you expect by participants.** Sometimes, they will react much more acutely to things that you, as a group facilitator, say than they would have done if the same words were used by fellow group members. Therefore, for example, if you happened to repeat something critical that one of them had said about another's ideas, it would be your words that produced the most damage. You are likely to be regarded as an authority, even if you don't feel yourself to be one.

- **Don't forget body language.** An exasperated sign, a grimace and a sigh are each a powerful 'putting-down' message of one sort or another. Your body language is observed quite acutely by members of your groups. Body language that is positive causes no problems; it is the critical body language that gets noticed.

Failing to invite equal contributions

Many parts of this book address the issue of facilitating group work in an equitable way. In the context of damaging facilitator behaviours, it is important to remember that participants themselves often include in their feedback notes failure to have the chance to make equal contributions to group processes. Sometimes this may indeed have been their own fault, but nevertheless their impression is often that the issue should have been addressed directly by the facilitator. Here are some reminders about a few of the processes whereby you can try to ensure that participants do not feel that they have been left out:

- **Use Post-its to allow group brainstorming.** This helps to ensure that it is not just the participants who speak out most readily who are seen to be the originators of ideas.

- **When taking oral comments from members of a group, give everyone the same opportunity.** For example, go round the whole group, giving the same time to each contribution. Next time, start with a different person, and so on.

- **Set out to give group members equal 'air time'.** This can mean gently stemming the flow from those who have too much to say, and equally gently encouraging the flow from those who are more reticent.

- **Use pairs sometimes to discuss things before they report to the whole group.** This can help to increase the confidence of the more reticent members of a group. When they have already sorted out their ideas in pairs, they often find it much easier to report back to a larger group.

- **Explore the causes of persistent 'passenger' behaviours.** Sometimes the cause can be pure laziness, but quite often there are other reasons why participants may find it hard to contribute equally to a group setting. Sometimes, once these reasons are identified, you'll be able to find ways of making it easier for the people affected to input equitably to the group. For example, some participants prefer to be scribes rather than spokespersons, and so on.

- **Allocate different tasks to different group members.** When everyone has a facet of the overall task to address, it becomes easier to achieve equality of contribution than when everyone has been thinking about exactly the same thing.

Lack of clear objectives

In education and training it is increasingly accepted that objectives, or intended learning outcomes, have a vital part to play in ensuring that learning takes place successfully. This is no less true of small-group work than of lectures. Moreover, the *absence* of clear objectives for group work is only too readily taken by participants as a signal that the group work can't really be an important part of their overall learning. The following suggestions may help you to put objectives or statements of intended learning outcomes to good use in facilitating group learning:

- **Work out exactly what you intend each group learning session to achieve.** It is best to express this in terms of what you intend participants themselves to gain from the session. Make sure that the learning outcomes are expressed in language that participants can readily understand, so that they see very clearly what they are intended to achieve.

- **Publish the learning outcomes or objectives in advance.** This allows participants to see where any particular group session fits in to the overall picture of their learning. It also helps them to see that their group learning counts towards their assessment in due course.

- **Maintain some flexibility.** For example, it is useful to have some further objectives for any group session, designed to cover matters arising from previous sessions or to address participants' questions and needs as identified on an ongoing basis through a programme of study. These additional objectives can be added to the original intentions for the session, and re-prioritized at the start of the session if necessary.

- **Don't just write the objectives or outcomes – use them!** State them (or display them on a slide or issue them on a handout) at the start of each and every group session, even if the session is continuing to address a list of intended outcomes that were discussed at previous sessions.

- **Assist participants in creating their own objectives.** From time to time ask them, 'What do *you* need to gain from the coming group session?', for example giving them each a Post-it on which to jot down their replies. Then stick the Post-its on a chart (or wall, door or white-board), and ask the group to shuffle them into an order of priority or to group them into overlapping clusters.

Chapter 3

Resource-based training

Rationale, benefits and choices

Creating flexible learning materials

This chapter is about getting trainees to learn by themselves, using learning resources of various kinds. It's about training using open or flexible learning, allowing trainees to tackle at least some parts of their learning at their own pace, in their own way, and when and where they choose to learn. The tips in this chapter are selected and adapted from *500 Tips on Open and Flexible Learning* (Phil Race, 1998, Kogan Page).

The chapter looks first at the big picture of open and flexible learning, and **how it can be adapted** for appropriate elements of training. Suggestions are given about the **benefits that flexible learning can deliver**, addressed respectively to trainees themselves, trainers, employers and training providers. There follows detailed advice to help you decide **how to choose off-the-shelf flexible learning materials** for your trainees, if indeed anything suitable already exists, and **how to go about adapting existing materials** that are not yet entirely suitable.

The remaining part of the chapter is about **creating your own open or flexible training materials**, should this prove to be the most sensible way forward with your own training area and your own subject material.

1. What are the characteristics of resource-based learning?

- **Resource-based learning can be considered to be open or flexible in nature.** Flexible learning packages are learning resources in their own right, whether they are print-based, computer-based or multimedia in design. The learning that happens in resource-based learning usually opens up some freedom of time and pace, if not always that of place.

- **Resource-based learning suggests that the subject content is provided to trainees through materials rather than via teaching.** The term 'resource-based' is often used as an opposite to 'taught'. Having said that, good practice in face-to-face teaching and learning often depends on trainees working with learning resources during sessions, as well as outside formal contact time.

- **Learning resources can be quite traditional in nature.** With suitable study guides or briefing notes, resources such as textbooks, videos, audiotapes and journals can all be part of resource-based learning programmes, either when located in learning resources centres or libraries, or when issued to or borrowed by trainees.

- **Learning resources can also be based on new technologies.** Large amounts of material can be stored on media such as CD ROMs. You could assemble suitable material and make copies available to your trainees (but be aware of copyright issues). You could also direct your trainees to suitable World Wide Web sites. You would need to make sure the information is still available at the Web addresses you give and to be aware that electronic information is easily copied into people's work.

- **Resource-based learning usually accommodates a considerable amount of learning-by-doing.** Resources should provide trainees with opportunities to practise, and to learn by making mistakes in the relative comfort of privacy. Resource-based learning also depends on trainees being provided with feedback on how their learning is going. This feedback can be provided by tutors, or by interactive elements within the learning resources, where feedback to trainees may be provided in print or on-screen.

- **Clearly expressed learning outcomes are important in all kinds of resource-based learning.** There may not be tutor support available at all times, and tone of voice, emphasis of tone, and facial expression may not be available to help trainees work out exactly what it is they are expected to become able to do as they work with the resource materials. This means that the wording of the intended learning outcomes is crucial.

- **Assessment criteria need to be clearly stated.** Trainees take important cues from the expected performance criteria. These can indicate to them the kinds (and extent) of the evidence they should accumulate to demonstrate that they have learnt successfully from resource-based learning materials.

- **Resource-based learning often needs appropriate face-to-face debriefing.** It can be very worth while to reserve a whole-class session to review an element of resource-based learning, and to answer trainees' questions about the topics covered in this way. Such group sessions can also be used to gain useful feedback about the strengths and weaknesses of the materials themselves.

2. What sorts of flexibility are there?

Whether we think about flexible learning as used in distance learning programmes, or for particular elements within training programmes, there are several different aspects to flexibility. The following descriptions may alert you to which aspects of flexibility you particularly want to address in your own provision:

- **Flexibility can mean freedom of start dates.** Many flexible learning programmes are described as 'roll-on, roll-off' systems. The key feature here is that trainees can start more or less at any time of the year, and finish when they are ready. There may be difficulties incorporating such an approach when flexible learning is being used for elements within college-based programmes, not least that most educational institutions don't operate on a 52-week year.

- **Flexibility can mean freedom of entry levels.** It is important to spell out clearly any prerequisite knowledge or skills, so that trainees can tell whether they are able to progress on to working with each package.

- **Flexibility can give trainees some choice about how much support they use.** Tutor support may well be available to all of the trainees on a programme, but some may make little use of this and still succeed without difficulty. Some prefer to work on their own, and rise well to the challenge of sorting out their own problems. Those trainees who most need tutor support can then be accommodated.

- **Flexibility can mean freedom of pace.** This is one of the most attractive hallmarks of many flexible learning programmes. Especially when studied by mature, part-time trainees, freedom of pace may be an essential feature, allowing them to fit their learning into busy or unpredictable work patterns.

- **Flexibility can allow freedom of location and learning environment.** Flexible learning can allow trainees to continue their studies while away from the institution on work placements, on vacation or even when confined to home by temporary illness. Trainees can have more choice about whether they work in a library or learning resource centre, or wherever they feel comfortable.

- **Flexibility can allow trainees freedom to determine how important a part information technology will play in their studies.** While sometimes it may be deemed necessary to involve trainees in using communications and information technology, for some trainees this can be a significant hurdle. With flexible learning, it can usually be arranged that there is more than one way of achieving most of the outcomes successfully.

- **Flexibility can mean freedom of end-points.** In some systems, trainees can go in for assessments (tutor-marked, computer-marked and even formal exams) more or less when they feel that they are ready for assessment. This can allow high-fliers to try the assessments without spending much time studying the materials concerned, or trainees who find the material more demanding to wait until they are confident that they can succeed with the assessed components.

- **Flexibility can allow trainees to work collaboratively or on their own.** Some trainees may not have much opportunity to work collaboratively, for example isolated trainees on distance learning programmes. For them, it may however be possible to use electronic communication to allow them to make efficient (and cheap) contact with each other. For college-based trainees working through flexible learning elements alongside class-based ones, it is worthwhile to encourage them to collaborate, as they can often give each other useful feedback and help each other to make sense of the more difficult ideas and concepts.

3. What lends itself to flexible learning?

It is worthwhile to think about which parts of the curriculum best lend themselves to an open or flexible approach. It is useful to start your flexible learning writing with such parts, and perhaps better still to first experiment with adapting existing resources covering such curriculum areas towards a flexible learning format. The following suggestions show that such starting-points can be based on several different considerations, and are often linked to ways that flexible learning can augment face-to-face training programmes:

- **Important background material.** In face-to-face programmes, a considerable amount of time is often spent near the start getting everyone up to speed with essential knowledge or skills, to the annoyance of the trainees who already have these. Making such information the basis of a flexible learning package can allow those people who need to cover this material before the whole group starts, to do so in their own time and at their own pace, without holding up the rest of the group.

- **'Need to know before...' material.** For example, when different trainees will be attempting different practical exercises at the same time, it could take far too long to cover all the prerequisite material with the whole group before introducing practical work. Designing separate, short flexible learning elements to pave the way to each practical exercise can allow these to be issued to trainees so that the practical work can be started much earlier.

- **'Remedial material'.** In many courses, there are problem topics that can hold up a whole class while the difficulties are addressed by trainers or tutors. This can lead to time being wasted, particularly by those trainees for whom there are no problems with the parts concerned. The availability of flexible learning packages addressing such areas can allow such packages to be used only by those trainees who need them, in their own time, so that the progress of the whole group is not impeded. Don't, of course, use a term as insulting as 'remedial' in the title of your package!

- **'Nice-to-know' material.** While 'need-to-know' material is more important, flexible learning elements can be particularly useful to address 'nice-to-know' material, and giving such material to trainees without spending too much face-to-face time on it. This allows contact time to be saved for helping trainees with the really important material, and for addressing their problems.

- **Much-repeated material.** If you find yourself often covering the same ground, perhaps with different groups of trainees in different contexts or courses, it can be worth thinking about packaging up such material in flexible learning formats. If you yourself get bored with things you often teach, you're not going to pass on much enthusiasm for these topics to your trainees, and it can be mutually beneficial to invest your energy into creating an alternative flexible learning pathway to cover such material.

- **Material that is best 'learnt-by-doing'.** Flexible learning is based on trainees answering questions, and doing tasks and exercises. Therefore it can be a useful starting-point to base a flexible learning package on the sorts of activities that you may already be giving your face-to-face trainees. Standard assignments and activities already in use in traditionally delivered courses and programmes may be adapted quite easily for flexible learning usage, and have the strong benefit that they are already tried and tested elements of the curriculum.

- **Material where trainees need individual feedback on their progress.** A vital element of flexible learning is the feedback that trainees receive when they have attempted to answer questions, or had a try at exercises and activities. The kinds of feedback that you may already give your face-to-face trainees can be packaged up into flexible learning materials.

- **Material that you don't like to teach.** It can be tempting to turn such elements of the curriculum into flexible learning materials, where trainees can work on them individually (or in untutored groups), and using face-to-face time more efficiently to address any problems that trainees find, rather than to teach them from scratch.

- **Material that trainees find hard to grasp first time.** In most subjects there are such areas. Developing flexible learning materials addressing these means that trainees can go through them on their own, as many times as they need. Effectively, the flexible learning material becomes their teacher. Trainees can then work through such materials at their own pace, and can practise with the learning materials until they master them.

- **Material that may be needed later, at short notice.** It is often the case that some topics are only really needed by trainees quite some time after they may have been covered in a course or programme. When such materials are turned into flexible learning formats, trainees can polish up their grip on the topics involved just when they need to.

4. Which trainees are particularly helped?

All sorts of people use flexible learning in distance learning mode. The following categories of trainees are included as those who can be particularly helped in different ways. Many parallels may also be drawn to the use of flexible learning elements in college-based programmes, where similar benefits can be delivered to a variety of constituencies of the trainee population:

- **High-fliers.** Very able trainees are often frustrated or bored by traditional class-based programmes, as the pace is normally made to suit the average trainee and may be much too slow for high-fliers. With flexible learning, they can speed through the parts they already know or the topics they find easy and straightforward. They can work through a package concentrating only on the parts that are new to them or that they find sufficiently challenging.

- **Low-fliers.** The least-able trainees in a group are often disadvantaged when the pace of delivery of traditional programmes is too fast for them. They can be embarrassed in class situations by being seen not to know things, or not to be able to do tasks that their fellow trainees have no difficulty with. With flexible learning, they can take their time and practise until they have mastered things. They have the opportunity to spend much longer than other trainees may take.

- **Anxious trainees.** Some people are easily embarrassed if they get things wrong, especially when they are seen to do so. With flexible learning, they have the opportunity to learn from making mistakes, in the comfort of privacy, as they try self-assessment questions and exercises, and learn from the feedback responses in an interactive learning package.

- **Trainees with a particular block.** Trainees who have a particular problem with an important component of a course can benefit from flexible learning, in that they can work as often as they wish through materials designed to give them practice in the topic concerned. It can be useful to incorporate self-assessment exercises, with detailed feedback specially included for those trainees who have problems with the topic.

- **Trainees needing to make up an identified shortfall.** For example, in science and engineering programmes, it is often found quite suddenly that some trainees in a group have not got particular maths skills. Rather than hold up the progress of a whole class, self-study components can be issued to those trainees who need to get up to speed in the areas involved. When the trainees have a sense of ownership of the need that these materials will address, they make best use of them.

- **People learning in a second language.** In class situations, such trainees are disadvantaged in that they may be spending much of their energy simply making sense of the words, with little time left to make sense of the ideas and concepts. With flexible learning materials, they can work through them at their own pace, with the aid of a dictionary, or with the help of trainees already fluent in the language in which the materials are written.

- **Part-time trainees.** These are often people with many competing pressures on their time, or with irregular opportunities for studying, perhaps because of shift work, work away from home or uneven demands being normal in their jobs. Flexible learning materials allow them to manage their studying effectively, and to make the most of those periods when they have more time to study.

- **People who don't like being taught.** Surprisingly, such people are found in college-based courses, but there are many more of these who would not consider going to an institution. Flexible learning allows such people to have a much greater degree of autonomy and ownership of their studies.

- **Trainees who only want to do part of the whole.** Some trainees may only want – or need – to achieve a few carefully selected learning outcomes that are relevant to their work or even to their leisure activities. With a flexible learning package, they are in a position to select those parts they want to study, whereas in face-to-face courses they may have to wait quite some time before the parts they are really interested in are covered.

- **Trainees with special needs.** For example, people with limited mobility may find it hard to get to the venue of a traditional course, but may have few problems when studying at home. Trainees with other problems may be able to work through flexible learning materials with the aid of an appropriate helper or supporter. Open and flexible learning is increasingly being used to address the particular needs of diverse groups, including carers, prisoners, mentally ill people, religious groups, socially excluded people and so on.

5. Benefits for trainees

'What's in it for me?' is a natural question for trainees faced with open learning to ask, especially if their previous education or training has been delivered using conventional or traditional teaching and learning processes. It is important that trainees are alerted to the benefits that can accompany open learning pathways. The following are some of the principal benefits open learning can offer trainees, written using wording you yourself could adapt to explain these benefits to trainees:

- **You can learn when you want to.** This means that you can make use of down time at work, or at any time of the day or night when you can find time to study. You don't have to wait for timetabled lectures or training sessions. You may even be able to start and finish your studies at dates of your own choosing, rather than have to fit in with course start dates and finish dates.

- **You can learn where you want to.** With print-based (and some computer-based) packages, you can choose your own preferred learning environment. Better still, you can have some of your learning materials with you everywhere you go, allowing you to do at least some studying in each of many different locations – at home, at work, in colleges, in libraries, on trains, in waiting rooms – almost anywhere.

- **You can learn at your own pace.** You don't have to worry about how fast you're learning, or whether other people seem to be faster than you. When you find something difficult, you can simply spend more time on it.

- **You know where you're heading.** Good open learning materials have well-expressed learning outcomes. You can go back and look again at these at any time to remind yourself of what you're trying to become able to achieve. You can read them as many times as you need to, so that you get a real feeling for what is involved in them.

- **You can see what the standards are.** Self-assessment questions and assignments will give you a good idea of the level you should aim to meet. You can scan these in advance to alert you to what is coming up.
- **You can get things wrong in the comfort of privacy.** Learning by making mistakes is a productive way to learn most things. With self-assessment questions and exercises, you can afford to find out which things you are confused about. When you know exactly what the problems are, you're usually well on your way to solving them.
- **You get feedback on how your learning is going.** The feedback responses to self-assessment questions will confirm whether you are getting the hang of the material. When you get something wrong, the feedback may well help you to find out *why* you did so, and won't just tell you what the correct answer should have been.
- **You can decide what to skip altogether.** For example, if you think you can already achieve a particular learning outcome, you can have a go straight away at the related self-assessment questions or exercises. If you know you can already do these successfully, you can skip them and go straight to the feedback responses to check that you would have succeeded.
- **You can keep practising till you master difficult things.** When you have problems with self-assessment questions and exercises, you can have another go at them a little later, to check whether you still know how to deal with them.
- **You can stop when you're tired or bored.** Successful learning tends to happen in bytes rather than megabytes. When you're flagging, you can have a break, or go backwards or forwards to some other part of your learning materials that you find more interesting.
- **You become more confident.** Open learning helps you to develop your own self-esteem and autonomy as a trainee, and this helps you to make the most of each and every learning opportunity you meet.

6. Benefits for trainers

If you're normally involved in delivering face-to-face training, you need to be able to see significant benefits for yourself as well as for your trainees if you are to move towards incorporating flexible or open learning elements. It's important to be able to convince yourself, as well as any traditionally minded colleagues, about the potential of open learning. This includes having replies for colleagues who may think, 'My trainees will never learn this way' or 'I love to teach, and my trainees always do so well. Why throw that away?' If you need to enthuse fellow trainers about the benefits of open learning, you need to be able to offer them something that they will appreciate. Here are some suggestions as a starting-point, written in wording you can adapt for fellow trainers – or indeed think about for yourself:

- **You won't have to teach the same things over and over again.** With open or flexible learning materials, the things that you teach most often (and perhaps sometimes get bored with teaching) are likely to be the first areas that you decide to package up into open learning materials or flexible learning options.

- **You won't have to explain the same things over and over again.** In face-to-face work with trainees, it often happens that you seem to be repeatedly explaining the same things to different people. The same mistakes and misconceptions occur frequently, and you may lose enthusiasm for putting trainees right about these. With open or flexible learning, such areas represent ideal development ground for self-assessment questions and feedback responses, where you are able to package up your experience of explaining such things to trainees into a form where they can benefit from your explanations without you having to keep delivering them.

- **Flexible learning can help you to deliver more curriculum.** With open learning, much of the actual learning will be done by trainees in their own time, and your task becomes to help them to navigate the course of learning resource materials rather than to go through all of the curriculum directly with them. This can be particularly useful if you already feel under pressure regarding getting through all of your curriculum with trainees.

- **Flexible learning can help your trainees to develop important skills beyond the curriculum.** Such skills include working with learning resources independently, practising self-assessment and evaluation, becoming better at time management and task management, prioritizing the relative importance of different parts of the syllabus, and using fellow trainees as a resource. All of these skills are useful in the world of work and are valued by employers. Flexible learning provides your trainees not only with a chance to practise and develop these skills, but opportunities to accumulate evidence of their development as autonomous learners.

- **Open learning can refresh your practice.** Getting involved in open learning causes staff to re-examine their approaches to teaching, learning and assessment. For example, fresh attention is often paid to identifying learning outcomes, and to expressing these in clear, unambiguous language that open learners can understand. This can lead to parallel refinements in face-to-face work with trainees. The key principles of good practice in open learning extend readily to face-to-face education.

- **You can focus your skills and experience on areas where trainees really *need* your help.** Since flexible learning materials can cover most of the anticipated questions and problems that trainees normally have, your role supporting open learners moves towards being an expert witness for those questions where they really need your experience to help them.

- **You can move towards being a learning manager.** This helps you to have more time and energy to focus on individual trainees' needs and difficulties, rather than simply delivering the content of the curriculum. Some of the most satisfying parts of the work of trainers are seeing that individuals have been helped and developed.

- **You may be able to escape from some things you don't enjoy teaching.** You can do this by packaging up into open learning formats those parts of your syllabus. This has benefits for your trainees as well as for you, as if you're teaching something you're fed up with, the chances of them becoming enthused by such topics diminishes, and their learning would not be likely to be very successful.

- **Open learning can make your job more secure.** Although many educators and trainers fear that they could make themselves redundant by moving towards open learning, in practice the reverse tends to happen. Staff who can generate or support open learning often find themselves even more valued. The diversification of their skills opens up new ways in which they can deliver learning and training.

- **It is less of a disaster if you're ill.** In face-to-face programmes, it can be a nightmare if you are not able to deliver important parts of the curriculum, or even if you lose your voice and can't give lectures. When open learning materials are available, it is often possible to use these at times when you are unable (for example) to give a lecture or run a training session. It is much easier to brief a colleague to give your class some briefings about using their learning resource materials than to hand over a lecture or presentation to someone else.

- **You can spend more of your time getting the assessment side of things right.** From your trainees' point of view, assessment may well be the most important dimension. Busy trainers often do not have as much time as they would wish either to design good, valid assessments, or to mark them. When flexible learning is used to reduce face-to-face delivery time, some of this time can usefully be diverted into paying more-detailed attention to assessment.

7. Benefits for employers and managers

The benefits of open learning are well appreciated by those employers or managers who have been successful open learners themselves – a rapidly increasing group. For some employers and managers, however, open and flexible learning seems rather different to the way that they remember their own education or training. Some of them still equate effective learning with attending classes. Since they may need convincing regarding the benefits of flexible learning before sponsoring their staff to participate in such programmes, the following benefits may be useful to you if your role includes justifying open learning provision to them. The wording here is directed at employers and managers:

- **Your staff will have a better chance of learning relevant things.** The flexibility provided by open learning means that it is often possible to choose training materials that are directly suited to learning needs relating to the workplace.

- **You can see the relevance of each learning programme.** Because open and flexible learning programmes are normally based on clearly stated intended learning outcomes, you can check how useful the achievement of these outcomes by your staff will be for your own organization.

- **Open learning is based on learning-by-doing.** Therefore, your staff will be learning more from practising and applying the skills, concepts and ideas that they are encountering than might have been the case if they had merely attended courses where trainers talked about the subjects being learnt.

- **Open learning materials provide feedback to each trainee.** In college-based programmes, trainees may have to wait for feedback on their progress; with open learning they get much of the feedback at once from the learning resource materials, while their attempts at tasks, questions and exercises are still fresh in their minds.

- **Most open learning programmes use trainer support.** At best, this support is focused towards those aspects of their studies where trainees need human judgement from an expert witness, and away from routine feedback on common problems, which can be built into the learning resource materials. In effect, this can mean that the human interventions of trainer support are much more significant and useful than they sometimes are on a taught course.

- **You can judge the standard of the training.** Open learning materials include self-assessment tasks and exercises, and trainer-marked assignments, all of which help you to see the standard to which your staff are being trained. The assessed components of open learning materials and programmes help you to monitor the actual level to which the intended learning outcomes can be expected to be achieved by your staff.

- **Employees will develop themselves as autonomous learners.** This is one of the most significant pay-offs of open learning. The skills that open learners necessarily develop or improve include time management, task management, taking charge of their own learning, learning from print-based or computer-based resource materials, as well as taking most of the responsibility for preparing themselves for assessment. All of these skills make people more employable and more resourceful.

- **There is less time off the job.** Open and flexible learning allows staff to learn in the workplace, during down time or quiet periods, as well as to extend their studies to home-based learning. The amount of travelling time to a training centre or college is reduced or even eliminated.

- **Open learning helps your organization to cope with the unexpected.** When urgent needs demand that staff cannot be released to attend timetabled training programmes, open learning allows them to catch up on their studies later. This allows you to reduce the occurrence of key staff being unavailable for unanticipated important work, due to being off-site on training programmes.

- **You can make further use of learning resource materials.** When some of your staff have successfully completed open learning courses or elements, the materials that they have learnt from may still be available to you to spread to other staff. The resource materials are much more permanent than the transient experiences of staff attending lectures or training workshops. It is much more difficult to cascade live training than open learning. That means, however, that the valuable trainer-support elements of open learning may not be able to be extended to other staff working through the learning materials on their own.

8. Benefits for training providers

Many institutions in further and higher education are moving towards making open and flexible learning a more important part of their operations. Similar developments have affected training centres in many organizations and industries. This trend, however, is not always being followed for the best of reasons. In particular, the view that flexible learning can reduce staff costs is fraught with danger. The following list of benefits of open learning may be useful to you if you need to inform senior managers or policy makers about *good* reasons for introducing flexibility in delivery:

- **Open learning widens the range of training needs that can be addressed.** At times when the viability of courses and programmes depends more sharply on economics, many useful programmes become untenable for financial reasons. Flexible learning can prove more cost-effective in such cases, while maintaining a desirable breadth of provision.

- **Open learning can make your organization more competitive.** This is more to do with the breadth of learning needs or training needs that can be addressed than about the unit cost averaged out over trainees. Competitiveness is also linked to your organization's ability to respond to diverse requirements regarding the timescales of provision, and the extent of support required by trainees.

- **Open learning meets accepted national agendas and targets.** In the UK and elsewhere, government policies are exhorting providers to address widening participation in learning, and to exploit communications and information technologies, as well as to address the professionalization of those involved in teaching and learning management. Open and flexible learning development can be directly relevant to achieving such targets.

- **Strategic commitment by senior managers to open learning can underpin success.** When open learning is supported top–down in an institution, the other requirements tend to fall into place, including appropriate information technology formats for flexible learning delivery, relevant staff training provision and well-thought-out resources deployment.

- **Open learning causes fruitful staff development.** One of the most significant pay-offs of becoming involved in delivering or supporting open learning is that staff look again at how best to support *learning*, rather than just how to teach or to train. Many staff report that things that they find out through supporting open learners change their practice significantly with face-to-face trainees.

- **Open learning helps develop a multi-skilled staff.** Trainers who get involved in designing or supporting open learning learn a variety of new skills that can pay dividends to the operation of colleges and training providers. For some staff, the new challenges and demands associated with designing and delivering open and flexible learning enrich their professional practice, and bring new enthusiasm to their work.

- **Open learning increases the variety of roles needed by college staff or trainers.** This can mean, for example, that someone who has problems delivering face-to-face sessions may be found a valuable role in some other aspect of supporting learning, designing new materials or spending time assessing open learners' work and giving them feedback in writing or by electronic communication.

- **Open learning is not about dispensing with people.** When used wisely, open learning can be a means of giving staff more opportunity to do the things that are best done by people. Much of the routine transmission of information to trainees can be achieved using learning resource materials. This gives your staff more time to concentrate on applying high-level human skills to support trainees, and to exercise their professional judgement.

- **Open learning can make more cost-effective use of your resources.** For example, open learning can continue for almost all weeks of the year, making good use of learning resource centres, libraries, computing facilities, as well as of staff. Care needs to be taken, however, to ensure that all staff have adequate opportunities both to plan and to take holidays and other kinds of absence, such as attending training programmes themselves, or participating in conferences and meetings.

- **Open learning can reduce peak-demand levels.** For example, with 'roll-on, roll-off' open learning programmes (or flexible learning elements in conventional programmes), trainees are not restricted to starting at a particular time of the year, or being assessed at another fixed time. There can be choices of start and finish dates, and fast-track possibilities for the most able trainees as well as 'crawler-lane' provision for trainees whose time may be very limited.

- **Open learning allows more opportunity to review assessment standards, instruments and processes.** Because the curriculum delivered by open learning is public, with clearly framed statements of intended learning outcomes, it is necessary to ensure that the assessment associated with open learning is not only reliable but also valid and robust. Some of the time saved from face-to-face delivery of information can usefully be diverted into refining and testing assessment formats.

- **Open learning helps move towards being a learning organization.** The learner-centredness of open learning can become a driving force extending throughout the organization, and transforming traditional face-to-face delivery as well as support offered to trainees. It can cause attitude changes that break down the barriers between managers, teaching staff and support staff.

9. Selecting flexible learning materials

One of the problems with commercially available flexible learning materials is that some look good but just don't work, and others work well, but don't look attractive. Much published material falls between these two positions. What really matters is that the materials cause your trainees to learn successfully, but acceptable standards of appearance and style remain on the agenda. The following two sections may be a useful start when reviewing existing published materials, while exploring the possibility of adopting them or adapting them for your own trainees.

10. How will they work?

- **Look first at the intended learning outcomes.** If these are well expressed and in language that your trainees will be able to understand easily, the materials are off to a good start in your interrogation.
- **Check how interactive the materials are.** There should be learning-by-doing opportunities throughout the materials. This is better than just having a collection of self-assessment questions or activities at the end of each section or module. Check whether the tasks and exercises are pitched at an appropriate level, so that they could give your trainees useful practice and the chance to learn from anticipated mistakes.
- **Check how well the materials respond to trainees' efforts.** Look particularly at the responses to self-assessment questions. These should be considerably more than simply answers to the questions. Your trainees should be able to find out not only whether their own attempts at the questions were successful, but also what might have gone wrong with their own attempts when unsuccessful.
- **Check the standards.** The standards to which the learning outcomes will be delivered should be most clearly evident from the levels of tasks in the materials. In particular, if tutor-marked assignment questions are included in the materials, see whether they are pitched at an appropriate level for your trainees, and decide whether you may indeed use them as they stand.
- **Think about the tone and style of the materials.** Most flexible learning materials work better when the tone and style are relatively personal and informal. The materials should be involving, with trainees addressed as 'you' and, when appropriate, the authors talking to

trainees as 'I'. Check, however, that the tone won't be found patronizing by your trainees. This is not necessarily the same as whether you may find the tone or style too informal – remember that you are not *learning* from the materials.

- **Think about the ownership issues.** For example, if the materials are designed for trainees to write all over them, filling in answers to questions, entering calculations, sketching diagrams and so on, trainees are likely to get a high degree of ownership of their learning from the materials. If the materials are more like textbooks, this ownership may be reduced, and trainees may not regard the materials as primary learning resources.

- **Think ahead to what you may wish to add to the materials.** For example, when materials don't yet contain sufficient self-assessment questions, or when feedback responses are not yet self-sufficient enough for your trainees, you may well be able to bridge the gap by adding questions and responses of your own. This can be well worth doing if there are other aspects of the materials that make them particularly attractive as a starting-point for your own fine-tuning.

- **Look at the layout and structure of the materials.** For trainees to trust them, the materials should look professional and credible. Trainees should be able to find their way easily backwards as well as forwards through the materials. There should be good signposting, showing how each section of the materials fits in to the whole, and linking the intended learning outcomes to the tasks and activities in the materials.

- **See whether you can get feedback on how well the materials actually work.** Check whether there are other colleges or organizations already using the materials, and try to find out how well the materials are doing their job there. Reputable sources of published flexible learning materials will normally be only too pleased to provide details of major clients.

- **Check the costs involved.** There are different ways of 'adopting' flexible learning materials. These range from purchasing copies in the numbers you require for your own trainees to acquiring a site licence to reproduce your own copies. If you are dealing with a minority specialist option, the economics will probably favour buying copies directly. Bulk discounts may be available for significant purchases, and it can be worth buying in supplies to last for more than one 'run' of the materials, but this should only be considered when you are really certain that these are the materials that you want to use.

11. Is the content right?

It is important that time is devoted to checking out the content of materials, and that such time is made available to those with this responsibility, or that someone appropriate is commissioned to evaluate the materials:

- **Check carefully the match between the published learning outcomes and those of your own programme.** It is normal to expect some differences. Some of your own learning outcomes may be absent from the published materials. The materials may at times go well beyond your own learning outcomes. It is important to establish what fraction of the published materials will be directly relevant to your own flexible learning programme. If it is less than half, this is normally a signal to continue searching elsewhere.

- **Check that the published materials are compatible with other parts of your trainees' studies.** For example, check that they use subject-specific conventions or approaches that will be familiar to your own trainees.

- **Seek out reviews of the learning materials.** Just as with textbooks, reviews can help you make decisions about which to adopt and which to reject. Reviews of flexible learning materials can be useful indicators of their quality. Reviews tend to concentrate more on the subject matter than the ways that the materials actually deliver successful learning, and are therefore useful in the context of establishing relevance.

- **Decide whether the materials are sufficiently up to date.** A quick way to do this is to look for references to 'further reading' or tasks briefing trainees to make use of other reference books or articles on the topics covered. You will normally know of the most respected source materials and any recent developments that should be encompassed within the flexible learning materials or referred to from them.

- **Check that any resources that the materials depend upon are available.** For example, if the flexible learning materials are written with one or more set textbooks or articles to be used alongside them, make sure that these materials are still available. Even important set texts go out of print, often between editions, and the next edition may not lend itself to the particular tasks for which it was referred to from the flexible learning materials.

- **Check the relevance of the learning-by-doing tasks in the materials.** Compare these with the sorts of tasks you would set trainees in conventional courses at the same level. Watch particularly for tasks that could be considered too basic, or 'missing the point' of important elements of learning. Also look out for tasks that may be too advanced, and that may stop your trainees in their tracks.

- **Estimate the expected time that trainees may need to spend using the materials.** There are often indications of this built into flexible learning materials, but you may need to work out upper and lower limits that would reasonably relate to your own least able and most able trainees. Match these timescales to the overall duration (or equivalent duration) of your flexible learning programme, and the relative importance of the topics addressed by the materials. For example, if a published workbook is expected to take the average trainee 12 hours to work through, but the topic concerned is only one-tenth of your 60-hour-equivalent module, you may need to look for a more concise package covering the same ground.

- **Check that you can live with the ways the materials address important topics.** This includes equal opportunities approaches. For example, check how the materials portray male/female roles in case studies and illustrations. Don't get into the 'not invented here syndrome'. If you really don't like the way the materials handle an important concept, you are probably well advised to look for other materials. Any distrust or reservations you have about learning materials may be quite infectious, and your trainees may quickly pick up doubts about the materials, and lose their confidence to learn from them.

- **Work out how much you may need to add to the materials.** It is quite normal for published materials not to cover everything that you would include if you were designing them yourself. It is relatively easy to bridge small gaps, by designing handouts or small workbooks to address them.

- **Work out how much you might wish to delete.** You don't want your trainees to waste their time or energy by doing things in published materials that are not connected to the learning outcomes of their own programmes, or that are not involved in their own assessment in some way. It is perfectly feasible to brief your trainees on such lines as 'Don't do anything with Section 9 unless you want to just for your own interest; it's not on your agenda.' In deciding which published materials you may wish to adopt, make sure that there is not too much in this category.

12. A quality checklist for flexible learning materials

The following checklist is presented as a summary of many of the main points made in *500 Tips on Open and Flexible Learning* (Phil Race, 1998, Kogan Page). It is adapted from criteria first published in *The Open Learning Handbook* (Phil Race, 1994, Kogan Page) and in *The Lecturer's Toolkit* (Phil Race and Sally Brown, 1998, Kogan Page). The checklist is particularly intended to help you make decisions about the strengths and weaknesses of published resource materials, but may well be useful as a framework to address the quality of materials you design yourself.

Objectives or statements of intended learning outcomes

- **Is there a clear indication of any prerequisite knowledge or skills?** If not, you may usefully compose a specification of what is being taken for granted regarding the starting-point of the materials. It is particularly important that when flexible learning elements are being used within college-based traditional courses, trainees should know where the flexible learning outcomes fit into the overall picture of their courses.

- **Are the objectives stated clearly and unambiguously?** This is where you may wish to 'translate' the objectives of particular learning packages, making them more directly relevant to the trainees who will use them. This can often be done by adding 'for example...', illustrations of how and when the intended outcomes will be relevant to their own situations.

- **Are the objectives presented in a meaningful and 'friendly' way** (ie *not* 'The expected learning outcomes of this module are that the trainee will...')? We suggest that it is preferable to write learning outcomes using language such as 'When you've worked through Section 3, you'll be able to...' It is important that trainees develop a sense of ownership of the intended learning outcomes, and it is worth making sure that the outcomes as presented to them make them feel involved and don't just belong to the learning package.

- **Do the objectives avoid 'jargon' that may not be known to trainees before starting the material?** It is of course normal for new terms and concepts to be introduced in any kind of learning, but it is best if this is done in ways that avoid frightening off trainees at the outset. It may remain necessary to include unfamiliar words in the objectives of a learning package, but this can still allow for such words to be explained there and then, legitimizing a starting-point of 'not yet knowing' such words. Adding a few words in brackets along the lines of 'This means in practice that...' can be a useful way ahead in such cases.

Structure and layout

- **Is the material visually attractive, thereby helping trainees to want to learn from it?** It is not always possible to choose the materials that *look* best, however. Sometimes the best-looking materials may be too expensive, or they may not be sufficiently relevant to learning needs. At the end of the day, it is the materials that *work* best that are cost-effective, so compromises may have to be made on visual attractiveness.

- **Is there sufficient white space?** In print-based materials this is needed for trainees to write their own notes, answer questions posed by the materials, do calculations and exercises that help them make sense of the ideas they have been reading about, and so on. A learning package that allows trainees to write all over it – or insists on them doing so – is likely to be more effective at promoting effective learning-by-doing.

- **Is it easy for trainees to find their way backwards and forwards?** This is sometimes called 'signposting' and includes good use of headings in print-based materials, or effective menus in computer-based materials. Either way, well-signposted materials allow trainees to get quickly to anything they want to consolidate (or 'digest') as well as helping them to scan ahead to get the feel of what's to come.

- **Is the material broken into manageable chunks?** Trainees' concentration spans are finite. We all know how fickle concentration is at face-to-face training sessions. The same applies when trainees are learning from resource materials. If an important topic goes on for page after page, we should not be surprised if concentration is lost. Frequent headings, subheadings, tasks and activities can all help to avoid trainees falling into a state of limbo when working through learning packages.

- **Does the material avoid any sudden jumps in level?** A sudden jump can be a 'shut-the-package' cue to trainees working on their own. It is just about impossible for authors of learning materials to tell when they have gone one step too far too fast. The first people to discover such sudden jumps are always the trainees who can't understand why the material has suddenly left them floundering. In well-piloted materials, such difficulties will have been ironed out long before the packages reach their published forms, but not all materials have waited for this vital process to happen.

Self-assessment questions and activities (learning-by-doing)

- **Are there plenty of them?** For example, I suggest that there should be one in sight per double-page spread in print-based materials, or something to do on most screens in interactive computer-based packages. If we accept that learning mostly happens by practising, making decisions or having a go at exercises, it is only natural that effective interactive learning materials are essentially packaged-up learning-by-doing.

- **Are the tasks set by the questions clear and unambiguous?** In live sessions, if a task isn't clear to trainees, someone will ask about it, and clarification will follow. With packaged learning resources, it is crucial to make sure that people working on their own do not have to waste time and energy working out exactly what the instructions mean every time they come to some learning-by-doing.

- **Are the questions and tasks inviting?** Is it clear to trainees that it's valuable for them to have a go rather than skip the tasks or activities? It is sometimes an art to make tasks so interesting that no one is tempted to give them a miss, especially if they are quite difficult ones. However, it helps if you can make the tasks as relevant as possible to trainees' own backgrounds and experiences.

- **Is there enough space for trainees to write their answers?** In print-based materials, it is important to get trainees writing. If they just *think* about writing something, but don't *do* it, they may well forget what they might have written. In computer-based materials, it is equally important to ensure that users make decisions, for example by choosing an option in a multiple-choice exercise, so that they can then receive feedback directly relating to what they have just done.

- **Collectively, do the self-assessment questions and activities test trainees' achievement of the objectives, and prepare them for any final assessments they may be heading towards?** Perhaps one of the most significant dangers of resource-based learning materials is that it is often easier to design tasks and exercises on unimportant topics than it is to ensure that trainees' activities focus on the things that are involved in them achieving the intended learning outcomes. To eliminate this danger, it is useful to check that each and every intended learning outcome is cross-linking to one or more self-assessment questions or activities, so that trainees get practice in everything that is important. The self-assessment questions should collectively prepare trainees for any other assessments that they will experience after completing their open learning.

Responses to self-assessment questions and activities (feedback)

- **Are they really *responses to what trainees will have done*** (ie not just answers to the questions)? We saw earlier how important it is for trainees to get the chance to learn through feedback on their efforts. If trainees can't get the correct answer to a question, telling them the answer is of very limited value. They need feedback on what was wrong with their own attempt at answering the question. In face-to-face training, they can get such responses from their trainer. In resource-based learning, such feedback needs to be available to them in predetermined ways, in print or in feedback responses that appear on their computer screens.

- **Do the responses meet each trainee's need to find out, 'Was I right? If not, why not?'** When trainees get a self-assessment question or activity 'right', it is quite straightforward to provide them with appropriate feedback. It's when they get it wrong that they need all the help we can give them. In particular, they need to know not only what the correct answer should have been, but also what was wrong with their own answers. Multiple-choice question formats are particularly useful here, as they allow different trainees making different mistakes each to receive individual feedback on their own attempts at such questions.

- **Do the responses include encouragement or affirmation (without being patronizing) for trainees who got them right?** It's easy enough to start a response with words such as 'well done'. However, there are many different ways of giving praise, and saying 'splendid' may be fine if the task was difficult and we really want to reward trainees who got it right, but the same 'splendid' can come across as patronizing if trainees felt that it was an easy question.

- **Do the responses include something that will help trainees who got it wrong *not* to feel like complete idiots?** Do the responses give them guidance on what an acceptable answer might look like? One of the problems of working alone with resource-based learning materials is that people who get things wrong may feel they are the only people ever to have made such mistakes. When a difficult question or task is likely to cause trainees to make mistakes or to pick incorrect options, it helps them a lot if there are some words of comfort, such as 'This was a tough one!' or 'Most people get this wrong at first.'

Introductions, summaries and reviews

- **Is each part introduced in an interesting, stimulating way?** There's no second chance to make a good first impression! If trainees are put off a topic by the way it starts, they may never recover that vital 'want' to learn it.

- **Do the introductions alert trainees to the way the materials are designed to work?** Learning resource materials should not assume that all trainees have developed the kinds of study skills needed for flexible learning. It is best when the authors of such materials share with trainees the way that they intend the optimum learning pay-off to be achieved. When trainees know where they are intended to be going, there's more chance they'll get there.

- **Are there clear and useful summaries or reviews?** Do these help trainees to digest what they have learnt? In any good face-to-face session, trainers take care to cover the main points more than once, and to remind trainees towards the end of the session about the most important things they should remember. When designing learning resource materials, authors sometimes think that it's enough to put across the main points well – and only once. Summaries and reviews are every bit as essential in good learning materials as they are in live sessions.

- **Do summaries and reviews provide useful ways for trainees to revise the material quickly and effectively?** A summary or review helps trainees to identify all the essential learning points they should have mastered. Once they have done this, it should not take much to help them retain such mastery, and they may well not need to work through the whole package ever again if they can polish their grasp of the subject just by reading summaries or reviews.

The text itself

- **Is it readable, fluent and unambiguous?** When trainees are working on their own, there is no one to ask if something is not clear. Good learning resource materials depend a lot on the messages getting across. Those people who never use a short word when they can think of a longer alternative should not be allowed to create learning resource materials! Similarly, short sentences tend to get messages across more effectively than long sentences.

- **Is it relevant?** For example, does the material keep to the objectives as stated, and do these fit comfortably into the overall picture of the course or module? It can be all too easy for the creators of learning resource materials to get carried away with their pet subjects, and go into far more detail than is reasonable.

- **Is the tone 'involving' where possible?** Is there plenty of use of 'you' for the trainee, 'I' for the author, 'we' for the trainee and author together? This is a matter of style. Some writers find it hard to communicate in an informal, friendly manner. There is plenty of evidence that communication works best in learning materials when trainees feel involved, and feel that the learning package is 'talking' to them in a natural and relaxed way.

Diagrams, charts, tables, graphs and so on

- **Is each non-text component as self-explanatory as possible?** In face-to-face training sessions, there are all sorts of clues as to what any illustrations (for example, overheads or slides) actually mean. Trainers' tone of voice and facial expressions do much to add to the explanation, together with the words they use when explaining directly. With learning packages, it is important that such explanation is provided when necessary in print.

- **Do the trainees know what to do with each illustration?** They need to know whether to learn, label or complete it, note it in passing, pick out the trend or even do nothing. In a face-to-face session, when trainers show (for example) a table of data, someone is likely to ask, 'Do we have to remember these figures?' If the same table of data is included in learning materials, the same question still applies, but there is no one to reply to it. Therefore, good learning resource materials need to anticipate all such questions, and clarify to trainees exactly what the expectations are regarding diagrams, charts and so on. It only takes a few words of explanation to do this, along such lines as 'You don't have to remember these figures, but you do need to be able to pick out the main trend' or 'You don't have to be able to draw one of these, but you need to be able to recognize one when you see one.'

- **'A sketch can be more useful than 1,000 words': is the material sufficiently illustrated?** One of the problem areas with flexible learning materials is that they're sometimes created all in words, at the expense of visual ways of communicating important messages. Sometimes the explanation is as simple as the writer of the materials not being confident about providing sketches or diagrams. However, good-quality materials overcome this weakness, by using the services of someone with the appropriate talents.

Some general points

- **Does the material ensure that the average trainee will achieve the objectives?** This of course is one of the most important questions we can ask of any learning package. If the answer is 'no', look for a better package.

- **Will the average trainee *enjoy* using the material?** In some ways this is the ultimate question. When trainees 'can't put the package down, because it is so interesting to work through it', there's not usually much wrong with it.

- **How up to date is the material covered?** How quickly will it date? Will it have an adequate shelf-life as a learning resource, and will the upfront costs of purchasing it or developing it be justified?

- **How significant is the 'not invented here' syndrome?** Can you work with the differences between the approach used in the material and your own approach? Can you integrate comfortably and seamlessly the two approaches with your trainees? (If you criticize or put down learning resource materials your trainees are using, you're quite likely to destroy their confidence in using it, and their belief in the quality of the content of the material as a whole.)

- **How expensive is the material?** Can trainees realistically be expected to acquire their own copies of it? Can bulk discounts or shareware arrangements be made? If the material is computer-based, is it suitable for networking, and is this allowed within copyright arrangements?

- **Can trainees reasonably be expected to gain sufficient access?** This is particularly crucial when large groups are involved. Could lack of access to essential resource materials be cited as grounds for appeal by trainees who may be unsuccessful when assessed on what is covered by the resource material? This particularly applies to information technology laboratories and personal computers, when they play an important part in flexible learning delivery. Are part-time trainees disproportionately disadvantaged in terms of information technology access?

- **What alternative ways are there of trainees learning the topic concerned?** What complementary ways are there of learning the topic that trainees can combine with the resource material in question?

- **How is the resource material or medium demonstrably better than the cheapest or simplest way of learning the topic?** There need to be convincing answers to this question, not least regarding expenditure.

- **Will it make trainees' learning more efficient?** How will it save them time, or how will it focus their learning more constructively?

- **Will the resource material or medium be equally useful to all trainees?** Will there be no instances of disadvantaging of (for example) trainees learning in a second language, women trainees, men trainees, mature trainees, trainees who aren't good with computers and so on?

- **What additional key skills outcomes will trainees derive from using the material?** Are these outcomes assessed? Could they outweigh the *intended* learning outcomes?

- **How can feedback on the effectiveness of the resource material be sought?** What part should be played by peer feedback from colleagues, feedback from trainee questionnaires, observations of trainees' reactions to the material, and assessment of trainees' learning?

13. Choosing and using computer-based learning resources

Computer-based packages are widely used in teaching, and play a valuable part in flexible learning programmes. There may well exist computer-based packages that will be helpful to your own trainees, and it could be more cost-effective to purchase these and adopt them as they stand (or adapt them) than to design new materials of your own. Many of the issues covered in the previous checklist continue to apply to computer-based learning resources, but the following additional suggestions may provide you with help in selecting computer-aided learning packages for your trainees:

- **Remember that it's harder to get a good idea of the effectiveness of computer-based materials than for paper-based ones.** This is not least because it is not possible to flick through the whole of a computer-based package in the same way as is possible with a printed package. It can be quite hard to get a feel for the overall shape of the learning that is intended to accompany a computer-based package.

- **Choose your packages carefully.** The best computer-based learning packages are not always those that look most attractive, nor are they necessarily the most expensive ones. The best indicator of a good package is evidence that they cause learning to be successful. Where possible, try them out on trainees before committing yourself to purchasing them. Alternatively, ask the supplier or manufacturer for details of clients who have already used the packages, and check that the packages really deliver what you need.

- **Prepare your own checklist to interrogate computer-based materials.** Decide the questions that you need to ask about each possible package before committing yourself to purchase. Questions could include:

  Are the materials supplied with workbook elements?
  Do trainees themselves *need* these elements?
  Can support materials be freely photocopied?
  What is the standard of the equipment needed to run the packages effectively?
  What level of technical support and back-up will be required?
  Does the software include individual trainee progress monitoring and tracking?
  Do the materials make good use of pre-test and post-test features?
  Can the materials run effectively on a network?
  Are there licensing implications if you wish to run the package on more than one machine?
  Can you afford multiple copies if the materials are multimedia, single-access packages?

- **Try to establish the pedigree of the software.** Some computer-based packages have been thoroughly tested and developed, and have been updated and revised several times since their launch. Such packages normally give some details of the history of their development. Beware of packages, however well presented, that have been published or disseminated without real trialling.

- **Find out about packages from colleagues in other institutions.** Use your contacts. Ask them what packages they know of that work well and really help trainees to learn. Also ask them about packages that they don't rate highly, and about the factors that led them to this conclusion.

- **Try before you buy.** Computer-aided learning packages can be quite expensive, especially if you need to purchase a site licence to use them on a series of networked computer terminals, or to issue trainees with their own copies on floppy disk. If you're considering buying a particular package, try to get a sample of your trainees to evaluate it for you. Their experience of using it is even more valuable than your own, as only they can tell whether they are learning effectively from it.

- **Look at how the medium is used to enhance learning.** If the material does no more than present on glass what could have been presented equally well on paper, it is probably not worth investigating further. The medium should do something that helps learning, such as causing trainees to engage in interaction that they might have skipped if the same tasks or questions were set in print.

- **Get familiar with the package, before letting your trainees loose with it.** There is a learning curve to be ascended with most computer-based packages, and it is best if you go up this ahead of your trainees. They will need help on how to make best use of the package, as well as on what they are supposed to be learning from it. Find out what it feels like to use the package. By far the best way to do this is to work through the package yourself, even if you already know the subject that it covers. Find out what trainees will *do* as they use the package, and check whether the tasks and activities are really relevant to your trainees, and pitched at an appropriate level for them.

- **Check the intended learning outcomes of the computer-based package.** The best packages state the intended learning outcomes clearly within the first few screens of information. The intended outcomes, and the level that the package is pitched at, should also be spelt out in supporting documentation that comes with the package. The main danger is that such packages address a wider range of intended outcomes than are needed by your trainees, and that they may become distracted and end up learning things that they don't need to, possibly interfering with their assessment performance.

- **If necessary, rephrase the learning outcomes associated with the package.** It may be useful to tell your trainees exactly what the learning outcomes mean in the context of their particular studies. You may well need to redefine the standards associated with the outcomes.

- **Think about access to equipment and software.** Some packages come with licence arrangements to use the package with a given number of trainees, either allowing multiple copies to be made, or the package to be used over a network. Ensure that the software is protected in order to prevent unauthorized copying, or unlicensed use on more than one machine.

- **Think how trainees will retain important ideas from the package, after they have used it.** Make sure that there is supporting documentation or workbook materials, as these will help trainees to summarize and remember the important things they gain while using computer-based packages. Where such resources don't already exist, you should consider the benefits of making a workbook or an interactive handout, so that trainees working through the package write down things (or record them) at important stages in their learning.

- **Ensure that learning-by-doing is appropriate and relevant.** Most computer-based packages contain a considerable amount of learning-by-doing, particularly decision making, choosing options and entering responses to structured questions. Some of the tasks may not be entirely relevant to the intended learning outcomes of your programme, and you may need to devise briefing details to help trainees to see exactly what they should be taking seriously as they work through the package.

- **Check that trainees will get adequate feedback on their work with the package.** Much of this feedback may be already built into the package as it stands. However, you may need to think about further ways of keeping track of whether your trainees are getting what they should from their use of the package. It can be worth adding appropriate, short elements to tutor-marked assignments, so that there is a way of finding out whether particular trainees are missing vital things they should have picked up from the package.

- **Check how long the package should take.** The time spent by trainees should be reflected in the learning pay-off they derive from their studies with the package, and this in turn should relate to the proportion of the overall assessment framework that is linked to the topics covered by the package.

- **Think ahead to assessment.** Work out what will be assessed, relating directly to the learning that is to be done using the computer-based materials. Express this as assessment criteria, and check how these link to the intended learning outcomes. Make sure that trainees, before working through the computer-based materials, know *what* will be assessed, *when* it will be assessed and *how* it will be assessed.

- **Explore software that tracks trainees' progress.** This can involve pre-testing and post-testing, and storing the data on the computer system, as well as monitoring and recording the time taken by each trainee to work through each part of the package. Such data can be invaluable for discovering the main problems that trainees may be experiencing with the topic, and with the package itself.

- **Seek feedback from your trainees.** Ask them what aspects of the package they found most valuable, and most important. Ask them also what, if anything, went wrong in their own work with the package. Where possible, find alternative ways of addressing important learning outcomes for those trainees who have particular problems with the computer-delivered materials.

14. Adopt, adapt or start from scratch?

A vast amount of material has been written to support open and flexible learning. Some of this material looks good but does not work. Some looks bad but does work. The following questions and suggestions offer some help towards reaching a logical decision about some of the factors involved in deciding whether to embark on creating new flexible learning resource materials, or to prepare to adopt or adapt existing materials:

- **Do you really want to start from scratch?** If your answer is a definite 'yes', this is probably a good enough reason for at least exploring in more depth the implications of creating new flexible learning materials. If the answer is a definite 'no', it is probably worth your while to look carefully at some of the possibilities there may be of adopting existing materials, or adapting them to meet the needs of your particular trainees.

- **Have you got time to start from scratch?** Designing open learning materials is a time-consuming activity, and usually takes quite a lot longer than is planned. In particular, materials need to be piloted and adjusted on the basis of feedback from trainees (and tutors, mentors and anyone else who sees how they work in practice), and such piloting should be done quite extensively, well before the materials are committed to their first 'published' form or made generally available. Starting from scratch can be really expensive if starting from a position of inexperience too.

- **Do you actually need to start from scratch?** Many institutions have developed their own policies, approaches and house styles relating to the production and support of open and flexible learning, and have staff development and training provision available. Such policies and training are often centrally resourced in the institution, and project management support may also be available. Before being tempted to start out on your own, it is important to make sure that you have checked out where your institution stands.

- **Have you got the skills to start from scratch?** If you have already developed highly successful open learning materials, you will not be in any doubt about your answer to this question. If, however, you have not yet gone up the learning curve involved in such development, you may not realize the diversity of skills that are involved.

- **Will you be a lone spirit, or a member of a cohesive team?** While it is indeed possible for one person to create and design an excellent open learning resource, the statistical probability of this happening is much less than when a committed team tackles the task. Members of such a team need to have broad agreement on the nature of most of the hallmarks of effective open learning materials, as well as time to work together on developing open learning alongside all the other things that they may be doing.

- **Will the right people be doing it for the right reasons?** When creating new open learning materials, everyone involved needs to believe in what they are doing, not just you! Team membership should not be dictated by who happens to have some slack in their timetable, or even by an identified need to establish a flexible learning pathway in a topic taught by particular people.

- **Have you got the resources to start from scratch?** Creating new open learning materials involves more than skilled writers who know both the subject involved and the problems that trainees have in learning it. Other things to consider include layout, production, reproduction, print runs, design of media-based elements, administration, communication to trainees learning independently, monitoring trainee progress, and the design and implementation of related assessment elements.

- **Are you in a position to find out what exists already?** There is a wealth of published open learning material, increasingly accessible through catalogues and databases. There is an even greater wealth of material that is unpublished, but working effectively locally in colleges, universities, training organizations and elsewhere. There is no easy way of tracking down some of this material or of finding out how useful or relevant some of it may be to the needs of your own trainees. Most colleges have staff such as learning resources managers, and links to consortia, whereby progress can be made in tracking down and evaluating suitable resource materials.

- **Are you in a position to buy in identified suitable resources?** Almost anything that exists can be purchased for use in your own institution, but the cost–benefit analysis needs to be considered carefully. Detailed negotiations may need to be undertaken with the owners of the copyright of the work concerned if you intend to mass-reproduce it. Site licences for local reproduction may need to be negotiated.

- **How important may the 'not invented here syndrome' be?** One of the biggest problems with adopting other people's materials is that the sense of ownership is lost. This may be reflected by a lack of trust in the materials. Reactions such as 'It's not the way I would have covered this topic' or 'This just isn't at the right level for my trainees' or 'This misses out some important points my trainees need to address' reflect genuine problems.

15. Planning how to adopt

Below are some practical suggestions about how to adopt materials that you have found to be suitable:

- **Work out whether trainees will be issued with their own personal copies.** Will trainees be able to keep their copies after they have finished working through them? If not, will there be a problem about trainees writing answers to self-assessment questions on the materials? It is obviously best where trainees can retain learning resource materials, as they can then relearn from them later when necessary. Is it feasible to offer a purchase-or-loan option to trainees themselves? If the materials are to be issued on a loan basis, how will you be able to get them back? What percentage can you expect to get back in a fit state for reissue? How many 'runs' may the materials survive?

- **Work out how many copies of the materials you will need.** This will normally be rather more than the flexible learners you expect in your first cohort. Even so, it can be quite difficult to estimate the number of copies to purchase, especially if your planning is for more than a single year.

- **Check out delivery dates firmly.** It is most unsatisfactory if at least the first parts of the materials you have chosen are not available at the start of your open learners' studies. Similarly, if the materials are bulky, you may not have space to store multiple copies for a long period of time.

- **Take particular care with computer-based materials.** Something you've seen working well on someone else's network may not work on your hardware. There may be bugs to iron out. There may be incompatibility problems with other software, or with printers, modems and so on. Almost all such difficulties are solvable, but sometimes solutions take time. Get the computer-based elements up and running well before your flexible learners may need them.

- **Protect at least one full copy of everything.** You never know when you will need that last available copy for an important purpose. The assignment booklet may be needed, for example, to show teaching quality reviewers or external examiners the level of the work expected from trainees. The installation instructions for computer software may be needed again when your system has to be cleared of a virus and programmes need to be reinstalled. Keep all the essential papers and data in a safe place, and file them well so everyone knows what is there.

- **Work out exactly how you intend your trainees to make use of the adopted materials.** Work out how long they can expect to spend with each element of these materials. Clarify which intended learning outcomes are most relevant to them. Prioritize which tasks and exercises they should regard as central, and which as optional.

- **Revisit the intended learning outcomes.** You will almost certainly need to restate these, fitting them in to the context of the overall outcomes your flexible learners are working towards. You may need to prioritize the published outcomes in the purchased materials, helping your trainees to see which ones are central, and which are more peripheral.

- **Think ahead to how you will assess the learning outcomes.** Work out what proportion of the overall assessment will be linked to learning achieved through using the materials. Maybe start straight away on designing tutor-marked assessment questions and related exam questions. Perhaps also design some indicative sample questions, which you can give out to trainees along with the materials, so they can see the standards they are expected to reach in their achievement of the outcomes.

- **Compose briefing instructions for your open learners.** Introduce the adopted materials, explaining where they fit in to the overall learning programme. If necessary write short notes explaining any differences between the approaches used in the materials and in other resources they may be working with.

- **Think about study-skills advice.** It can be particularly helpful to flexible learners to have tailored suggestions for 'how to get the most out of…' both for print-based materials and computer-based ones. Such briefings can also suggest additional ways that trainees can make opportunities to practise the most important things you intend them to learn using the materials.

16. Planning how to adapt

Adapting existing flexible learning materials happens more frequently than adopting them as they stand. It is, not surprisingly, rare that someone else's package is exactly appropriate for your own trainees. If you are adapting published materials for use by your trainees, you will need to think about most of the suggestions in the preceding section. Moreover, there will be the adaptations themselves to think about. Although this task may seem daunting, it becomes more manageable if broken down into the elements described below:

- **Regard adaptation positively.** It's a lot of work adapting a flexible learning package to make it directly meet the needs of your trainees, in the context of their overall study programme. However, there are benefits for you too. For a start, you will feel a stronger sense of ownership of the materials after you've done your work with them than if you had used them in their original state.

- **Start with the intended learning outcomes.** If these are published within the package, rank them in terms of which are essential, which are desirable but not central and which are optional for your own open learners. Then look carefully for anything important that is missed in the published outcomes. Look for outcomes that have not been stated, but that could be achieved using the materials as they stand. Then look for outcomes that are not covered by the materials, as these will become the focus of some of your adaptations.

- **Think early about other resource materials you may intend your trainees to use alongside the adapted ones.** For example, there may be sections of textbooks, handouts you already use or key articles that you would prefer them to work from rather than from parts of the materials you are adapting. Start clarifying in your own mind the parts of the materials that you are adapting that you *don't* want your flexible learners to work through.

- **Look carefully at the interactive elements.** Examine the learning that occurs through the self-assessment questions, exercises and activities. Decide which of these are really useful, as they stand, for your own trainees. Aim to keep these as they are. Then start looking for intended learning outcomes that are not yet matched by opportunities for learning-by-doing, and draft out further self-assessment questions and tasks as necessary. Adding such interaction is normally the most important stage in adapting materials for your own purposes.

- **Look at the quality of the responses to self-assessment questions and activities.** The feedback that trainees receive after engaging with the interactive elements is crucial for their learning. You may well decide to recompose the feedback components for a significant proportion of the self-assessment questions, particularly those you have already identified as central to the learning outcomes.

- **Think about adding some completely new self-assessment questions and feedback responses.** Consider how much practice your own trainees may need to make sense of the most important ideas, concepts and procedures covered by the learning materials. It is better to have too many good interactive elements, and then to whittle them down to realistic amounts, than to have too restricted a range at the outset.

- **Review any tutor-marked assignments already in the materials.** You may well want to change these, fine-tuning them so that the tutor-marked agenda fits in with other such elements in different parts of your trainees' overall programme. You may be able to use tutor-marked assignments that you already use in face-to-face programmes instead.

- **Consider writing a commentary to talk your trainees right through the materials as they use them.** This could be in a small booklet that they keep alongside them as they work through the materials. It is useful to use this as a guided tour through the materials. Specific comments such as 'I suggest you skip the exercise on page 34 unless you had a problem with the question on page 30' or 'Only aim to remember the three most important factors listed on page 51' can be very helpful to your trainees.

- **Think about whether to do a 'cut-and-paste' job on the package being adapted.** Whether you can do this may depend upon the conditions on which you purchased or licensed your use of the package. However, it is worth if necessary negotiating with the authors, or owners of the copyright, of the material that you are adapting. A cut-and-paste job begins to become a preferred option when the changes, additions and deletions you decide to make reach more than a third of the original material. Be particularly careful, however, not to infringe copyright legislation regarding the material from the original package that remains intact.

- **Plan a careful pilot of your adaptation.** It is quite likely that after the first 'run' you will wish to make substantial further adaptations, not least to the parts that you introduced yourself to the package. Beware of going into production of large numbers of copies of the first version of the adaptation. Even though it is more economical to do fairly large reprographic runs, it is false economy if you end up binning the lot because you have to make further changes.

17. Writing new flexible learning materials

The most difficult stage in starting out to design a flexible learning resource can be working out a logical and efficient order in which to approach the separate tasks involved. These suggestions should help you to avoid wasting too much time, and particularly aim to help ensure that the work you do is directly related to composing learning material rather than writing out yet another textbook:

- **Think again!** Before really getting started on designing flexible learning resource material, it's worth looking back and asking yourself a few basic questions once more. These include:

  - Am I the best person to write this material?
  - Is there a materials production unit in my institution that can help me?
  - Are there any experienced materials editors there whose expertise I can depend upon?
  - Is there graphics design help and support?
  - Is there already an institutional house style?
  - Can someone else produce the flexible learning materials, while I simply supply the raw material and notes on how I want it to work in flexible learning mode?

  If after asking these questions you decide to press ahead with designing your own materials, the following steps should save you some time and energy.

- **Don't just start writing subject material.** A flexible learning package is much more than just the subject matter it contains, and is something for trainees to *do* rather than just something to read.

- **Get the feel of your target audience.** The better you know the sorts of people who will be using your flexible learning material, the easier it is to write for them.

- **Express your intended learning outcomes.** It is worth making a skeleton of the topics that your material will cover in the form of learning outcomes, at least in draft form, before writing anything else. Having established the learning outcomes, you are in a much better position to ensure that the content of your flexible learning material will be developed in a coherent and logical order.

- **Seek feedback on your draft learning outcomes.** Check that they are seen by colleagues to be at the right level for the material you are designing. In particular, check that they make sense to members of your target audience of trainees, and are clear and unambiguous to them.

- **Design questions, tasks and activities firmly based on your intended learning outcomes.** Some of the outcomes may require several tasks and activities to cover them. It is also useful to plan in draft form activities that will span two or three learning outcomes simultaneously, to help pave the way towards integrating your package and linking the outcomes to each other.

- **Test your draft questions, tasks and activities.** These will in due course be the basis of the learning-by-doing in your package, and will set the scene for the feedback responses you will design. It is extremely useful to test these questions and tasks first, with anyone you can get to try them out, particularly trainees who may be close to your anticipated target audience. Finding out their most common mistakes and difficulties paves the way towards the design of useful feedback responses, and helps you adjust the wording of the tasks to avoid ambiguity or confusion.

- **Plan your feedback responses.** Decide how best you will let your trainees know how well, or how badly, they have done in their attempts at each of your tasks, activities and questions.

- **Think ahead to assessment.** Work out which of the questions, tasks and activities you have designed will be self-sufficient as self-assessment exercises, where feedback responses can be provided to trainees in print in the learning package, or on-screen if you're designing a computer-based package. Work out which exercises need the skills of a tutor to respond to them, and will usefully become components of tutor-marked assignments.

- **Map out your questions, tasks and activities into a logical sequence.** Along with the matching learning outcomes, this provides you with a strong skeleton on which to flesh out the content of your flexible learning material.

- **Work out your main headings and subheadings.** It is wise to base these firmly on the things that your trainees are going to be doing, reflecting the learning outcomes you have devised. This is much better than devising headings purely on the basis of the subjects and topics covered, or on the original syllabus you may have started out with.

- **Write 'bridges'.** Most of these will lead from the feedback response you have written for one question, task or activity into the next activity that your trainees will meet. Sometimes these bridges will need to provide new information to set the scene for the next activity. It is important to ensure that these bridges are as short and relevant as you can make them, and that they don't run off on tangents to the main agenda provided by the skeleton you have already made. This also ensures that you make your writing really efficient and save your valuable time.

- **Write the introductions last.** The best time to write any introduction is when you know exactly what you're introducing. It is much easier to lead in to the first question, task or activity when you know how it (and the feedback associated with it) fits into the material as a whole, and you know how and why you have arranged the sequence of activities in the way you have. Although you may need to write draft introductions when first putting together your package for piloting, it is really useful to revisit these after testing out how trainees get on with the activities and feedback responses, and to include in the final version of each introduction suggestions to trainees about how to approach the material that follows, based on what was learnt from piloting.

18. Tone and style for open learning

Whether writing new open learning materials, adapting existing resources or writing study-guide elements to support trainees working with learning resource materials, the tone and style of your writing may need to be different from that which you would use for other purposes. One of the principal differences between material designed for open learning, and textbooks, journals and manuals, is that open learning material is considered best when written in an accessible, user-friendly style. The following suggestions should help you to pitch your level of informality appropriately, and avoid your trainees being intimidated or patronized:

- **Remember that you are 'talking' to people.** They may well be working alone while reading your materials. Remind yourself of the sorts of people that you anticipate addressing, and try to write in a way that will capture their interest, gain their involvement and motivate them to learn actively from your materials.

- **Think about what your trainees find comfortable to read.** Find out what kinds of magazines and newspapers they prefer. Look at the tone and style of the writing in these materials. Academics are often surprised at the simplicity of style of skilled journalists, who can be describing complex situations, but using simple language structures.

- **Remember that you've not got tone of voice, facial expression or emphasis to help you out.** The words you choose need to be able to convey as many as possible of the more subtle nuances that you would unconsciously use in speech.

- **Think carefully about how to address them.** The most natural way is to talk to them as 'you'. This is preferable to talking about 'students', 'learners', 'trainees' or even subject-specific terms such as 'accountants', 'managers' and so on. Everyone is 'you'! It is, however, often useful to mention other labels in such contexts as 'One of the biggest problems accountants have with... is...' or 'Trainees who have not met the concept of... will find a useful source is...'

- **Be particularly careful to make task briefings and instructions personal.** This is where the use of 'you' is most helpful. In self-assessment questions, tutor-marked assignments and any other occasions where you want your trainees to do something, they are less likely to skip the task if there's at least one 'you' in your briefing.

- **Try to make the material itself involving.** There is an abundance of third-person passive material in textbooks, journal articles and maybe also in the reference materials you are briefing your open learners to work with. The briefings or adaptations you are writing are the most important parts for your trainees, so try to ensure that they get the most out of them by feeling involved and included.

- **Think about who the author is.** It is normally best, when appropriate, to refer to yourself as 'I' in briefings, instructions and explanations. Phrases such as 'I found the best way into this was to...' and 'I think you will find it helpful to...' do much to keep your trainees' attention, and to make them feel less lonely, even when working alone.

- **Be careful with 'we'.** This is a particular problem when you may be co-authoring your open learning materials (or study guides). Then it seems natural to write 'we', but it sometimes does not come across as sincerely as you intend it to. In such cases it may be worth thinking about occasionally slipping in phrases such as 'Both of the authors found that the...'

- **Use short words when possible.** The meaning of a sentence is much more likely to get across unambiguously if you avoid unnecessary long words. This is particularly important with briefings for tasks, exercises and assignments. You may well *need* to use long words relating to the subject you are writing about, if your trainees are expected to use them too, but check that there is a genuine purpose every time you use a long or unusual word or phrase. There is a tendency in academic writing to demonstrate one's sophistication in the application of linguistics, sometimes to the detriment of the intended message that is to be communicated. Some writers seem to be under the misapprehension that if anyone can understand their writing without having to pause to consolidate each idea in turn, they must be failing to reach the standard required. The preceding two sentences in this tip are meant to illustrate the point!

- **Keep sentences as short as you can.** This is most crucial when difficult ideas or concepts are involved, or when giving briefings to self-assessment questions, tasks, exercises or tutor-marked assignments. People are much more likely to make assumptions, possibly dangerous ones, about long sentences than about shorter ones. Even when writing *about* topics where long sentences are part of the discipline (for example, law and sociology) it is important to keep *your* sentences short, and leave the lengthier ones for the subject-matter extracts themselves.

- **Think about contractions.** In everyday speech, most of us use contractions such as 'I've', 'let's', 'you'll', 'we've', 'it's' and so on. Some people, unfortunately, regard such language as sloppy. Make your own decision as to whether your trainees will learn better from material that presents ideas in an informal way.

- **Watch your punctuation.** A series of ideas separated by commas in a long sentence is more difficult to grasp than a list of bullet points. With such a list, readers can immediately see how many factors are involved, rather than having to count them up along the length of a sentence.

- **Ask rather than tell.** The question-mark key is probably the most powerful one on your keyboard when it comes to helping people to think rather than just to read. Asking a question brings the chance for trainees to think about their own answers before reading yours.

- **Don't overuse exclamation marks!** They lose their impact if used too often. While you may mean to convey a wry smile with such a device, if your readers have already become irritated by the frequency with which they occur in your writing, they will prove counter-productive. Try just deleting them, and see if your point still comes across. The first one in this tip is not necessary!

- **Test out your tone by listening to it.** Consider getting someone to tape-record an extract of your open learning writing. Then sit back and listen. Any problems someone else had reading it into the recorder, or problems you have in hearing what you meant to write, may help you to see how you could adjust your style.

- **Use the sentence starter 'What I *really* mean is…'** Saying this to yourself before writing a sentence often means that what you write comes across rather better than it otherwise might have done. Imagine your reader asking 'So what?' and respond to this too, maybe in your next sentence.

19. Writing self-assessment questions

Self-assessment questions, activities and exercises are one of the most important features of flexible learning materials, as they allow learning-by-doing, through practising, and also provide valuable opportunities for learning by trial and error. It is normally safer to use structured question formats rather than open-ended ones for self-assessment questions, as it is then much more possible to respond to exactly what your trainees *do* with each task. The following suggestions may help you to ensure that the self-assessment exercises you design are serving your trainees well:

- **Write lots of them!** Writing self-assessment questions gets quicker and easier with practice. Like most things, it is learnt best by doing it. The more you write, the more you can select only the good ones to include in your material.

- **Make good use of existing materials.** If you are already teaching the topic concerned, you are likely to have accumulated quite a stock of class exercises, homework assignments, practice questions and so on. These have the great advantage that you already know they are relevant and important tasks. Many of these will lend themselves to being translated into self-assessment questions and feedback responses.

- **Look at as many samples of flexible learning material as you can.** This helps you see a variety of types and styles, and enriches your own writing of self-assessment components.

Look at the examples you see from the trainee's point of view. In particular, look at the kinds of question where you feel that you are getting useful feedback if you make mistakes or don't actually choose the best or correct option in multiple-choice formats.

- **Keep your intended learning outcomes firmly in mind.** These should provide the agenda for all of the questions, tasks and activities that you set in your flexible learning material. If you find yourself tempted to use a question or exercise that is not directly related to the learning outcomes, check whether it would be a good idea to add new learning outcomes to your agenda to link such a question into your material properly.

- **Keep your tutor-marked assessment ideas firmly in mind.** Trainees who successfully work through all of your self-assessment questions, exercises and activities should be able to expect confidently that they will succeed in any other kinds of assessment they will encounter. The self-assessment components should provide them with all the practice they reasonably need, as well as allowing them to learn from mistakes in the comfort of privacy, before mistakes count against them.

- **Work out exactly what each question is intended to test.** There needs to be a good answer to 'What's this question for?' Sometimes the answer will be to allow trainees to confirm that they have mastered an idea, sometimes to introduce something new and at other times to alert them to something that they may have a problem with. It is important that trainees don't view the self-assessment questions as trivial – they may not even attempt them then.

- **Don't test too many things at once.** It is usually best to keep self-assessment tasks relatively straightforward and not too complex. This makes it much easier to design feedback responses, addressing anticipated problems that trainees may have found.

- **Have a feedback response in mind.** To work as a self-assessment activity, it has to be possible to respond to what your trainees actually do with it. This usually means that you will need to structure your questions carefully, so that you can *know* what your trainees are likely to do with them, and respond appropriately to trainees who succeed and to trainees who don't.

- **Try multiple-choice formats, where they are suitable.** For example, with multiple-choice questions you can respond directly, and differently, to trainees choosing different distractors (wrong or less-good options) and to trainees who choose the correct or best option (the 'key').

- **Don't just use multiple-choice formats.** While these are very versatile, it can become tedious for trainees if this is the only kind of self-assessment question they meet. Ring the changes. Try some prioritizing or sequencing questions, where you ask your trainees to put given things in the best order of priority or the most logical sequence. Try some completion or filling-blanks questions, to help your trainees see whether or not they know what words should be added to complete the sense of sentences, definitions or statements.

- **Consider the use of at least some open-ended tasks as self-assessment questions.** While you can't guarantee to be able to respond to exactly what your trainees may have done with open-ended questions, there are ways of helping them to self-assess their own answers to these. The biggest danger is that trainees are quite likely not to go to the trouble of critically assessing their own answers, unless you make the self-assessment part of the exercise really valuable – and interesting – to them.

- **Try your questions out on trainees (and anyone else!).** The best way of finding out whether a question, task or activity will make a good self-assessment exercise is to see how people get on with it. You will find that this helps a great deal when you come to write the feedback responses, as you will be much more aware of the sorts of things that trainees may do incorrectly, or the most likely errors that they could make.
- **Discard lots of self-assessment questions.** Having gone to the trouble of designing self-assessment components, it is tempting to leave them in your materials even when you know from piloting and testing them that they are not too effective. It is better to start with a large number of possible questions, and select only those that work well. You can always recycle the discarded ones for usage in other contexts in which they will work better, such as in-class questions or tutorial exercises.

20. Writing multiple-choice questions

As already hinted at above, one format of self-assessment question that can work particularly well in flexible learning materials is multiple-choice. The greatest advantage of multiple-choice questions is that (when well designed) they can provide appropriate feedback to trainees whether or not they make correct (or best) selections from the options offered to them. A multiple-choice question has three main ingredients: the 'stem' setting the context; the 'key', which is the best option or the correct one; and 'distractors' – options containing faults or errors. The following suggestions should help you to get all three parts of multiple-choice questions working effectively:

- **Make sure that the key is definitely correct.** It should not be possible for trainees to find anything wrong or arguable in the key. It is often the most able trainees who spot something wrong with the key, and this can be frustrating to them when they see a response that does not acknowledge the level of thinking they exercised.
- **Make sure that the key does not stand out for the wrong reasons as being correct.** The key should not be given away by containing leading wording from the stem, nor should it be of significantly different length from the other options. Also make sure that any grammar links between the stem and the key don't give the key away. You may think such matters would rarely arise, but the last person to spot them is usually the author of the question!
- **Take care with 'definites' versus 'indefinites'.** It is all right to have sets of options including indefinite words such as 'sometimes', 'often', 'usually', 'rarely', *or* sets of definite words

such as 'always', 'never', 'all', 'none', but it is not wise to combine the two kinds of words in a given question, as the indefinite options are more likely to be chosen as correct by anyone who is just guessing – and are probably correct too!

- **Make sure that the stem provides a clear task.** For example, be clear about whether 'which?' means 'which one?' or 'which one or more?'. There is no harm in asking 'Which *two* of the following...?' when you really want trainees to pick two options, and are going to respond accordingly in your feedback.

- **Avoid options that may let your trainees think too little.** It is best to avoid options such as 'all of these' or 'none of these'. These tend to be chosen as cop-out selections by trainees who are not thinking deeply enough to identify the best option. Having expressed this reservation, either of these options can be valuable if used *occasionally* where you really want to make a point about 'all of these' or 'none of these' being the best answer.

- **Be careful with negative questions.** For example, if asking 'Which one of the following is *not* true?' or 'Which is an *exception* to the rule?' make it really stand out that it is a 'wrong' option that has to be selected in such questions; candidates become accustomed to looking for correct options.

- **Make sure that there is something wrong with each distractor.** Remember that when you write a feedback response to a distractor you need to be able to explain convincingly what is wrong with it, or why the key is better.

- **Choose distractors that represent likely errors.** There is no point in having distractors that are not chosen as 'correct' by at least someone. Distractors need to be as plausible as you can make them. That said, it is fine to inject a note of humour occasionally by using an 'unlikely' distractor.

- **Let trainees help you to find better distractors.** It is worth posing the stem as an open-ended question to a face-to-face class if you have such an opportunity, and finding out what the most common wrong answers are. These can then form the basis of your distractors.

- **Try questions out on a large group if you can.** For example, in a presentation put the question up on the screen, and ask for a show of hands for each option in turn. When everyone chooses the correct (or best) option, your distractors may need to be made a bit more appealing! If you don't have the chance to work with large groups of trainees, it is still worth trying out your questions on as many people as you can, even if one at a time and at a distance (or electronically).

- **Remember that multiple-choice questions are not restricted to simple formats.** For example, an extended set of options can be used, with the question asking trainees to decide which *combination* of options is correct or best ('a, d, e' or 'b, c, e' and so on). Browse through some flexible learning materials to explore the range of multiple-choice formats that is possible. The science foundation course of the Open University in the UK has many excellent examples of sophisticated (and difficult!) multiple-choice questions.

21. Writing feedback responses to multiple-choice questions

Whatever form your multiple-choice questions take (print, computer-based or test), trainees want (and need) to find out two things every time they make a choice: 'Was I right?' and 'If not, *why* not?' The following suggestions may help your responses provide useful, quick feedback to trainees:

- **Think about when your response will be seen.** For example, trainees may see your response immediately on-screen after picking an option in a computer-based package, or at the back of a print-based package in the self-assessment question responses, or they may see it in print after completing a series of questions in a multiple-choice test.
- **Make it immediately clear whether the option was correct or not.** Instant feedback can be very useful, particularly when you can remind trainees of why they were right, or show them why they were wrong. Even if your trainees receive the response somewhat later, their first priority will still be to establish whether their choice was successful.
- **Give appropriate praise for the choice of correct options.** A few well-chosen words can be encouraging for trainees who made the correct choice. But make sure that 'well done' messages don't get boring or out of control! There are hundreds of ways of responding 'Well done.' Save the 'Splendid!' responses for right answers to really tricky questions. Milder forms of 'Well done' include 'Yes', 'Right', 'Of course' and so on.
- **Respond to trainees who choose distractors.** It's little use just saying to them, 'Wrong; the correct option was A.' Trainees want (and need) to find out why the distractor was not the best option. If you can't respond to a distractor, take it as a sign that it was not a good distractor in the first place. Good distractors are wrong for a reason, not just wrong!
- **Acknowledge trainees who choose options that are partly correct.** When part of a distractor is correct, use words to remind trainees who have chosen it that they did indeed have some good reasons for their choices. For example: 'While it is true to say that…, it is not right to conclude that…'
- **Let trainees choosing distractors off the hook gently.** They may well be working on their own, so don't leave them feeling that they must be the only people ever to have made such mistakes. Words like 'This was a tricky question' or 'Most people find this hard at first' can go a long way towards making it more acceptable to choose distractors. This can also help to build trainees' trust in the value of making mistakes in the comfort of privacy, and then finding out why.

- **Give trainees the opportunity to give you feedback on your feedback.** Check particularly when you explain what was wrong with distractors that trainees get your messages clearly. Ask your trainees to mark on to their materials any feedback responses that they cannot understand. Often the understanding will be about to dawn, and slowing down to identify exactly what it is that is not yet understood is all it takes to put things right. When this does not happen, it could be that the fault lies in the question or in the feedback, and some editing may be needed for the next edition.

- **Think of visual ways of responding.** Some trainees may wish to be responded to visually rather than with words – at least sometimes. Try to arrange coffee with a computer-graphics expert if you're designing responses for a computer-based package.

- **Keep the language of responses familiar and friendly.** Responses should address the trainee as 'you' and should use simple, accessible vocabulary. A sense of humour usually helps, but excessive humour (especially feeble puns!) can be counter-productive.

22. Writing open-ended questions and responses

It is much harder to write feedback responses to open-ended questions. In particular, you cannot be certain what your trainees have done in answer to the questions; you can only guess. In general, open-ended questions serve a more useful role in tutor-marked assignments, when human judgement and comment can be used to respond to trainees' answers. The following suggestions, however, may help you to include at least some open-ended questions in the self-assessed parts of your open learning materials. In the first few suggestions, I concentrate on ways of turning open-ended questions into ones that have at least some degree of self-assessment potential, and I end with some suggestions for open-ended tasks that are more to do with getting trainees to reflect on their own studies:

- **Have a good reason each time you decide to use an open-ended self-assessment question.** In other words, don't just use open-ended questions because they are much easier to set. The best place for open-ended questions is normally tutor-marked assignments, where human response can be available to whatever interpretations open learners place on the meaning of the questions.

- **Include a few open-ended self-assessment questions as 'dry runs' for tutor-marked components.** Some open learners can be quite anxious about tutor-marked assessment. It may be some years since they have had authoritative feedback on their written work. Giving them some practice at writing out more-extended answers can help increase their confidence, and can illustrate the standard of answers that may be expected from them. To make best use of these 'dry runs', trainees need to write down their own answers to the open-ended questions, and *then* self-assess their answers using guidance notes and marking criteria provided in their learning materials. These may need to be 'hidden' away from the questions, so that trainees really have the chance to answer the questions themselves before seeing upon what basis to self-assess their answers.

- **Include open-ended questions as a means of helping open learners discover much more about the assessment criteria that will be used in tutor-marked elements.** Such questions can be used with the self-assessment dimension as their main purpose, with detailed briefings about how trainees should evaluate and mark their own answers.

- **Use open-ended questions to extend the comfort of privacy to free-form answers.** One of the advantages of structured self-assessment questions is the opportunity they provide for open learners to learn from their mistakes in the comfort of privacy. This dimension can be extended to open-ended questions, especially when you have a good idea of the possible kinds of mistakes that you want to bring to the attention of your open learners.

- **Make the questions, and your responses, as interesting as you can.** Open-ended questions will normally take your trainees a lot more time to attempt than structured questions, and the temptation to skip open-ended self-assessment questions is always there. If the task looks fascinating and important, this temptation is reduced.

- **Explain *why* you are setting each open-ended self-assessment question.** For example, flag them as dry runs for tutor-marked assignments, or practice for typical exam questions and so on, with the real purpose of helping your trainees to see what counts in their answers, and to find out about how the assessment criteria will work in practice.

- **Compose feedback responses carefully.** Work out exactly what you want your open learners to *do* to self-assess their answers. Give detailed briefings about how they should go through their answers, including what to be looking for in them that would score marks, or that would lose marks in a formally assessed answer.

- **Consider getting open learners to apply a 'real' marking scheme to their own answers.** You could base the marking scheme on one that is tried and tested from a previous exam or assignment, and where you already know the most likely difficulties and areas of weakness. You will almost certainly have to recompose the marking scheme in learner-friendly language, however.

- **Think about the value of model answers.** These are not in themselves sufficient as responses to open-ended self-assessment questions, but can be part of an illustration of what is really being looked for in terms of standard and content of answers. Model answers work best as feedback to trainees when they are accompanied by a commentary (maybe in a separate column down the right-hand side of the model answers).

- **Think about the possibilities of responding to open-ended questions on audiotape.** For extended open-ended tasks, it can be useful to talk open learners through their own work, by recording a short audiotape that helps them go about self-assessment. The benefits of this include tone of voice, emphasis and the fact that trainees can be briefed to stop the tape and do something with their own answers, then restart the tape and continue. Such usage of audiotape can be particularly useful for *any* self-assessment questions, and also for tutor-marked assignments, where trainees are studying in a second language. Audiotape also comes into its own as a feedback medium for partially sighted trainees.

- **Bear in mind that it may not be possible to respond completely.** Open-ended self-assessment questions are unlikely to be entirely self-assessable, even with model answers and marking schemes. The self-assessment only goes as far as trainees' own comparisons of their answers with the response framework provided in the materials. It is useful to legitimize follow-up face-to-face or e-mail discussions with trainers, for trainees who may still have problems self-assessing their own answers to such questions.

- **Consider using some completely open-ended questions.** For example, it can be productive to ask open learners to make entries in their own personal learning logs or reflective journals or diaries. Think of designing specific questions as the basis for such reflection and consolidation. It could be that trainees' answers are not assessed at all, or alternatively you could set a tutor-marked assignment question asking trainees to process further some of the thinking they may have done for open-ended questions of this sort.

23. Writing an introduction that works

The importance of the first page or two in an open learning package (or the first few screens in a computer-based one) cannot be overestimated. Your trainees' attitudes are formed by the first few minutes they spend with your materials. The following suggestions may help you to get them off to a successful start:

- **Beware of trying to start at the beginning.** The problem is that to start most things at the beginning takes you so far back that most people already know most of it, and become bored by reading it. You may well have to backtrack to make sure that each trainee can make sense of the starting-point, but choose something more important to be the focus of your attitude-forming introduction.

- **Use the introduction to explain how the package will work best.** It can be useful to explain any conventions used in the package, and to let trainees know in advance about any equipment or other resources they will need to have available as they work further into it.

- **Start as you mean to go on.** If you are writing in an informal, friendly style in the body of your material, don't preface it all by an impersonal stolid introduction. It is worth capturing your trainees' interest right from the start. Also, this means that they won't be 'thrown' by a sudden switch to a less formal approach when you start to involve them in self-assessment questions and other activities.

- **Don't write the introduction too early.** The best time to write the introduction (or the final version of it) is when you know everything towards which it is leading. When you know exactly what is in your package or study guide, and *how* the material is designed to work, you are in a much better position to write an introduction to the learning package, and not just to the topic concerned.

- **Think twice about calling it 'Introduction'.** There is something about the word that implies for many people 'This is not really important; it's only a lead-in, and I can skip it.' In its own way, use your introduction to address the question 'So what?' that may be in the minds of at least some of your trainees.

- **Don't try to introduce too much at once.** Even when you know the whole of what will follow, it is usually best to lead into only a manageable amount of it. Remember that you will have many more lead-in sections throughout the material.

- **Ask yourself, 'What does this introduction actually do?'** Think about turning your answer to this into a question heading. See if you can use this to explain to your trainees *why* it will be worth their while to look at it carefully. For example, 'Why is thermodynamics important?' will work better than 'An introduction to basic thermodynamics'.

- **Consider breaking your introduction up into separate elements.** When there is more than one purpose to be served by your introduction, work out the objectives it will serve, and maybe pose these in the very first part of it; then deal with each under a different, appropriate subheading.

- **Consider making your introduction interactive.** Starting with a setting-the-scene task, or a 'find out how much you already know' quiz, can be a good way of getting your open learners involved right from the start. It can be useful to start with a pre-test or diagnostic test, particularly if prior knowledge of something in particular will be important later in the material. It is however important not to make pre-tests too intimidating, and to introduce them in a way that makes it clear that your trainees are not *expected* to answer all the questions correctly.

- **Seek particular feedback on drafts of your introduction.** Ask colleagues and trainees alike how they *feel* about the introduction. Ask them whether you're taking anything for granted and perhaps need to add a sentence here and there to clarify matters. Consider asking someone else to draft an introduction for you (with, or without, sight of yours), and see whether they come up with something about which you have not thought.

- **Don't expect your introduction to be remembered by your trainees.** For example, even when you make important points in your introduction, such as about how best to make use of the learning materials, your trainees will probably not return to it again. You may well need to reinforce or repeat important points at various stages throughout your materials.

24. Finishing well: reviews and summaries

As with most kinds of creative writing, to generate a good impression an open learning package should not just fizzle out. Introductions may be your one chance to make a good *first* impression, but how the package ends makes important last impressions. The following suggestions may help you decide how best to bring your open learning materials to a successful, robust conclusion:

- **Design your conclusions as a revision aid.** A well-designed set of conclusions should be a useful reminder of the main things you intend your trainees to be able to do, or to know, when they have completed their work on your package.

- **When you think you've reached the end, don't feel you have to ramble on.** It sometimes takes some courage to decide to end. If you put off the moment of coming to a conclusion for too long, you're almost certain to be losing your trainees' interest.

- **Plan your ending quite early.** It helps to know where you're heading towards, and to marshal your arguments and tidy up any loose ends as you get nearer to your conclusions. It is sometimes quite difficult to decide exactly where to finish, and it often helps to aim towards ending with a particularly important point or idea.

- **If you write 'Conclusions', make them short.** Trainees often look at conclusions while working through materials, and sometimes before starting, to check out the destination towards which they are working. For this to work well, it is best if the conclusions are no more than half a page in text-based materials, or one screen in computer-based ones. Whatever form your conclusions take, try to end with a short sentence, which is likely to have more impact than a long one.

- **Beware of saying 'Well done.'** This can work with computer-based materials, where to reach the final screen you *know* that each trainee has worked through all of the package. In print-based materials, trainees can look at the conclusions at any time, and seeing 'Well done' is somewhat artificial, especially if they haven't yet done any real work on the package. 'Well done' messages are probably best reserved for responses to self-assessment questions, for example to trainees who have chosen the correct (or best) option in multiple-choice tasks.

- **Check that your conclusions have a close relationship with the intended learning outcomes.** If there is any discrepancy here, it could be that you need to go back and adjust the intended learning outcomes.

- **Use conclusions to point forwards as well as to look back.** If the materials are a stepping-stone towards further packages, it can be useful to explain briefly those that follow on most directly from the present one. It can be helpful in such cases to give your trainees a little advice along the lines, 'The one thing from this package that you will most need for the next one is…'

- **Think of ways of ending with an activity.** Think about the merits of a test-yourself quiz, or a 'rate-yourself' exercise that compares progress against the intended learning outcomes. Try not to *end* the whole package with an exercise, however, without some form of wrapping up and summarizing the main content first.

- **Consider ending with a short feedback questionnaire.** This in its own way flags the end of the material. Remember to thank your respondents in advance for their feedback; this helps to ensure that you will receive it! Use at least part of the questionnaire to cause your trainees to think back through some of their learning. For example, ask them which self-assessment question response they found most valuable in terms of feedback, or ask them to prioritize half a dozen topics in terms of most difficult to least difficult.

- **Think about the last thing in your package.** This may not in fact be your conclusions, due to the structure of the materials. For example, in print-based materials, the responses to the self-assessment questions could be at the end of the package. There may also be appendices such as a glossary, an index or some supplementary, remedial or optional information about an earlier part of the package. You may still want to have something at the very end of the package that carries a sense of completion. In such cases, one option is to consider repeating the intended learning outcomes, this time phrased, 'Now that you have completed your work on this package, check that you can…'

25. Writing study guides

Sometimes the quickest, and best, way to implement a flexible learning pathway is to collect and organize some relatively traditional materials, and to write a study guide to take trainees through them in a planned, structured way. Study guides are particularly useful for academic subjects where it may be necessary to get trainees to review a lot of case study or research-based material. Writing study-guide material involves many of the processes considered already in this section, but it is also important to think carefully about how trainees are briefed to use the traditional resources. The following suggestions should help you to ensure that your study guide helps trainees to make the most of such resources:

- **Make each study guide attractive and motivating.** The study guide may be the central document that trainees work with all of the time on your module, while they refer out from it to different books, articles, Web sites, videos and multimedia resources. Explain to trainees how the study guide is intended to help them balance the various activities of their studies.

- **Link the intended learning outcomes to the resources.** For example, when different textbooks or articles contain the reference material for your trainees' learning, it helps to indicate which learning outcome is addressed in each different resource material.

- **Link self-assessment questions to the respective resources.** One of the most important components of an effective study guide is the interaction that plays the same part as self-assessment questions and feedback responses in self-standing flexible learning materials. With study guide materials, the subject matter is likely to be located in supporting texts or articles, and it helps to specify which source material(s) should best be used by trainees when working on the questions.

- **Link feedback responses to the respective resources.** Rather than write out detailed feedback responses, it is often possible to refer trainees to particular sections or paragraphs in their resource materials. However, it remains best to write the main response feedback, and to confine such references to 'Further explanation' or 'See also the discussion in...'

- **Don't refer trainees to large amounts of material at once.** For example, suggesting that trainees should read Chapter 4 of a textbook is not likely to cause them to learn much from their reading. It is better to brief them to focus their reading on particular pages or sections, and to legitimize the process of merely scanning less relevant or less important material.

- **Use the study guide to suggest reasonable timescales.** For example, when referring out to textbooks or computer-based learning packages, it can be useful to give your trainees a rough idea of the maximum and minimum times you expect them to spend with each source. This can help your trainees to avoid becoming sidetracked and, for example, spending too much time working with one particular source.

- **Give trainees an agenda *before* they read extracts from other resources.** For example, suggest, 'You should read Chapter 3, Sections 3.3–3.5 next, looking for answers to the following five questions...' When trainees have already got questions in their minds, their reading becomes considerably more active, and when they discover some information that answers one of their questions, they tend to learn it more successfully.

- **Advise trainees on what *not* to read.** One of the problems with using external sources such as textbooks is that there is usually a significant amount that is not directly relevant to the intended learning outcomes of the flexible learning module. It can be helpful to advise trainees along the lines, 'There is no need for you to look at Chapters 4–5 of this source, unless you happen to be particularly interested in the content; this will not relate to any assessments in the present programme.' Most trainees are quick to take such hints!

- **Consider setting tasks that cause trainees to compare and contrast different sources.** When the same topic is addressed in different ways in different sources, it can be valuable for trainees to make their own minds up about which approach they like best rather than glossing over the differences. Compare-and-contrast tasks may be better as part of tutor-marked assignments than as self-assessment exercises, as tutor feedback may add further value to trainees' own decisions about the different approaches they encounter.

- **Include study-skills help.** Writing a study guide is about helping trainees with the *processes* they should aim to use to make the most of the resources with which they are working. It can be useful to have a separate commentary, including practicable suggestions about how to approach working with each different source or resource.

Chapter 4

Computer-based training

The vast field of computers and information and communications technology is the fastest changing part of our modern world. You may be already well immersed in the world of technology, or you may be looking anxiously towards taking your first steps into this world. You may even have decided that computers are not for you!

The tips in this chapter were written by Steve McDowell and myself, and have been adapted from the two books we've written on computing: *500 Computing Tips for Lecturers and Teachers* (2nd edn, 1999, Kogan Page) and (to a greater extent) *500 Computing Tips for Trainers* (1998, Kogan Page).

The first part of the chapter is for you if you're just starting to embrace the world of technology. It contains down-to-earth tips about all the bits and pieces you are likely to need **to get started**.

The chapter continues with tips that aim to help trainers whose work involves **getting their trainees working effectively with computers**, keyboards, mice, multimedia learning packages and so on.

The chapter then turns to **electronic mail, computer conferencing and the Internet**, and is written both to help you to get started with these if necessary, and to help you to pass these skills on to your own trainees.

After that come tips on **looking after your stress levels**. This overlaps a little with the tips on looking after yourself from Chapter 1, but here the emphasis is on dealing with the things that technology can do to increase stress.

I've added a final section on **jargon busting** to this chapter, adapting a glossary written by Steve Higgins, and first published in *500 ICT Tips for Primary Teachers* (Packard, Higgins and Race, 1999, Kogan Page). Although the worlds of primary education and training are some distance apart, this often-amusing glossary might count towards reducing your stress levels!

1. Organizing your workspace

People often sit at a computer for hours at a time and are surprised when they feel tired and have aches and pains afterwards. If you find you are unexpectedly tired or stressed after each session with your computer, take steps to put things right before they worsen. Most desks and chairs were designed for writing and are at the wrong height for computer use. If you can choose your furniture, bear in mind the points below. If, like most people, you have to use the desk and chair you are given, take steps to adapt them as far as possible:

- **Make sure your monitor is at a suitable height.** As a general guide, the top should be slightly below eye level. Working with the monitor too low is very common and results in back and neck strain due to the weight of the head being unbalanced.

- **Looking down at the keyboard causes neck and back strain.** If it is a serious problem, try to learn to touch type. There are computer programs available to help you with this, and the time spent learning will soon be repaid.

- **The keyboard should be at the correct height.** When you are typing, your forearms should be at about right angles to your upper arms and your wrists should be straight. An adjustable height chair can help achieve this. If you use a mouse, make sure your hand is relaxed when you use it. Ergonomic mice are available to help with this. Repetitive strain injuries (RSI) can result from working with bent wrists for prolonged periods. These injuries can be disabling and should be taken seriously.

- **Your arms should be supported when you are typing.** This can be done by an adjustable wrist rest. If you haven't got one, experiment with a piece of wood wrapped up in some towelling or other thick material. If it helps, buy a proper rest.

- **Make sure that your feet are flat on the floor.** If your knees are lower than your hips when the chair is at the correct height for everything else, use a footrest.

- **When copying from a source document, have it in a good position.** Have it at the same level and distance as the screen to avoid looking up and down and refocusing all the time. Document holders are available for this purpose.

- **Minimize eyestrain problems.** If you have headaches, blurred vision or itchy eyes, see your optician. Contact lens wearers should make a conscious effort to blink, as computer use encourages staring at the screen, which can dry lenses out.

- **Take care with reading glasses and bifocals.** These can cause problems with focusing on the screen. Bifocal wearers may suffer neck strain from tilting their heads. Your optician will be able to advise you and possibly prescribe special glasses for computing.

- **Lighting is very important.** You must have good lighting to work effectively, but there mustn't be any glare on the screen. Situate your computer so that you avoid reflections, or use screens to block light from the screen. Anti-glare screens are available to fit to the front of a monitor. A desk lamp can be useful, as it can be adjusted according to your needs.

- **Take plenty of rest breaks away from the computer.** Make sure you rest your eyes and body. Some simple stretching exercises can help. Try to plan your work to incorporate a variety of tasks and to avoid long, continuous spells at the keyboard.

2. Health and safety

There are risks in doing anything, and using IT is no exception. There are some real hazards, and some hype. Common sense will help you to avoid most hazards, but there are some hidden dangers that you need to be aware of:

- **All electrical devices are potentially dangerous.** If you suspect that your computer may have an electrical fault, seek expert help. Watch out for damaged leads, broken cases, unusual 'hot' smells and crackling or fizzing noises. If you are worried, switch it off at the wall socket and unplug it.

- **Many computers, monitors and printers are heavy.** If you want to move one, check its weight carefully before you go too far. Move one component at a time and disconnect all leads to avoid tripping over them. Be particularly careful about steps when you are carrying something that blocks your view.

- **Most computers have a large number of wires connected to them.** Make sure they are located so that they can't trip anybody. Pulling a lead out of the computer can cause it to stop working and you could lose your work. If leads are a hazard, tie them up in a bundle and secure them out of the way. If your computer is against a wall, you could put up a narrow shelf just below desk height. All the leads and power supplies can be held on this shelf.

- **Think about radiation emissions from monitors.** These have been a source of worry for many years, particularly in the case of pregnant women. There is a lack of proof about whether or not this is a real problem. Modern monitors are constructed to strict standards for radiation emissions to minimize any hazard to the user, but it has been suggested that they produce dangerous levels of radiation from the rear. Until proof is established, it would be prudent to avoid risks as far as possible by checking the specifications for monitors and for pregnant women to avoid spending long periods near them.

- **There have been reports of a link between computers and facial dermatitis.** This may also be linked to low humidity and the static electrical field generated by the monitor. If you have any problems of this kind, try using a humidifier and reducing static by the use of anti-static rugs or carpets. There are also anti-static screens to fit to monitors to help with this.

- **Check that monitors will not cause epilepsy.** People who suffer from photosensitive epilepsy can have attacks triggered by a flickering screen. Sufferers will almost certainly know about this problem and should avoid poor-quality monitors that flicker.

- **Beware of ozone.** This is a highly desirable gas in the upper atmosphere, but acutely toxic to people. It can be given off by laser printers and photocopiers. New laser printers have filters fitted, but these can lose efficiency. Fortunately, ozone can usually be detected by smell, usually described as 'the smell of electricity'. If you have a laser printer (or photocopier) near you, make sure there is adequate ventilation. If you are concerned, check with the manufacturer about its maintenance schedule. If you are not happy, arrange to have the exhaust vented outside by an extractor fan.

- **Remember that toner used by laser printers can be hazardous.** Check the manufacturer's safety guidance before changing a toner cartridge and avoid any contact with the toner. Use disposable plastic gloves to provide extra protection.

- **Cleaning materials used on computer equipment can cause allergic reactions.** Follow the health and safety rules on packaging carefully. Once again, disposable plastic gloves will provide extra protection.

- **Don't hit your computer, however justified you may feel!** It will hurt you more than it hurts the computer. Invest in one of those foam bricks to hit or throw against the wall!

3. Panic page (technophobia)

Even the most experienced computer users will have major problems once in a while. It is easy to feel total panic when something goes wrong (normally stable people may even cry!), but if you keep a clear head, you may be able to avert disaster:

- **My work has all disappeared from the screen!** Make sure you haven't accidentally scrolled down or across the page. Have you started a new document by accident? Have you moved to a different spreadsheet workbook? If so, your work is there, but you can't see it. Check the scroll bars and try moving to different windows.

- **My system won't work at all!** Check the obvious things first. Make sure it is plugged in and the socket is switched on. Is the socket working? Will another machine work from the same socket? If so, has the fuse in the plug blown? If there is no life at all after checking these, you have a serious problem. Or it could be (as frightened one of your authors silly once) that the screen illumination has accidentally been turned right down!
- **The computer seems to work, but there is nothing on the monitor!** Is it plugged in and switched on? Monitors often take their power from a socket in the back of the computer and these connectors often come loose. Is the signal lead (the other lead from the monitor) plugged in to the computer? If these all fail, is there another monitor (of the same type) that you could try on your computer, to find out whether it is the monitor or the computer that is at fault?
- **My keyboard/mouse won't work!** Make sure they are plugged in. If they still won't work, can you try someone else's on your machine?
- **My computer gives an error message when it starts up!** Have you left a disk in the floppy drive? If so, the computer might try to use instructions on it to control how it operates. If the disk is not a 'boot' disk that has been specially formatted, it won't work.
- **My work won't print out.** Try the obvious things, like leads and power switches. Is the printer full of paper? Have you got a paper jam? Has the printer got toner or ink? If you are on a network, are you printing to the correct printer? Is the network working? Have you got enough memory left on your hard disk for printing to occur? When hard disks get too full, failure to print is sometimes the first warning you get.
- **My computer reports problems with the hard disk or memory when it starts up.** Write down the message on a piece of paper so that you can report exactly what has happened. You will probably need professional help – or rather, your computer will need this!
- **Is there anything else I can do before having my computer taken away for repair?** If you are of a practical (and brave) nature, you could take the lid off your computer and make sure that nothing has worked loose inside it. Before you start, make sure you are not charged up with static electricity, by touching an earthed metal object (such as a radiator pipe). Check that leads are connected tightly and that memory modules are seated properly. If there are any chips on the computer board that are in sockets, make sure they are properly seated. Don't use excessive force and don't guess where any loose leads go (there are often a few spare leads inside a computer anyway). If in doubt, leave it alone, especially if it is still under guarantee.
- **My machine needs to go away for repair and it has sensitive data on its hard disk.** This could be a problem. If it isn't a disk problem, can it be removed before sending it away? Speak to whoever is going to repair it and seek advice.

- **What shall I do?** My computer has gone off to be repaired and I need some work that's on it! Use your back-up disks on another computer. That's what they are for. What do you mean, you 'didn't think you needed to bother'? What will you do if the problem is a hard disk failure?

4. Learning to use a new program

With modern computers, once you have learnt to use one program, you will recognize many features in other programs. For example, you will probably find that many of the headings in the menu bar are the same on all the programs you use. This means that many common operations, such as loading, saving or printing your work are very easy and familiar when you start to learn a new program:

- **Allow enough time.** Learning to use a program can be very time-consuming. Be prepared to invest some time in learning the program thoroughly. This will mean that you save time when you use the program in the future.

- **Use tutorials.** Most programs come with tutorial materials and these are an obvious starting-point. Usually these are hands-on interactive sequences that lead you step by step through the main features of the program. Their quality varies but, if nothing else, they will give you an overview of what is possible.

- **Don't try to learn too much.** Modern programs are often extremely complex, and many users will only ever use a small part of them. Work out which parts will be useful to you and learn them. Keep a mental note of what else is available, however, because you might need more facilities in the future.

- **Find a 'real' task to try.** Tutorials can be very helpful, but you will only start to learn to use the program properly when you try to use it for a task of your own choosing. Trying to complete your own tasks will help focus your learning and will force you to confront new problems.

- **Choose your tasks carefully.** Don't be too ambitious about what you can achieve in the early stages. Try to select tasks that will be based on what you already know, but that will also need you to develop some new skills.

- **Don't be afraid to experiment.** If you want to try something new, go ahead! The worst you can do is to destroy all the work you have just done. Your computer will survive, though your temper may not.

- **Save your work often.** If you save your work before trying anything new, and use a new number on the end of the filename, you can reload your work in the event of a disaster, so virtually eliminating all risks.

- **Practise regularly.** Like all skills, using a computer program well takes practice, particularly in the early stages. Try to keep using programs regularly so that you don't forget too much between sessions.

- **Find out about 'undo' facilities.** Many programs allow you to undo the last thing you did, or even to undo a series of operations. You can also often 'redo' things. These facilities give you even greater freedom to experiment.

- **Review your knowledge.** When you have used a program for a while, and you feel comfortable with it, review the skills that you learnt at the beginning. You may well find, in the light of your experience, that you can see more effective methods of working. You may also now understand areas that you skimmed at the beginning. Your program may have a 'Quick preview' or 'Examples and demos' as part of its 'Help' facility. Look at these occasionally, to make sure you are making the most of your program. Things you ignored when you first started with the program may make a lot of sense (for example, 'short cuts') once you are experienced enough to make use of them.

5. Where to find help

If you are learning to use computers on your own, it is easy to feel isolated. There is help available and someone else has probably solved the problem that you are struggling with. All you need to do is to find the help:

- **Build up your own help notes.** As you're learning to use new programs or new machines, you'll learn so much that it's easy to forget important steps if you've not written them down somewhere. It can take ages to backtrack to where you found key instructions. It could be worth having a small pocket-notebook, where you jot down things that you are particularly keen to be able to find again quickly.

- **Look in the 'Help' section.** There is normally 'online' help available within programs. Find out where it is and how to use it. Help facilities often include demonstrations of how to carry out tasks. There may also be other forms of help available, such as a 'tips' window or help 'balloons'. Find out how to turn them on and off, as they can be an annoyance as well as a benefit.

- **Look in the manual.** Computer manuals are notorious for their complexity, but many programs come with a 'getting started' manual that is targeted at beginners. The full manual may be large and intimidating, but it will contain a vast amount of vital information. Start to use it soon so that you have some familiarity with its contents and layout.

- **Find a book.** The complexity of computer manuals has resulted in the publication of books on all aspects of computer use. Many of these are targeted at novices and leave out the more complex information. You may find some of these books insulting in tone, but 'Sticks and stones...' These books are often fat and expensive, so try to borrow one from a library or from a colleague.

- **Read a magazine.** Newsagents' shelves are bursting with a huge array of computing magazines. Some of these are very good and it is worth investigating them. They are very up to date and are the best source of current information. They are often packed with advertisements, but this keeps the price down to a reasonable level. Find one that is at the correct level (ie it teaches you something, but isn't too advanced) and consider subscribing to it.

- **Try a video or computer-based training package.** These are available for computers in general and for a wide range of programs. They can be quite expensive and they don't suit everybody but, if you can find one, try it and see if it helps.

- **Ask for help.** If you know someone who uses the program you want to learn, make contact with that person. It is probably better to have some specific questions ('Do you know how to...?'), rather than just saying, 'Will you teach me to use this program?' You will be respected for having tried for yourself before seeking help.

- **Start a 'self-help' group.** Test out the old saying, 'Two heads are better than one.' If you can find other people who are in the same position as yourself to discuss problems with, you may all be able to supply different pieces of the jigsaw.

- **Use the Internet.** There are newsgroups where people discuss all kinds of topics, and many of these deal with problems people have with computing. Before asking questions, read the discussions to get some idea about the level of the topics that are being discussed. If your questions are very basic, you might find that there is a section for FAQs (frequently asked questions), which might contain the answers you need.

- **Teach someone else.** It may sound bizarre, but this will force you to examine your knowledge and you may gain sudden enlightenment while explaining something to someone else. It will also let you see the tasks that this person is attempting and it may spark off new ideas for your own future work.

- **Go on a course.** Take advantage of any training that is available. There may be 'in-house' training available, or a local college may offer a suitable course. Commercial computer courses can be expensive, but if they save you enough time they may be worth the money.

6. Printing

Despite dreams of the 'paperless office', computer systems are incomplete without printers. It is important to choose the right printer to make sure that you can do exactly what you need without spending too much money. Before you choose, look below at which printers are best used for which purposes:

- **Use a dot matrix printer for cheapness.** These printers are slow, low-quality and noisy. They are, however, very cheap to buy and run. You can even re-ink ribbons to save more money. They can usually use fanfold paper (with tractor holes down the edges, which helps it keep aligned during long print runs).

- **Daisywheel printers offer very good quality – if all you want to print is made of letters.** They are rather noisy and can only produce a limited range of fonts. Extra fonts can be produced by changing the type wheel. They cannot produce graphics. Because of these restrictions, they are not popular nowadays.

- **Inkjet printers are fairly cheap and can offer good quality.** They are very quiet and can be cheap to run, especially if you refill the ink cartridges. They can produce a wide range of fonts and graphics.

- **Laser printers are very high-quality and can be fast.** They are also quiet and are becoming cheaper. Running costs can be high but some suppliers will recondition and refill toner cartridges, which will save money. However, look carefully at the balance you need between speed and quality – some laser printers are very slow!

- **Think hard about whether you really need colour printing.** Don't forget that colour photocopying is very expensive, so colour handouts are not usually feasible. If you do need colour, an inkjet printer will be the best option. Colour dot matrix printers are poor quality and colour laser printers are expensive to buy and run. Paper and other stationery can be bought pre-printed with colour borders or backgrounds if you want to have a colour 'corporate image' on your work. One reason you might want colour is for producing colourful overhead transparencies to support major conference presentations, if you give such things.

- **Colour inkjets should also have a black cartridge.** If a printer tries to produce black by mixing colours, the result is a muddy brown. The expensive colour cartridges are also used up rapidly. Some of these printers allow you to change between colour and black cartridges, but the best have both fitted and use the correct one automatically.

- **Inkjet inks are often not waterproof.** This can be disastrous, so check yours and take appropriate measures. If you produce address labels, the ink may run in the rain; if your presentation goes badly, your sweat or tears might make your transparencies splodgy!

- **Inkjets are sensitive to the type of paper used.** With some papers, the ink 'bleeds' into the paper, causing blurring. Experiment with different papers if you are disappointed with the results. Try to test a sample before buying reams of paper. You could also find that one side of the paper is better than the other. For the best possible results, special coated papers are available (at a price).

- **You can print on to overhead projector transparencies.** Make sure you are using the correct kind of transparency material. If you use a normal transparency in a laser printer, it can melt inside the machine and severely damage it. Inkjet ink will not dry on ordinary transparencies, but it will on special ones. Try to test samples before you buy, as they are expensive. Making mistakes while printing will be expensive, so do a test print on paper before printing on transparencies.

- **Use a bureau for really high-quality work.** There are bureaux that will print computer files to your specification for you. They have expensive machines to produce high quality, but discuss the process with them thoroughly before you produce your work so that you can provide it in the correct format for them. Careful proofreading is even more important than usual in these circumstances.

7. Maintenance

Your computer system doesn't need a great deal of care and attention, but a little will help it last longer and make it more pleasurable to use:

- **Be careful about using water or solvents on the equipment.** Read the instructions and only use what is recommended. If in doubt, test your cleaning process on part of the system that is normally not in full view.

- **Cleaning the screen will improve your view.** Buy some screen wipes and use them regularly. This will really help. They should also reduce the build-up of static electricity on the screen.

- **Clean your mouse regularly.** If your cursor moves in jerks, your mouse probably needs cleaning. Most mice can be cleaned by turning and removing a plate so that the ball can be taken out. Wipe the ball clean and gently remove any dirt from the rollers inside. Cotton buds can help with this. Using a mouse mat will help your mouse work smoothly and help keep it clean.

- **Keyboards can be cleaned too.** This is a fiddly job, but you can use screen wipes to clean the key tops if they become disgustingly dirty and sticky. You may need moistened cotton buds to remove stubborn deposits. You can also turn the keyboard upside down and shake it to remove crumbs, paperclips and other debris. Keyboards can also be vacuumed gently.

- **Desperate measures can be tried.** If you (for example) spill a cup of coffee in your keyboard and it won't work any more, you may have to buy a new one anyway. As a last resort, before spending money, try washing it out in a bowl of water with washing-up liquid. Drain it and let it dry thoroughly before trying it. If it still doesn't work, you haven't lost anything. Do not try this on anything that plugs directly into the mains, such as the computer itself, monitors or printers. Better still, don't spill coffee in your keyboard.

- **Floppy disk drives can be cleaned too.** If a drive becomes unreliable, it is worth trying to clean it with a special kit. Don't do this as a matter of routine, though, because it causes extra wear.

- **Keep equipment covered.** Dust and general dirt will harm all equipment. It is worth buying or making covers, particularly for keyboards. Thin membrane covers can be bought for keyboards that allow them to be used with the cover fitted, giving protection to the keyboard all the time.

- **Clean your printer too.** After much use, printers can build up accumulations of dried ink and paper dust. Follow the manufacturer's instructions to keep them clean.

- **Keep your computer in the correct conditions.** Heat, liquids and dust are bad for your computer. Make sure you follow the manufacturer's recommendations about the conditions your computer works in.

- **Consider using a 'screen saver'.** If your computer is left switched on all day, every day, there is a risk that images could be permanently burnt into your screen. This is particularly likely if there is always a menu bar in the same position. Screen savers put a constantly moving picture on the screen after a few minutes of disuse, preventing this burning while showing that the computer is still switched on. When you press a key or move the mouse, the computer returns to normal operation. Make sure, however, that a screen saver does not constantly access your hard disk, or prevent any power-saving measures from operating.

8. Computing on the move

If you travel a lot, particularly by train or plane, you may want to be able to carry on working during your journeys. You could also take a computer with you so that you can give presentations or so that you can communicate using a modem:

- **Laptop computers are expensive.** In order to justify the cost of a sophisticated laptop computer, you will need to use it a great deal. You may be able to compromise with a less sophisticated model for travelling, with a more powerful desktop computer for use at work.

- **Laptop screens can be hard to work with.** You may find it tiring to look at the screen for long periods. In particular, it can be hard to see the cursor when it moves. This may be worse in poor light and you won't have control over lighting when travelling. Check out the screen and cursor aspects before buying. Programs are available to change the shape and size of the cursor, which may help.

- **Battery life can be limited.** Laptop computers will need to be run on their own rechargeable batteries when there is no mains supply available. Check on how long the computer will really run for (not what the manufacturer claims). You may need to budget for extra batteries as part of your purchase.

- **Laptop computers can feel heavy.** Even a few pounds can be tiring if you have to carry the laptop a long way. Remember you may need to carry extra batteries and a mains supply as well as the computer.

- **Check the keyboard carefully.** Laptop keyboards are small and usually incorporate some compromises to provide the same range that is available on a full-size keyboard. This may mean some alterations to your typing, which will need practice. Laptops don't always have a separate numeric keypad, so if you're used to using one for entering data for calculations, you may have to learn to be equally adept with the numbers on the QWERTY keyboard.

- **The mouse can be a problem.** When you are travelling, there is often nowhere to operate a mouse. Various solutions have been tried, such as trackballs and trackpads. Make sure you are happy with the alternative provided on any laptop you consider. Don't forget that it's more difficult to use trackballs on moving vehicles than when sitting at a stationary desk. You could use external devices, but this will increase the amount that you have to carry.

- **Some laptops have 'docking stations'.** When you're not actually travelling these enable you to use a full-size monitor, connect easily to a printer or network and use a full-size keyboard by putting your laptop into a module. This means you use the same computer, whether on the road or at work.

- **Consider alternatives to full-powered laptops.** If your needs while travelling are simple, you could buy a cheap device that would let you (for example) take notes. You could transfer these notes to a desktop computer when you are back at work and finish them using a word processor. Investigate the possibilities of 'palmtop' computers, 'message pads' and even the better 'electronic organizers'. Some of these are very powerful and surprisingly small and light, and have long battery life.

- **Be careful about battery charging.** Follow instructions on battery charging very carefully as incorrect use can shorten battery life considerably. In particular, don't charge a NiCad (nickel cadmium) battery until it is completely flat to avoid the 'memory' effect that can reduce the amount of charge a battery can hold.

- **Use a timer to avoid overcharging batteries.** When batteries are charged for too long, they can be damaged by overheating. It is easy to forget to turn the charger off, so use a cheap mains timer to turn off the power after the recommended time.

9. Writing on the move

The following tips are intended for people who do quite a lot of writing on the move, and are based on experience learnt by trial and error:

- **Choose suitable writing tasks for your travels.** Writing on the move is usually best with jobs where it's all right to do a little at a time and then return to it (like writing this book!).
- **Write, but don't edit much.** While in motion on trains, for example, it's much easier just to type material in than it is to go backwards and forwards making amendments and corrections. Getting the cursor to exactly the bit you want to change is not too easy when the journey is a bit bumpy!
- **Save the fiddly jobs for later.** Editing, spell-checking, adjusting the layout and so on are best done when you're on terra firma. Another reason for this is that such operations run your battery down faster than just typing in new material.
- **Choose jobs where you don't need lots of reference materials to hand.** There's not usually much room when writing on trains or planes to spread books and papers out around you. It's normally possible to accommodate a single document, but not a pile of papers and books.
- **Choose your company?** People tend to be fascinated by the sight of people working on laptops, and this may put you off. It is better, for example, to sit in the 'airline-style' double seats on busy trains than at a table designed for four people. Some trains have one or two single seats, which are ideal even on very busy trains – if you can find them!
- **Have a multimedia journey?** It's worth having your Walkman or Discman with you – if you're already carrying a laptop, spare battery and mains lead, it won't make much difference to the weight. Listening to something of your choice while you write saves you from being put off by children being normal children or by football fans, or even from being distracted by those fascinating conversations you only hear on trains!
- **Call in for a pint and a watt!** On long journeys, you may not be able to find somewhere to give your battery a top-up, but you can usually find a power point in a hotel lounge or even the station buffet. It's best to be a valid 'consumer' when you're consuming just a little bit of electricity too!
- **Keep saving to floppy disk as well as to the hard disk.** When travelling, you never know when you may suddenly be interrupted (for example, when told to change to a train that isn't broken down!). In the rush of gathering up your bits and pieces, it's only too easy to forget to save that last bit you've written.

- **Carry a three-way mains adaptor.** Your hotel destination will probably have rooms where there's a shelf or other hindrance that stops you plugging in your mains connector directly into the power. With a three-way adaptor, there's much more chance you can apply some suitable geometry, and get charging again. It may also mean you can both write and boil the kettle for that coffee you need.

- **Consider having a backpack.** This can be a better way of carrying relatively heavy laptops and accessories around, and means you have hands left for other luggage and train doors, and to hang on when lurching to a stop!

10. Security

As you make more use of your computer, you will gather increasing amounts of data. In time, the data may become more valuable than your computer system. If you were to lose the data, it might not be possible to re-create them. Even if it were possible, it could be very time-consuming. In some cases, the data could be confidential and in need of protection from prying eyes:

- **One day, your computer will fail.** All machines will break down. What you don't know is when this will happen. It is vital that you have some strategy in place to protect your data from loss. In an emergency, you could always use your data on a different machine.

- **Back up important data.** It is usually most convenient to save your data on the hard disk of the computer that you normally use. If you don't want to risk having to re-create the data, save them somewhere else as well.

- **Think about how much data you can afford to lose.** If you back your data up once a day, you could lose a whole day's work. If this sounds like too much to risk, back up more frequently.

- **At the very least, use a simple back-up strategy.** The simplest method is to save your work to a floppy disk (or a recordable CD ROM) as well as to the hard disk a few times a day. For extra security, you could use two floppies as well as the hard disk. Have a number on the end of your file name (such as number 1 to start with) and use 'Save as' when you save your work. Each time you save, increase the number by one. If you do this, you prevent the computer writing over older versions of the file and you will have a series of files you could go back to. You might decide, at the end of the day, that you preferred the version you produced at lunchtime. You will, of course, fill your disks more rapidly, but you can delete old versions when you are sure they are no longer wanted.

- **Store your back-ups somewhere safe.** If there were a fire or a theft, you could lose your computer and your back-ups. Keep a back-up somewhere away from your computer. Take it home, or swap back-up disks with a colleague for mutual safety.

- **Consider a more systematic back-up strategy.** The simple strategy above will probably be satisfactory for many people, but there are still risks. What if a disaster strikes while both copies are together? What if a computer error (or a virus) damages both copies of the data? One strategy is to keep several 'generations' of important files. Only the oldest is brought to the computer at any time, to be overwritten with the latest copy. These techniques are sometimes called 'grandfather, father, son'.

- **Are your system and program files safe?** You should be able to reinstall your operating system and all your programs in the event of a major failure. This will be time-consuming and annoying. If you have 'customized' your system by changing large numbers of settings, it could take a very long time to redo all this. If you do a complete system back-up, you could restore the whole system if you need to.

- **Consider a special back-up device.** Floppy disks are fine for backing up small amounts of data but are very time-consuming (and expensive) to use for larger back-ups. There is a variety of devices designed for larger back-ups, including tape streamers, exchangeable hard disk units, CD ROM writers and digital audiotape drives. If you want to do large back-ups regularly, investigate these.

- **Use appropriate back-up software.** Most operating systems include software for backing up. Other software is available for the job. It may be faster, use less storage space for the back-ups, allow a wider range of options or help with automating the process.

- **Test your back-up devices and strategies.** It would be very upsetting to back your system up regularly only to find that you couldn't restore it when a problem arose. Make sure that it works before disaster strikes by testing the system's ability to restore from the back-up device.

- **Use passwords to protect your data.** Many computer systems allow you to use passwords to prevent unauthorized use. Check up on this and, if you use it, keep your password safe.

- **Sometimes you can password-protect data files.** When you save your work, there may be an option to password-protect it. On some systems you can lock files so that they can't be accidentally overwritten.

- **Don't use passwords that can be guessed easily.** Avoid your names, or those of your family, friends and pets. Don't use 'password' or 'testing'.

- **Don't forget your passwords.** This is embarrassing and counter-productive. You should, however, avoid writing them down and leaving them near your computer!

- **Be careful about 'deleted' files.** When files are deleted from a disk, they are still there! What happens is that the space that they used is marked as available for reuse and the file names are removed from the directory. Someone with a moderate level of computer knowledge could 'undelete' files and gain access to their contents. Software is available to destroy deleted files properly.

- **Power supply problems can destroy data.** It is fairly obvious that a power failure can cause you to lose work that you have just done. It may also corrupt complete files and disks. Less noticeable problems, such as power surges or spikes, can cause similar problems. Try to avoid plugging your computer into a supply near heavy machines or other sources of sudden power demand.

- **Power conditioning devices are available.** These vary from simple special plugs that smooth the worst of the surges from the supply to complete back-up power systems that switch in to power your computer in the event of a major power supply problem. You can even buy software that, in conjunction with a back-up power supply, will automatically save your work and close the system down safely. When the power is restored, your work will be returned to its previous state.

- **Protect your computer against theft.** Even if it is insured, you will suffer great inconvenience if it is stolen. You could also lose your data with it, if you don't have a good back-up strategy. Lock the room where it is kept and consider using alarms. Make sure it can't be seen from outside the building. Security devices are available to fix it to an immovable object with cables or to lock it inside a steel case.

- **The ultimate back-up is a print-out.** Despite the desire expressed elsewhere for a 'paperless office', one way of protecting your work from system failures or viruses is to print it out and store the paper copy somewhere safe. In the event of disaster, your thoughts are not lost. They can be retyped or scanned into the computer when it has been repaired or replaced.

- **Exchangeable hard disks can improve security.** These devices enable you to remove one hard disk and insert another. You can use them to back up your main hard disk to store in safe places for security purposes. You could also use different disks for different projects.

- **Don't rule out a safety deposit box.** If you're working on something that your whole career may depend on, it's not unreasonable, for peace of mind, to store both an interim disk copy and a paper copy somewhere as safe as possible.

11. Expressing intended learning outcomes

Over and above the suggestions about using learning outcomes made earlier in this book, there are some additional considerations when such outcomes relate to learning with technology. The following tips should help you show your trainees where the goalposts lie:

- **Remember that some of the language may be quite alien to your trainees.** If they've not already been mouse-trained, some may find the whole prospect of learning about computers quite daunting. Work out what your trainees should be able to do by the end of your training session, keeping in mind that some may be struggling.

- **Find out whether similar learning outcomes have already been laid down.** The syllabus content of many education and training courses has been expressed in terms of learning outcomes, for example in colleges that teach similar subjects. It can be useful to scan through a range of different interpretations of the learning outcomes associated with the subject matter you are handling.

- **Express your outcomes in a user-friendly way.** Don't use wording like 'The expected learning outcomes of this session are that the trainee will be able to...' It's much better to bring the word 'you' into your learning outcomes. For example, 'By the end of this morning, you'll be better able to do...' is much more involving for your trainees.

- **Don't be limited by a prescribed training programme.** If you're starting from an existing formal specification of learning outcomes, translate it into user-friendly language for your trainees. As long as the net result is that your trainees gain the same competences and skills as were indicated in the formal specification, it does not matter if you express your learning outcomes in a much more friendly way. You can show your trainees the formal version of the intended outcomes *after* their learning has been successful, when they won't be put off so much by formal language.

- **Don't use words like 'know' or 'understand' in your learning outcomes.** The problem with these words is that they mean different things to different people. It is difficult for people to tell whether or not they really understand something. The only way of measuring understanding is to find out what people can *do* with their understanding, so you might as well recognize this from the start, and express your learning outcomes in terms of the things your trainees will be able to do by the end of your session.

- **Start with some relatively straightforward learning outcomes.** If the very first learning outcome that your trainees see is frightening, they are likely to be put off right from the start. Leave the tricky ones for towards the end of the list, and perhaps don't reveal these until you know your trainees' performance well enough to judge whether they will accept them without being scared off.

- **Remember that some of your trainees are likely *already* to have achieved some of your intended outcomes.** When introducing the intended learning outcomes, give credit for existing experience, and confirm that it is useful if some members of the group already have some experience and expertise that they can share with others.

- **Be ready for the question, 'Why?'** It is only natural for trainees to want to know why a particular learning outcome is being addressed. Be prepared to illustrate each outcome with some words about the purpose of including it.

- **Be ready for the reaction, 'So what?'** When trainees still can't see the point of a learning outcome, they are likely to need some further explanation before they will be ready to take it seriously. Work out your answers to 'What's in this for me?' When trainees can see the short-term and long-term benefits of gaining a particular skill or competence, they are much more likely to try to achieve it.

- **Make sure that the learning outcomes, as expressed, cover any assessment that trainees may be heading towards.** The whole point of learning outcomes is letting learners know exactly what it is that they should become able to do. If your trainees achieve all of your learning outcomes, they should automatically be in a position to demonstrate their achievement if their learning is to be measured. What's more, they should *know* that achieving the outcomes equates to success in assessment, increasing their confidence when taking assessments.

12. Bringing trainees round to learning from a machine

Some trainees take to computers like ducks to water. Other trainees, however, are likely to believe that they need a human being to train them, and that they can't learn from mere machines. The following suggestions may help you to win them over, so that they are more receptive to letting computers train them too:

- **Remind them that there's always a human brain behind the machine.** When necessary, explain to trainees that the computer is merely a vehicle for storing human expertise, and that it's not actually the computer that will be planning what they should learn.

- **Tell them that the computer may be better than you are!** In other words, the expertise that will have gone into the computer-designed training packages is likely to be broader than that of any one person. The people who put together good-quality training packages are normally very experienced in their field, and are likely to be expert trainers in their own right.

- **Explain that working with computers is a transferable skill.** Gaining confidence and competence with computers is likely to spill over into future careers and lives, and will make your trainees easier to update and retrain as further advances are made in their fields. Also, young people at school are increasingly highly mouse-trained, and many of your trainees may welcome the chance to keep up with their own kids!

- **Try to convince your trainees that learning from computers can be great fun.** Once they are over any fear that they will break the equipment or that the computer will 'think' that they are silly, most people actually take pleasure in getting a computer to work for them.

- Remind your trainees of the comfort of making mistakes in privacy. When trainees get tasks or exercises wrong, in computer-based training only the computer knows – and computers don't mind! Therefore, it is much better to learn from one's mistakes using a computer than when human beings can see each and every slip.

- **Point out that, when using computers, your trainees don't have to waste time on things they already know.** In face-to-face training sessions, the whole group is often held up until someone catches up. With computers, anyone who already knows something can press on to something more demanding, without having to wait for anyone to catch up. Computer-aided training can allow trainees to work at their own individual pace.

- **Computers don't mind the plea, 'Run that by me again.'** Some things are not learnt properly first time round. It's not always convenient (or possible) to ask a human trainer to go once more through something that a trainee might find difficult, but a computer will go through it as many times as it takes to get the message firmly home.

- **Remind your trainees that they learn most things by having a go at them.** When they learn-by-doing using a machine, they're being supported every step of the way, and most computer-based packages are highly interactive, and force trainees into making decisions, working things out, selecting the best answers to questions from a range of alternatives and so on. This means that these aspects of their learning can be much more focused and efficient than in a group training situation.

- **Suggest that human trainers are there for more important roles.** While trainees can learn things from machines, human beings are better at helping to measure and evaluate their learning, and explaining in other ways any parts that the computer was unable to teach them.

- **Remind them that they don't have to work alone with computers.** While it may be intended that the computer-based training materials are for individual use and independent learning, it can be very useful for clusters of trainees to explore a training package together. This allows them to compare notes on what they find out, and to learn from each other and explain things to each other. This can be a useful first step before setting out to work through a package in depth, independently.

13. Helping trainees to learn-by-doing using computers

Learning happens by practice and trial and error. Learning happens by having a go. Not much learning happens when trainees simply watch an expert doing something. They are not then in a good position to do it for themselves. The following suggestions should help you to make your trainees' learning more productive and more enjoyable:

- **Plan your training session around things that your trainees will actually *do*.** This is more important than simply trying to get together all the things that you might wish to tell them or show them. Map out the tasks that your trainees will do during a session, rather than simply mapping out the structure of the content that you intend them to cover.

- **Share your intention to get trainees learning-by-doing.** Tell them how much more they will learn by having a go with computers (or anything else) than they would if they just sat listening to you talking about them. When trainees can see the point of doing practical tasks, even when they don't feel that they know enough to get started on them, they become more receptive to the idea of jumping in at the deep end (with plenty of lifebelts and floats around them).

- **Remind your trainees that they're not going to break the computer.** Trainees who haven't used computers before are often afraid of damaging them, knowing that they are expensive pieces of equipment. They're extremely *unlikely* to damage them unless they are moving them physically.

- **Tell your trainees about the benefits of learning-by-doing.** It helps when they know that this is the best way to make sense of the things that they are learning. It is useful to move their expectations away from simply listening to you explain things to them.

- **Plan to let your trainees learn from their mistakes.** This is one of the best ways to learn most things, when mistakes can be made in a safe environment and with help available for anyone who does not understand why a mistake happened.

- **Remind your trainees that computers don't care about mistakes!** They may give error messages when instructed wrongly, but a computer does not get angry or frustrated even when the same mistake is made several times in succession (unlike typical human reactions!).

- **Make good use of anticipated mistakes.** Think of all the things that are known to be the most common problems with the subject matter you are handling, and set up learning-by-doing situations that will precipitate these likely errors. Let your trainees know that this is your intention, so that they themselves can be looking out for the errors and trying to avoid them.

- **Build in practice and repetition.** For the most important things that your trainees will learn-by-doing, make sure that they consolidate their learning by repeating the steps involved two or three times during the training session. Structure these repeats differently, so that they don't get bored by the repetition.

- **Remind your trainees that speed comes with practice.** They sometimes feel that their efforts are unbearably slow, especially if they see an expert like you gliding effortlessly through long sequences of steps at great speed. Let them see how much faster they do a task the third time through than on the first attempt.

- **Get your trainees to talk each other through the steps that they have taken.** This helps them to take on board consciously the sequences that they followed; putting it into words deepens their understanding of what they have done.

14. Getting trainees used to working with mice and keys

Becoming good at using computers, like most other things, is best learnt by doing it. The following suggestions may help you to make the processes of gaining skill with keyboards and mice more enjoyable and efficient for your trainees:

- **Encourage your trainees to learn to touch-type.** They may not have time to do this during your training sessions but, if they really want to do it, there are good computer-aided training packages for just such a purpose. Explain that if they use computers a great deal, it is perfectly possible for them to become much faster at keyboarding than they may be at handwriting. Also explain that using the right fingers for the right letters makes keyboarding easier in the long run, even though it has to be learnt in the first place.
- **Remind your trainees that, in most computer operations, not all of the keys need to be used.** The most important keys tend to be the 'enter' key (for commands), the letter keys for text entry and the number keys for number entry or calculations. The function keys may be much more rarely used, especially when first starting to use computers.
- **Make the most of 'undo' facilities in software.** In many word-processing packages, for example, it is possible to 'undo' a series of keyboard entries. This can be particularly useful when trainees can't remember exactly what they actually did but know that something has gone wrong. They can also try using the 'redo' command, to find out, step by step, what they may have done when something went wrong.
- **Consider the possibility of having at least one machine where plastic covers or stick-on labels obscure some or all of the letters on the keyboard.** This is one of the techniques used to help people to develop touch-typing skills. Tell trainees using such machines not to look at their fingers at all, but to watch the letters on the screen as they type. Remind them that it does not matter if they type incorrect letters; they can always delete them and try again until they get what they are trying to get on the screen.
- **Give your trainees computer-based exercises that require them to enter words or numbers from the keyboard.** Many computer-based training packages, and also computer-managed assessment programmes, require trainees to use text entry and number entry for their answers to at least some of the interactive elements.
- Help your trainees to become mouse-trained. The best way for them to do this is simply to work through computer-based packages that require quite a lot of mouse work, such as using

drop-down menus, double-clicking icons and so on. Explain that it's a bit like learning to drive a car. While there are various kinds of mouse (including roller-balls, trackpads and various other ways of manipulating the position of the cursor on the screen), once competence has been gained using one system, different systems are relatively easy to learn.

- **Don't forget the left-handed.** It should be easy to move the mouse to the left side of the keyboard, but it is usually also easy to configure the buttons so that the most-used one is under the index finger. When you have done this, however, instructions like 'Press the left mouse button' will need to be changed. At the end of your session, you might need to reconfigure the mouse buttons for right-handed use.

- **Suggest to your trainees that they may benefit from varying the sensitivity of the mouse.** When they get really competent with a mouse, they are likely to prefer using fast speeds, but using slow speeds can help them gain confidence on the way.

- **Get trainees to experiment with the size and shape of the on-screen cursor.** The biggest source of anxiety, when learning to use a mouse, tends to be associated with 'losing' the cursor on the screen. Altering the colour and size of the cursor, to make it easier to spot, takes away much of this anxiety.

- **Get your trainees to do some exercises using just the cursor keys on the keyboard.** These can normally do all the cursor movements that are normally done using a mouse, but are usually much slower and more cumbersome. Trainees are then more likely to appreciate the benefits of getting themselves mouse-trained.

- **Choose some exercises that develop mouse-skills.** It can be productive to get your trainees to play with a 'painting' programme, both to draw shapes and objects using the mouse, and to select and fill different areas of their drawings. People who have hang-ups about their artistic skills often find that they exceed their own expectations when trying to draw in a completely new medium.

15. Language, visuals and numbers: international dimensions

The suggestions in this set may apply to you yourself if you are likely to travel to different countries to run training programmes, or could involve your work with trainees from abroad who may find unexpected differences in the computers. Keyboards are not always what they seem to be. You may already have discovered this, but you still may need to alert your trainees to some of the wrinkles. You may work with trainees from several different countries, and it could be useful to be aware of some of the other keyboard possibilities that may be familiar to them. Furthermore, if you yourself train abroad, there may be some surprises in store for you; perhaps there may be one or two points below that you have not yet discovered:

- **There are many more characters available on the computer than there are on your keyboard.** If you want to type other characters, you may be able to use the menu bar in your application to insert characters or symbols. This option usually shows you a table and you can select the character you want from this.

- **Set up 'short cuts' for symbols that you use frequently.** You can set up a combination of key presses that will give you a symbol quickly. These usually involve using the 'Ctrl' or 'Alt' keys, together with one of the main keys on the keyboard. It is useful to pass on to your trainees examples of short cuts that you find useful, and encourage them to experiment with their own.

- **Some typefaces have a wide range of different characters.** If you can't find a character that you want in the typeface you have been using, try other typefaces. Many computer systems have typefaces that contain special symbols that you can use. The most common of these typefaces is called 'Symbol'. Help your trainees to practise finding any special characters they are likely to need in their own work.

- **Make sure that other computers you wish to use have the correct typefaces.** If you produce a document using a special typeface, the symbols will look correct on your computer. If you view the same document on a computer that doesn't have that typeface, the computer will not display the symbols correctly and they may not appear at all. Point out to your trainees the sorts of problems that this may cause, if they use computers from a different country.

- **You can buy special typefaces for producing extra characters.** If the characters you want are not available on your computer, you may be able to buy an extra typeface that has them. As above, this typeface will need to be on all computers that are to use your document. Explain the possibilities to trainees, but remind them that the chances of them actually *needing* unusual characters in their everyday work with computers or word processors are likely to be quite low.

- **'Foreign' keyboards may have letters in different places.** This can lead to difficulties when you try to type. On some keyboards the differences are fairly small, but on others they are fundamental. For example, French keyboards aren't QWERTY; they are AZERTY! If trainees from abroad seem to be having particular difficulties with the computers they use on your courses, it is worth finding out from them more about the particular differences they notice, so that you can build up your personal store of advice that you can offer to future trainees.

- **Operating systems can be in other languages.** It can be a bit of a shock to start up a computer and see all the menu items appear in a different language. If you are travelling, it is a good idea to try to familiarize yourself with appropriate computer terms in the language of the country you are going to visit. You might be expected to deliver training in English, but your interactions with the computer could be in a different language. Conversely, be patient with trainees from abroad who encounter an operating system in English for the first time.

- **Make sure that you know how to set software to handle numbers correctly.** Numbers are represented differently in different countries. You may need to change currency symbols, the number of decimal points displayed and the use of commas to show thousands and millions. You may therefore need to point out local conventions to trainees from abroad.

- **Dates and times may be displayed differently.** Find out what is done in your destination country and how to set these correctly. Share with trainees from abroad the local conventions and preferences regarding showing or printing dates and times on documents.

- **Check up on the use of punctuation marks.** These vary throughout the world, so make sure you are familiar with local practice in any country you are visiting, and let trainees from abroad know about your own local conventions. Make sure any notes you produce use these correctly and, if possible, ask a native of the country to check them for you.

16. Using computers to give feedback to trainees

Feedback is a vital step in successful learning. Human beings can get bored when giving the same feedback repeatedly to different trainees; computers don't have this problem! In the suggestions that follow, we look at computer-generated feedback, where you programme the feedback messages you wish trainees to receive in anticipated circumstances, such as replying to options in multiple-choice questions. Later in this chapter, we explore in more detail the use of computer-delivered feedback, where your individual comments are e-mailed directly to individual trainees or put up on a computer conference where trainees can all see such comments. The following suggestions may help you to use computer-generated feedback to make your training more effective for your trainees, and more enjoyable for yourself:

- **Look for those occasions where you frequently need to give the same feedback message to different trainees.** Work out exactly what the gist of your feedback message is on such occasions, and consider whether it will be worth packaging up this feedback so that trainees can get the same help from a computer instead of from you.

- **Listen to yourself giving live feedback to trainees after they have attempted a task.** It can be worth tape-recording some examples of the way you talk to fellow human beings. The little 'asides' that you slip in to make sure they understand you are very important, and it's worth incorporating such asides in the feedback you get the computer to give them.

- **Devise a task relating to the planned feedback message.** Normally, the feedback will be reserved for those trainees who don't get the task right first time. Check out with live trainees that the planned feedback is self-sufficient, and that they don't need any further explanation from you in person to get the task right next time.

- **Don't forget to provide feedback to trainees who get the task right first time.** It is just as important to give positive feedback for successful work as it is to give helpful feedback when trainees encounter problems. Remind them exactly what they got right, in case it was a lucky accident.

- **Let trainees who get things right know about some of the things that might have gone wrong.** Learning from mistakes is useful, and people who don't make any mistakes can miss out on some valuable learning. Trainees are often quite hooked on finding out more about what they *might* have done wrong, even when they got it all right.

- **Be sympathetic to trainees who get it wrong.** When you programme feedback into a computer-based learning package, it is important that your trainees feel that the computer is treating them like human beings. Don't include blunt messages such as 'Wrong!' or 'Wrong yet again!' It is better to come across almost apologetically, with feedback messages starting perhaps, 'Sorry, but this doesn't work out in practice…'

- **Remind trainees about *what* they get wrong.** It is important that mistakes can be linked firmly to the task that brought them about. The danger is that when your trainees read your feedback messages, as programmed into the computer system, they may have forgotten exactly what they were trying to do when things went wrong.

- **Try to devise feedback that explains *why* trainees may have got something wrong.** It isn't enough just to know *what* was wrong. Whenever you can, devise feedback messages about mistakes along the lines, 'For this to have happened, you may have been thinking that…, but in fact it's like this…'

- **Road-test your feedback messages with small groups of trainees.** Ask them if they can think of any better ways of getting the feedback message across. Get them to put into words what *they* might have said to someone sitting next to them who attempted the same task and got it wrong. If their words are better than your original ones, steal theirs!

- **Explore the possibilities of using e-mail for 'later' feedback.** When you know how well (or badly) trainees have tackled a computer-based exercise, you may be able to give them feedback through the system of networked computers. This means that only the trainees concerned see each feedback message, and they have the comfort of privacy in which to read the feedback and think about it, without you seeing their expression or body language.

17. Interrogating multimedia for training

Training packages can contain, or refer out to, an increasing range of other kinds of material. We explored the use of videotapes in a separate set of suggestions, but the present set aims to alert you to the questions you should be asking yourself about *any* medium. This could include CD ROMs, the Internet, intranets, interactive videos and anything that adds sounds, still pictures, moving images or graphics to the experience of trainees working through training materials:

- **How does the medium help trainees' motivation?** Ideally, any multimedia component should help trainees to want to learn from them. If there are too many steps to getting going with the multimedia elements, there is the danger that trainees can be put off and may be stopped in their tracks.

- **Can the medium be used to provide some learning-by-doing?** Perhaps the biggest danger with some multimedia packages is that however sophisticated the media used, trainees may be only spectators rather than players. Where it is not possible to cause trainees to interact directly with the materials, it remains possible to get them to make decisions, answer questions and summarize conclusions, and to write down these for later reference.

- **Can the medium be used to give trainees feedback?** The danger is that the information presented using multimedia is often fixed, and cannot then respond to what trainees may be thinking about it, or to the problems or misunderstandings that may be in their minds. It is best to ensure that some self-assessment questions address directly any important information presented in multimedia formats, so that feedback responses addressing the difficulties can be designed for trainees.

- **How does the medium help trainees to make sense of things?** There are often excellent answers to this question. For example, sounds, pictures, moving images and colourful graphics can all play useful parts in helping trainees to get their heads round things with which they have been grappling.

- **Why is this medium better than other, cheaper media?** For example, why is a computer-based package better than a print-based one? There are many good answers to this question. The best answers are when the medium chosen does something that just cannot be done by other media, for example moving pictures showing body language and facial expression where such dimensions are crucially important for getting particular messages or attitudes across to trainees.

- **How relevant will the medium-based element be to the overall training programme?** One of the dangers with media-based training is that too much 'nice-to-know' material may be involved, with not enough emphasis placed on 'need-to-know' material, and that trainees may not easily be able to distinguish the two categories.

- **How will the choice of medium affect trainees' opportunities to learn?** For example, will they only be able to study the particular elements concerned when they are sitting at a networked computer terminal, or when logged on to the Internet? Will this mean that they have frequently to stop learning until they can gain such access? Will there be alternative coverage of these elements of training for any trainees who have not got easy access to the medium, and can it be guaranteed that they will not end up disadvantaged?

- **How easy will it be to edit and change the medium-based elements?** Training materials are never 'finished'. There are always adjustments and changes that are indicated from piloting, feedback from trainees, and assessments measuring how well trainees actually succeeded in their learning. Some media are much easier to edit and change than others. Changing a CD ROM or videodisk is a much more complex (and more expensive) business than changing a file in a computer-based package.

- **What *other* media could have been used?** There is rarely just one way to package up a particular element of learning. It is useful to explore at least two or three alternative ways of using media to deliver each element of training, and then to make an informed decision about *why* a particular medium is chosen.

- **How will trainees revise and consolidate what they have learnt from the medium?** What will they have to take away? Will they be able to make a structured summary of what they learnt while working with the medium that will bring all the important points back to their minds when looking at it later?

18. Helping trainees to work together with computers

Using computers is often thought of as a solitary activity. Many of us use PCs (personal computers), and this name suggests that they are meant for individual use. Computers can, however, be very useful for group activities. Group working can have many advantages, ranging from the interchange of ideas to providing social contact. It can also lead to problems, as some groups do not perform well and some people do not thrive in group work situations. When the group is widely dispersed, it is even more important than usual that steps are taken to help groups to function properly. Working together at a distance may sound paradoxical, but sometimes it is easier to arrange group activities in this way. Because of computer communications, barriers of distance and timing can be lowered. In order for your trainees to participate, they will need e-mail facilities as a bare minimum. For even more effective communications, computer conferencing will be needed. The following suggestions may help you to get groups to work together productively, whether as part of your training programmes or using computer conferences at a distance:

- **Think carefully about the number of people who should be in each group.** If groups are too small, the trainees may have to work too hard and they may not have all the skills needed for the task. If the groups are too large, they may be unwieldy and it might be difficult for decisions to be made. In large groups, there is a risk that skills can be duplicated so that some people are underutilized. When you decide on a size for each group, bear in mind that you might not have exactly the right number of trainees to divide up, so you will have to have a range of sizes in mind.

- **Decide whether you will choose who is in which group or whether the trainees will organize themselves.** If you choose, you have more control over the whole process of group working. If the trainees organize themselves, they will feel more empowered and will be taking more responsibility for their work.

- **Think about the task the groups will have to tackle and how it affects the composition of the 'ideal' group.** Some tasks require special skills and it may be necessary to distribute skill holders among the groups. These skills could be related to the task in hand, or they could be group skills such as leadership. Some thought may also need to be given to whether the groups need to be balanced so that they have a roughly equal chance of doing the task effectively.

- **Carry out some group-building tasks before the main group task starts.** If the groups are to work effectively from the beginning of a task, they must be functioning effectively as groups first. The members also need to be familiar with the computer conferencing system, if you are using one. Set up some minor tasks first so that the trainees can gain experience and so that roles within the groups can be established.

- **Develop group tasks that enable individuals to use their particular skills.** Your trainees may not all have learnt about the same computer skills, or some may be more proficient in some areas than others. Carefully chosen group tasks can involve real teamwork in distributing tasks among the group so that people can use their skills effectively.

- **Use group tasks to help distribute skills.** Someone who is particularly proficient in a skill can help other members of a group to improve their skills. This has an additional benefit of making the skilled person think hard about what he or she can do in order to show another person how to do it.

- **Encourage negotiation skills in distributing tasks among group members.** When a group is given a task, people will have to take on different roles. Some of these roles may be unpopular; others may be everybody's first choice. Help the group to negotiate so that they all feel that they are performing a useful role and that the allocation of tasks is fair.

- **Set group tasks that involve the group meeting new challenges.** When individuals are faced with a task that goes beyond their current knowledge, it is easy for them to feel overwhelmed by its difficulty. The dynamics of a group can help with this as the interactions between group members will often lead to new avenues of thought that can find ways round blockages.

- **Plan group activities that build on skills that have been developed elsewhere.** It is useful to use group work to help trainees to consolidate things they have already learnt, and to give them the chance to see how useful it can be to learn by explaining things to each other. This can save you time too.

- **Use group activities to help people appreciate each other's work.** If trainees who work in different fields tackle work-related problems together, it will also give them some appreciation of each other's work. This can help develop team building that will continue when their computer training is over.

- **Encourage computer communications between trainees as soon as possible.** In order to make effective use of computer communications, regular use is needed. If trainees can develop a culture of frequently checking e-mail and conferences, they will make very effective use of these media. If they only check occasionally, there will be a struggle to establish their effective use.

- **Set some simple tasks early on.** You could pair trainees up and give them a simple task that requires them to exchange ideas. They could then produce a joint word-processed report on what they have done. This would mean that they would need to communicate with each other and they could also need to exchange files attached to e-mail messages.

- **Give everyone some practice at using computer conferencing.** If you plan to use computer conferencing to keep trainee group work going after a face-to-face course, or between elements of such a course, it is useful to use part of the course time to get everyone talking to each other electronically. Ideally you will need a room with networked terminals for each trainee. It can be useful to start everyone off with a common-interest topic, even one that has no relationship to your training programme, and allow your trainees to concentrate on the process of communicating with each other electronically, rather than thinking too hard about the content of their practice communications.

- **Put out information by e-mail or in conferences to make people check for it.** Rather than sending out all the documents by mail, use computer communications for some of it. Warn your trainees that you are going to do this and keep doing it so that they continue to check their e-mail and conferences.

- **Make sure some kind of back-up is available.** If someone didn't receive a computer message because of technical problems, it could cause major problems for that person. Some sort of safety net could be used, for example you could send out a message to all trainees every week. Anybody who didn't receive the message would know to contact you so that you could try again or send a paper copy by post.

- **You might need to consider geographical location when setting up groups.** If your trainees are widespread, there is no need to consider where they live and work. If some of them live or work near to each other, they could meet occasionally. This might help the group work well, but it could also give them an unfair advantage over other groups who couldn't meet face to face.

- **Make sure groups have ways of communicating apart from electronic means such as computer conferencing or e-mail.** As with all technological systems, computer conferences can fail to work. It is very important that some back-up communication system can be used. Ideally, group members would exchange telephone numbers, fax numbers and addresses. Check what rules your institution has about releasing personal details, however, as there are often controls on this.

- **Set up private conferences for each group at an early stage.** Each group will need a conference where they can exchange messages that cannot be seen by members of the other groups. Set these up for them early in the process (or, better still, appoint a member of each group to do it). Make sure that the conferences contain suitable topics and remember to include a 'chat' area so that there is a suitable place for general conversation.

- **Decide on your own access to group conferences.** The groups' conferences could be closed to you, so that you cannot read them and trainees can discuss any topic freely. This may help trainees to feel uninhibited about what they say in messages. Alternatively, you could have access to them so that you can monitor progress. Make sure that the trainees know what you have decided so that they can behave appropriately!

- **Encourage trainees to take part in group activities regularly.** The group work will be taking place not only at a geographical distance, but also at different times. It is very important that all group members access their conference regularly and that they leave messages to show that they are doing so.

- **Include a group work topic in the main conference.** It will be very useful for members of different groups to have a common area where ideas and problems related to the group task can be discussed.

- **Make use of any facilities the software has for tracking who has done what.** Some packages (particularly word processors) have features that show who has written or revised different parts of a file. These enable some checking that trainees have done what they were supposed to.

- **Make sure that somebody is in charge of the group.** It is easy for a group to encounter serious problems if there is no control over its activities. One person needs to take on the role of co-ordinating the whole group to make sure that all the tasks are progressing properly. When groups undertake several successive tasks, encourage the groups to decide who will co-ordinate their work on a rotating basis.

- **Watch out for particular problems that can arise from computer use.** When groups are using computers, it is possible for out-of-date documents to become confused with current versions. If there is a failure of any kind, the consequences affect the whole group, so back-ups are particularly important. Somebody needs to be in charge of this area to make sure problems don't develop.

19. Setting out computers in your training room

A problem with computers as training tools is that they are designed for interaction with one person, not a group. This means that it is very difficult for more than two or three people to see the same computer screen clearly. It is even more difficult for a few people to sit comfortably around a computer screen for any length of time. The following suggestions aim to help you set out your training room to minimize visibility problems:

- **Position computers carefully to avoid reflections on the monitors.** If light is reflected shining on the screens of the computers, it can make it very hard and tiring to read the data. One person may be able to find a suitable position in order to avoid this problem, but it can be difficult for several people to do this.

- **Anti-glare screens can improve screen visibility.** You can reduce reflections on monitor screens by adding a special screen in front of the monitor. There are several types available, but if you want to use a screen to help with group work, check that it allows clear viewing from a range of angles. Some of these screens are even designed to restrict the viewing angles in order to improve security.

- **Close blinds to reduce glare from outside light.** It can feel a bit claustrophobic to be in a room with no natural light, but you may need to close some or all of the blinds or curtains to help with glare problems. If some windows aren't contributing to this problem, don't cover them.

- **Avoid using laptop screens for group viewing.** The screens in most laptop computers are small and not very bright. Even more importantly, they usually only allow viewing from straight in front, so they are not at all suitable for viewing by several people at the same time. If you want to use a laptop computer, see if you can connect it up to a full sized desktop monitor or a projection system.

- **Try to avoid the 'computers around the wall' layout.** Because it is the simplest way of routeing the cables of the computers, a common layout is to put all the computers around the walls. The trouble with this is that all you see, as a trainer, is the back of people's heads. This layout also makes it difficult for your trainees to look at you or at anything else in the room.

- **Make sure that all the cables are safe.** Make sure that cables aren't anywhere near people's feet to avoid any danger of them tripping over them. It is also easy for people to pull leads out of the back of computers with their feet, without realizing that they have done so.

- **It may be possible to use a large computer monitor, mounted fairly high up.** It is possible to connect more than one monitor to a computer, if the right hardware is available. This means that you could work at a computer, looking at its screen, while your trainees see the same information on a large screen. Large computer monitors are expensive, but there are adaptors available that allow televisions to be used in this way. This is cheaper, but the quality of the image can be poor.

- **Information can be displayed on several ordinary computer monitors simultaneously.** There are devices on sale that plug into a computer and several monitors to allow several people to see the information simultaneously. Using these requires some changes to the wiring of the computers in the room, so you will need to check if this is possible and if it would interfere with the normal operation of the computers.

- **A computer network might be able to display the same information on several monitors at once.** If your computers are linked together in a network, this is a possibility worth checking. You will need to ask your network manager if this is possible and to ask for help in setting it up.

- **Overhead projection 'tablets' are available.** These devices connect to a computer and duplicate its display on a transparent liquid-crystal display. This can be put on an overhead projector and projected on to a screen. These devices can be expensive and you will need to make sure that outside light can be reduced to help make the projected display clear. It is usually even better if you can hook up the computer directly to a projection set-up, such as used for projecting videos. These normally give a brighter and better-focused display than liquid-crystal tablets.

20. Now you see it, now it's gone!

This is one of the most significant pitfalls of computer-aided presentations or demonstrations. Trainees may well understand something while they are watching you show it to them, but their understanding may slip away quite quickly when they can't see it any more. The following suggestions may help you to overcome the problem:

- **You know it all already!** This is always the case when as an experienced trainer you have the problem of not being quite able to imagine not knowing the topic. With computer-aided presentations, the problem is in trying to work out which parts of your presentation are likely to go over trainees' heads first time through. Once you have identified the elements that you really want trainees to remember, you are in a much better position to take positive steps to help them to remember those elements.

- **Be a trainee yourself for a while.** It can be really useful to sit in on someone else's computer-aided presentation, or to work through a computer-based training package on something that you don't know anything about, and then to look at what was memorable and what was all too easily forgotten. This can inform the way you help your trainees to maximize their learning from your own presentations and materials.

- **Plan for them to *do* something, fairly quickly.** Relatively little learning happens just by watching something passively. More significantly, trainees' expectations of what they should be learning are mostly based on what they are asked to do. Look carefully at which parts of your computer-delivered presentation lend themselves to being the basis for fairly immediate tasks for trainees, and make sure that your trainees know what they will soon be required to have a try at for themselves before they watch your presentation, so that they will do so more attentively.

- **Design triggers that will bring back trainees' memories of things they have seen.** This is quite easy to do in the case of PowerPoint slides, where you can provide trainees with handout pages to remind them of both the content of individual slides and the sequence of the whole presentation.

- **Stop and switch the presentation off every now and then.** Design tasks to get your trainees recalling and consolidating what they have just seen and heard. Think about short tasks that they can do in twos or threes where they are sitting, so that they can be reminded of the main things that you wish them to remember from the episode of presentation that they have just seen.

- **Consider turning a presentation into a question-and-answer session.** You can brief trainees with the questions on-screen, and then turn off the presentation while they try to work out (or guess) answers to the questions. When you resume the presentation, they will be more receptive to the answers that your presentation already contains than if they had not been trying to answer the questions themselves for a while.

- **Get trainees to annotate copies of what they see.** If you issue print-outs of computer-presented slides, it can be useful to make many of the slides bullet point questions, and to encourage trainees to write summary answers to each question as you work through the presentation with them.

- **Get trainees to do things with what they see.** For example, ask them to complete a pro forma while watching a video sequence or a software demonstration. Brief them in advance about the main things they should be watching out for, and the questions already on the pro forma. Stop the demonstration or video quite frequently, to give them time to make sense of what they have been seeing, and to record it in their own words on the pro forma.

- **Use screen dumps to illustrate your handout materials.** This can be an effective way of helping trainees to recall important stages of demonstrations they have watched on-screen. Make sure that screen dumps are clearly legible – don't print them too small!

- **Don't illustrate indiscriminately.** Each illustration in your handout materials should have a definite purpose. It is best if you can give your trainees something to *decide* each time they see an illustration in their handouts, so that they really look at the illustrations.

21. Making effective use of e-mail

E-mail is the simplest form of communicating by computer. Electronic communication is addictive! To most people who have already climbed the learning curve of finding out how to use e-mail, the apprehension they may have experienced on their first encounters fades into insignificance. E-mail can be an important medium in training. Computers can be linked up to a network and the users issued with e-mail addresses. A user can use e-mail software to type a message and send it to any other user. The message is stored on a central computer until the recipient collects it. This can be on a computer network within a company or it can be via the Internet. The Internet will enable users anywhere in the world to exchange messages. Once you are connected to the Internet, sending e-mail is cheaper than sending a letter or making a telephone call and is much quicker. The following suggestions may help you to get started with e-mail yourself, and to maximize some of the benefits that it can offer to you and to your trainees:

- **Find out what e-mail facilities your institution has available.** If you work in an organization, it may already have access to e-mail facilities. It may be possible for you to use these facilities, saving you the effort of organizing your own.

- **Arrange to have your own e-mail address.** It is much better to be able to collect your e-mail separately from the rest of your organization. This will help avoid e-mail being lost within the organization and will help others feel that they are communicating with you directly.

- **Choose your e-mail address carefully.** You may be able to choose the first part of your own address. Make sure that it uses the name you usually use for your communications. It is common for IT managers to issue e-mail addresses to people based on their names from a personnel file. As an example, if your name is Keith Robert Simpson, the first part of the e-mail address you are issued might be KR Simpson. If you are generally known as Bob, people may not recognize you from the e-mail address. If it is possible, insist that the name part of your e-mail address is what you want it to be.

- **Include your e-mail address on written communications and tell people it when you are on the telephone.** Make the e-mail address part of your letterhead to make it widely known. Encourage people to e-mail you, rather than writing to you or telephoning you.

- **Take care to let people know if your e-mail address changes.** If you move from one service provider to another, for example, or if your institution changes its address details, your e-mail address will change. It can be worth the time spent to e-mail everyone in your address book with details of any forthcoming change, and then to e-mail them from your new address again as soon as the change is implemented.

- **Ask other people if they have e-mail and what their addresses are.** Most e-mail software includes an electronic address book. You can enter the e-mail addresses into it when you are told them. When you want to send an e-mail message, you can just select whom you want to send it to and the computer will fill the address in for you.

- **Make sure that trainees get started with e-mail.** Write careful, step-by-step briefing instructions for your trainees. The computer-literate people may hardly do more than glance at these before getting into the swing of using e-mail. However, for those people who lack confidence or experience with computers, these instructions can be vital and comforting until they become familiar with the medium.

- **Decide what you really want to do with e-mail.** There are numerous purposes that e-mail can serve, and you need to ensure that the purpose is always clear to your trainees. If they know *what* it is being used for, and *why* e-mail has been chosen for this, they are much more likely to get more out of it.

- **Make the most of e-mail.** Although you may just want to use e-mail for routine communication with (and between) trainees, there are many more uses that the medium can lend itself to. Think about the possible uses of sending attached files, such as documents, assignments, digitally stored images, sounds and video recordings. All of these can be edited or marked, and returned to trainees, in the same ways as simple messages.

- **Collect your e-mail frequently and reply quickly.** If you don't collect your e-mail frequently and respond promptly, you will lose out on the benefits of fast communications and other people will be less inclined to send you e-mail in future.

- **Make the most of the lack of time constraints.** One of the most significant advantages of e-mail as a vehicle for feedback is that trainees can view the feedback when they have time to make sense of it. They can store it until such time becomes available. They can also look at it as often as they wish to, and you can keep copies of exactly what you said to each individual trainee.

- **Be available.** When trainees are accustomed to e-mail, they expect quick replies to their queries. If you're going to be away from your access to the system for more than a day or two at a time, it is worth letting all your trainees know when you will be back online.

- **Make the most of the speed.** Giving feedback by e-mail to trainees at a distance obviously reduces delays. The sooner trainees get feedback on their work, the more likely it is that their own thinking is still fresh in their minds, and the feedback is therefore better understood.

- **Keep e-mail messages simple.** Most e-mail systems have very limited editing facilities and can only handle straightforward text. They don't allow different fonts or typestyles and diagrams are not possible, so messages tend not to look attractive. The reason for this is to let a very wide variety of systems communicate in a very simple way.

- **Make most messages really brief and to the point.** Few people take much notice of long e-mail messages. If something takes more than one screen, most readers either dump it or file it.

Encourage your trainees also to make good use of the medium, and to send several short messages rather than try to cram lots of points into a single missive.

- **When you send a long e-mail, explain why and what to do with it.** For example, from time to time you may want to send trainees something that you don't expect them to treat as a normal e-mail message, but perhaps to print out and study in depth. It makes all the difference if they know what they are expected to do with longer messages.

- **Send more detailed messages as attached files.** If you want to send more detailed communications, you can produce them in another, more flexible computer package. If you save the file you produce, you can then send this with a short e-mail message explaining what you are sending. If file sizes are large, it may take a long time for them to download. Packages are available to compress files (or 'zip' them) so that they take less time to transmit. If you zip files, the recipient will need to have software to 'unzip' them.

- **Make sure the recipient has software to read attached files.** If you send a complex file such as a word-processed document or a spreadsheet, make sure the recipient can read it. Ideally the recipient would have the same version of the program that you used to create it, but it may be possible to send a file that is saved in a format compatible with the recipient's software even if it isn't the same.

- **Make use of mailing lists to send copies to more than one recipient at the same time.** Most e-mail software makes it very simple to send extra copies of a message to other people. It is also often possible to create lists, or groups, of people and to send messages to all the members of the groups at the same time. These groups can also be saved for future mailings.

- **Encourage trainees to reply about your feedback.** When you are using e-mail to give specific feedback to trainees, it is important that you know that you have got through to them all. Asking them to reply to you gives them the chance to let you know how they *feel* about the feedback you have given them, or the mark or grade that you have awarded them.

- **Use e-mail to keep a dispersed or distant group of trainees together.** Sending out circular notes not only helps individuals to feel part of a community of trainees, but also reminds them about important matters such as assessment deadlines, problems that have arisen with course materials, or updates to interesting materials that have been discovered on the Internet.

- **Remember those trainees whose access to e-mail is difficult or impossible.** One of the disadvantages of using e-mail as a means of communication on training programmes is that, if some trainees have problems with access, they can become significantly disadvantaged. You may need to find ways of compensating through other means for those things they miss out on.

- **Take particular care with your e-mail message titles.** It can take ages to search for a particular e-mail if it is not clear what each message is about. The computer software can sort messages by date and by sender, but it is more difficult to track down topics. Two or three well-chosen keywords make the most useful titles.

22. Helping trainees to get started with e-mail

The use of electronic mail has accelerated rapidly in the last few years. We've already explored how *you* can get started with e-mail, and next we look at ways you can help your trainees to take the plunge. People who would not have been thought to be computer-literate often take their first steps into the area because they are attracted by the benefits of e-mail. Some, perhaps many, of your trainees are likely to be up to speed with computers and e-mail, but the following suggestions may help you to whet the appetites of those who have not yet become 'mouse-trained':

- **Mention how unlikely it is that trainees will break the computer!** For those trainees who are reluctant to get into computer usage, there is often a concern that they may do something drastic and irreversible to expensive equipment. Remind trainees that the only thing they are likely to risk when using computers is losing some of the work they have done with the machine, and even this risk is quite small, with 'undo' commands in most computer software, and with good habits about saving work to disk every few minutes.
- **Point out that e-mail is a way of practising useful written communication skills.** Getting trainees to communicate with each other and with you using e-mail helps them to develop their written command of the language. Seeing their own words on-screen rather than on paper can make them more aware of their strengths and weaknesses with the language.
- **Promote the benefits of computer literacy.** The information technology revolution has meant that a much greater proportion of people need to use computers in their everyday work and lives. Being computer-literate also means that people don't have to rely on other people to perform various tasks for them. For example, trainees who have mastered word processing don't have to pay someone to process their reports or memos, and can keep editorial control over them, making it much easier to change them whenever they receive some useful feed-back about draft versions.
- **Remind trainees that an e-mail message need not be sent until they are completely happy with it.** This allows them to edit and polish their writing. If they were to attempt so much editing on a handwritten message, it could either look very messy or have to be written out several times before the same number of adjustments had been achieved.
- **Remind trainees that e-mail can be viewed as environment-friendly.** The saving of paper can be significant. If the computing facilities are already available, it can be argued that using e-mail incurs negligible costs.

- **Point out to trainees that they can save and keep their own e-mail communications.** By copying each e-mailed message to their own files or disks, they can keep track of all the messages they have composed and sent. Keeping similar track of handwritten messages is less likely, or would involve the trouble and expense of photocopying. Trainees looking back at a range of e-mails they have composed can see for themselves how their skills with the language are developing.

- **Remind trainees that e-mail can be a way of them keeping in touch with their friends elsewhere.** Most libraries or colleges have Internet facilities available to trainees, making it possible for them to send messages to anywhere in the world. Such facilities are sometimes free of charge to library users, and in any case the actual costs are insignificant once the equipment has been installed.

- **Help trainees to get started.** Probably the best way to do this is for you to *require* all of your trainees to e-mail something short to you, with a time deadline. It can be worth thinking about using a short written exercise for this purpose, in which case you can attach at least some marks to the task. This can make all the difference to trainees who might otherwise not get round to finding out how to log in to the system and send an e-mail.

- **Make trainees' efforts worthwhile.** If you've asked all members of a group to e-mail something to you, try to respond *immediately* (within a day or two) to each message as it arrives. The fact that trainees get a little individual feedback via e-mail from you, and quickly, helps them to see for themselves the potential of e-mail as a communication medium.

- **Encourage trainees to write very short e-mails.** One of the problems with e-mail communication is that people only tend to read the beginning of a message. If an incoming message is too long for immediate reading, people tend either to file it away for later reading (and forget it!) or simply delete it.

23. Giving trainees feedback using e-mail and computer conferencing

Computer communications are very fast and cheap, so they are very useful for providing feedback to trainees. Once you have established a culture of using computer communications for aspects of your training, develop its use for feedback as well. E-mail is particularly useful as a vehicle for giving trainees individual feedback on assessed work, whether as stand-alone e-mail communications, or alongside or within a computer conferencing system. Electronic feedback can apply to computer-mediated coursework (where the work is submitted through a computer system), but can also extend usefully to giving trainees feedback on handwritten or hard-copy work that they have submitted for assessment. The following suggestions may help you to exploit the benefits of e-mail, not least to save you time and energy in giving trainees feedback:

- **Encourage trainees to send you assessments or samples of work as e-mail attachments.** If work is being produced on a computer, it is easy and quick to attach a saved file to an e-mail message. It will arrive very quickly and it is very cheap to send it.

- **Make the most of the comfort of privacy.** When trainees receive feedback by e-mail (as opposed to face to face or in group situations), they have the comfort of being able to read it without anyone (particularly you!) being able to see their reactions to it. This is most useful when you need to give some critical feedback to trainees.

- **Remember that you can edit your own feedback before you send it.** For example, you may well want to adjust individual feedback comments in the light of trainees' overall performance. It is much harder to edit handwritten feedback on trainees' written work. E-mail feedback allows you to type in immediate feedback to things that you see in each trainee's work, and to adjust or delete particular parts of your feedback as you go further into marking the work.

- **Exploit the space.** Inserting handwritten feedback comments into trainees' written work is limited by the amount of space that there may be for your comments. With e-mail feedback, you don't have to restrict your wording if you need to elaborate on a point.

- **Acknowledge receipt of assessments.** Trainees will be worried that their work hasn't arrived safely, so tell them when it has. An e-mail message is best for this because it is private.

- **Provide specific feedback to individuals by e-mail.** As this method of communication is private, it is suitable for giving comments on work to individuals. It is much easier to write this kind of communication by computer than by hand, so use the technology for the whole process.

- **Investigate word-processing software to help with assessment of written work.** If work is produced by word processing, it is often possible to add comments to it. You can use this to provide comments on the work as part of the feedback process.

- **Consider combining e-mail feedback with written feedback.** For example, you can write on to trainees' work a series of numbers or letters, at the points where you wish to give detailed feedback. The e-mail feedback can then translate these numbers or letters into feedback comments or phrases, so that trainees can see exactly what each element of feedback is telling them. The fact that trainees then have to decode each feedback element helps them to think about it more deeply, and learn from it more effectively, than if they had seen it directly on their work.

- **Spare yourself from repeated typing.** When designing computer-delivered feedback messages, you should only have to type each message once. You can then copy and paste all of the messages where you need to give several trainees the same feedback information. It can be useful to combine this process with numbers or letters that you write on to trainees' work, and build up each e-mail to individual trainees by pasting together the feedback messages that go with each of the numbers or letters.

- **Consider the possibilities of 'global' feedback messages.** For example, you may wish to give all of the trainees in a large group the same feedback message about overall matters arising from a test or exercise. The overall message can be pasted into each e-mail, before the individual comments addressed to each trainee.

- **Check that your e-mail feedback is getting through.** Most e-mail systems can be programmed to send you back a message saying when the e-mail was opened, and by whom. This can help you to identify any trainees who are not opening their e-mails. It can also be useful to end each e-mail with a question asking the trainee to reply to you on some point arising from the feedback. This helps to make sure that trainees don't just open their e-mail feedback messages, but also have to read them!

- **Keep records of your e-mail feedback.** It is easy to keep copies on disk of all of your feedback to each trainee, and you can open a folder for each trainee if you wish. This makes it much easier to keep track of your ongoing feedback to individual trainees than with handwritten feedback, which is lost to you when you return trainees' work to them.

- **Make the most of the technology.** For example, many e-mail systems support spell-check facilities, which can allow you to type really fast and ignore most of the resulting errors until you correct them all just before sending your message. This also causes you to reread each message, which can be very useful for encouraging you to add second thoughts that may have occurred to you as you went further in your assessment of the task.

- **Use e-mail to gather feedback from your trainees.** Trainees are often bolder sitting at a computer terminal than they are face to face. Ask your trainees questions about how they are finding selected aspects of their studies, but don't turn it into an obvious routine questionnaire. Include some open-ended questions, so that they feel free to let you know how they are feeling about their own progress and about your teaching too.

- **Use a computer conference to provide subtle pressure on trainees to submit work on time.** Publish lists of work you have received from trainees, but without names. This will make those who haven't submitted work realize that they could be falling behind.

- **Create a new conference topic for discussion of each assessment.** Trainees may want to exchange ideas after they have received feedback on assessed work. If you provide a topic for this, they will know where to discuss this without affecting the structure of the rest of the conference.

- **Seek permission from participants to use their work to give general feedback to the group.** If the work of one of the trainees includes something that you could use to illustrate a useful point to the whole group, ask the trainee's permission to use it. An e-mail message is the appropriate medium to use for this. The work could remain anonymous. Once you have permission, you can copy the appropriate sections to the conference and discuss it there.

- **Use the conference system to provide general feedback to groups.** When assessing work, there will be common points that need to be raised for several people. If these are discussed on the group's conference without naming anybody, participants can learn from each other's mistakes.

- **Consider putting assessment statistics on the conference.** You could make some basic information (such as average scores) available to the group. Some people might find it helpful to see how their performance compared with others in the group. On the other hand, some people might find this demoralizing, so this issue needs careful thought.

24. Thinking about using computer conferencing for training

There are several parallel names for this, including computer-mediated communication (CMC), computer-supported cooperative learning and, more simply, online learning. Whatever we call them, computer conferences can be of great value in training programmes, especially where the trainees are geographically dispersed but working on similar timescales. Many of the suggestions made about e-mail continue to apply, but in this section I would like to alert you to some of the additional factors to consider with computer conferences. Computer conferences are very similar to e-mail, but the messages are sent to all the people who are members of a conference. Conferences allow groups to discuss ideas together and, if the Internet is used, members can be anywhere in the world. The person who runs the conference is called the moderator. The moderator has control over who is a member of the conference and can set up sub-conferences (or topics). This person can also delete messages and so has some editorial control over the conference. The following suggestions may help you to plan whether to use computer conferencing, and point you towards maximizing the benefits that your trainees can derive from it:

- **Note the differences between computer conferencing and other forms of electronic communication.** The distinguishing feature of computer conferencing is that many people can see the same contents, from different places and at any time. The contents 'grow' as further notes and replies are added by participants. Most systems automatically alert participants to 'new messages' that have been added since they last viewed the conference, and allow these messages to be read first if desired.

- **Regard computer conferences as virtual classrooms, seminar rooms and libraries.** Computer conferences can be each of these. They can provide a virtual classroom, where the whole trainee group can 'meet'. They can be used to provide a virtual seminar room, closed to all but a small learning group of around six trainees. They can function as virtual libraries, where resource banks and materials are kept. They can also function as trainee-only gossip areas. Each of these ways of using computer conferences can emulate electronically the related best practice in face-to-face training environments.

- **Work out definite purposes for each computer conference.** Conferences are much more successful where they are provided to relate to identified needs or specific intended outcomes. It is worth working out how best you may use computer conferencing with your own trainees well before starting one up.

- **Get involved in computer-conferencing situations yourself first.** If you have access to e-mail or the Internet, one of the best ways to pave the way towards putting computer conferencing to good use with your trainees is to participate yourself. For example, join some discussion lists, and experience at first hand the things that work and the things that go wrong with such means of communication.

- **Explore the computer-conferencing systems from which you can choose.** There are several systems available round the world, each with their own formats, features and idiosyncrasies. If most of your trainees are not particularly computer literate, go for a system that makes it as easy as possible to log on and to add messages.

- **Investigate what computer-conferencing facilities your organization has available.** If there is already a mechanism for computer conferencing, it makes sense to see if you can use that, rather than starting from scratch on your own. You may also be able to tap into existing expertise in your organization.

- **Carefully evaluate computer-conferencing facilities offered by other organizations.** There will be a range of companies that are keen to sell you facilities based on their computer systems. You will need to investigate them thoroughly to make sure that you choose the best for your needs.

- **Question potential conference providers thoroughly.** Find out about prices for setting up the conference and for providing space for storing messages. Is there a limit on message storage and how much does it cost to buy more? Check the software that the systems use. Which is the easiest to use, and are essential facilities included? Are good help facilities provided in case you have problems setting up conferences? Is the conference system accessible via the Internet? If conference members will be connecting to the system by modem, are there plenty of telephone access points to the system so that calls are charged at local rates? Also check that the modems at these telephone access points are reasonably fast.

- **Make sure that conference members have good help provision.** Ordinary conference members do not need help with setting up or moderating conferences, as they will use the ones you set up. Make sure that any manuals or help facilities are correctly targeted to provide an appropriate level of support for ordinary conference users.

- **Check up on the levels of security and privacy provided.** It is important that conference members are happy that their messages can only be read by the intended audience. It may also be useful to enable sub-groups within the conference to communicate privately from the main conference.

- **Find out about the e-mail facilities offered by the conference providers.** E-mail is a very useful addition to conferences, as it enables private messages to be sent to individuals. The ability to communicate separately from the conference can be very helpful.

- **Make sure that all of your trainees will be able to access all the conferences that you want them to.** Ideally, you may also intend them to be able to download and/or print chosen extracts from the conference for their own personal study purposes. You can only build a computer conference into a training programme as an essential component if all of your trainees are able to participate. If the conference is just an optional extra for those able to join it, other trainees who aren't able to join may be able to claim to have been disadvantaged.

- **Try to practise setting up and moderating conferences before the real one starts.** A few colleagues may be willing to take part in a pilot exercise so that you can develop your skills by practising on them. Start this well in advance of your first real conference so that you can overcome problems and gain confidence.

- **Make sure that trainees will have sufficient access to networked terminals.** In particular, if contribution to a computer conference may be linked in any way to assessment, it is essential to ensure that trainees cannot appeal against assessment decisions on the grounds of not having been able to contribute because of lack of opportunity.

25. Getting a computer conference going

The success of a computer conference depends upon its value to trainees, and how well they can make good use of it. This in turn depends significantly on the design and structure of the conference, and on the degree of ownership trainees develop about it. The following suggestions may help you to tread sensitively regarding moderating a conference, while setting it up so as to maximize its value to trainees:

- **Explain to trainees the benefits of participating in computer conferences.** Trainees can exchange a lot of information, both study-related and social, through such conferences. They can get peer feedback on their own ideas and even on selected parts of their work. Participating in computer conferences helps trainees to develop computer-related skills, and can quickly help them to speed up their keyboarding skills.

- **Provide good 'start-up' pages.** These are the initial notes, to which trainees can append their replies. Each 'start-up' page should have a definite purpose, so that replies and ensuing discussion are focused rather than rambling. These are essentially the main topics of the conference, and are listed sequentially in the main directory of the conference. Conferencing takes place when participants add 'replies' to these pages. The replies are normally listed in the sub-directory of each start-up page in the order in which they are received.

- **Make each screen speak for itself.** Especially with 'start-up' pages, which introduce each topic in the conference, it is best that the essence of the main message takes up less than a single screen. Further detail can be added in the next few pages (or 'replies'). Encourage trainees contributing their own replies to keep them to a single screen whenever possible, and to send several replies with different titles rather than one long reply addressing a number of different aspects.

- **Aim to get the essence of a 'start-up' page on to a single screen of information or less.** If trainees have to scroll down more than one page before finding out what is being addressed, they are less likely to read the 'start-up' page, and therefore unlikely to reply.

- **Choose the titles of 'start-up' pages carefully.** When trainees are looking at the directory of a computer conference, they will see the titles of these pages arranged as an index, in the order in which the pages were originally entered. Aim to make these titles self-explanatory, so that trainees can tell what each section of the conference is about directly from the directory, rather than having to read the whole of a 'start-up' page before finding out whether they wish to explore the topic further.

- **Don't cover too much in a 'start-up' page.** It is better if each section of the conference is relatively self-contained, and prescribed, rather than having topic pages that cover several different aspects. As new matters arise from trainees' replies to 'start-up' pages, decide whether to introduce new 'start-up' pages to carry these matters forward separately. Add your own responses directing trainees who may be following the conference themes regarding where in the conference each theme is being developed further.

- **Choose the topics within your conference carefully.** Think about the structure you want the conference to take and set up a topic for each main area. Topics that are too general may end up with messages that are not clearly focused and discussions may not develop well.

- **Start with a small number of topics and only add more when they are needed.** It is confusing to have too many topics at first, so only have a few at the beginning. As the training develops and new subjects become relevant to your trainees, add new conference topics to provide discussion areas.

- **Make sure messages are put into the correct topic.** If messages are put into the wrong topic, the structure of the discussions will suffer. Encourage conference members to think about where to put messages at a very early stage and try to establish a culture of well-organized discussion. If some members consistently place messages in the wrong place, send them an e-mail explaining what they have done and what would be better. If they persist in doing this, you may need to use your moderating powers to move messages to the correct place.

- **Encourage trainees to reply with messages that are short and only contain one point.** Long messages are difficult to read on computer screens, so discourage any that are more than one screen long. If messages contain discussion of more than one point, the structure of the conference can break down, so encourage members to send several short messages, addressing one point each.

- **Leave a message every time you log on.** One of the concerns that computer conference users have is that nobody is reading their messages. Use the conference as frequently as you can and always leave some kind of message to show that you have been logging in. Ideally your messages should answer questions or raise some important issue, but a trivial message in the 'chat' topic is better than nothing.

- **Use the conference as a noticeboard.** Get into the habit of making the conference the best way to keep up with topical developments in the field of study, as well as administrative matters such as assessment deadlines, guidance for trainees preparing assessments and so on. Try to make it necessary for trainees to log on to the conference regularly; this will result in a greater extent of active contribution by them. A conference can provide you with a quick and efficient way to communicate detailed information to the whole of a class. Trainees themselves can print off and keep anything that is particularly important to them.

- **Use the conference as a support mechanism.** This can save a lot of tutor time. Elements of explanation, advice or counselling that otherwise might have had to be sent individually to several different trainees can be put into the conference once only and remain available to all. Whenever your reply to an enquiry or problem raised by a trainee warrants a wider audience, the conference is there to do this.

- **Make the conference a resource in its own right.** Add some screens of useful resource material, maybe with 'hot-links' to other Internet sources that are relevant. It is useful if some such material is *only* available through the computer conference; this ensures that all your trainees will make efforts to use it.

- **Try to get trainees discussing and arguing with each other via the conference.** The best computer conferences are not just tutor–trainee debates, but are taken over by the trainees themselves. They can add new topics, and bring a social dimension to the conference.

- **Set up a 'chat' topic for general conversation.** Conference members might want to discuss matters that are less serious than the training aspects of the conference. Set up an area for them to do this and encourage them to 'chat' in that area. Other names for 'chat' conferences might be 'café' or 'pub': choose a name to suit the tone you are trying to establish for your conference.

- **Encourage members to use e-mail where it is more appropriate.** E-mail is more private and so it should be used for messages that are for individuals rather than for general distribution to all conference members. There is also no point in making others read messages that are not relevant to them.

- **Try to moderate with a light hand.** If people are putting messages in the wrong topic or are not using e-mail appropriately, provide gentle guidance about what to do in future. As far as you can, keep the ownership of the content and structure of the conference with the participants themselves, rather than being tempted into editing the conference too much.

- **Be prepared to moderate rigorously if necessary.** For example, remove anything offensive or inappropriate before it is likely to be seen by many trainees. If particular trainees misuse the conference, treat the issue seriously, and seek them out and warn them of the consequences of such actions, for example loss of computer privileges. It is useful to recruit trainee moderators from those trainees who are particularly computer literate, and who may be only too willing to become conference moderators, editing and rearranging contributions to keep the structure of the conference fluent and easy to follow.

- **Consider having some assessed work entered on to the conference.** If trainees *have to* make some contributions, they are more likely to ascend the learning curve regarding sending in replies, and to do so more readily in non-assessed elements too. One advantage in having an assessed task 'up on the conference' is that each trainee can see everyone else's attempts, and the standards of work improve very rapidly.

- **Consider allocating some of the coursework marks for participation in a computer conference.** This is one way of ensuring that all the trainees in a class engage with a class conference. Once they have mastered the technique of contributing to a conference, most trainees find that they enjoy it enough to maintain a healthy level of participation.

26. Using the Internet for training

Trainees may be able to use the Internet at times of their own choice, in their own ways, at their own pace, and from anywhere that access to it is available to them. That said, this does not mean that it is automatically a vehicle for productive and effective learning. Indeed, it is very easy to become sidetracked by all sorts of fascinating things, and to stray well away from any intended learning outcome. The suggestions which follow are not intended as starting-points for setting out to *deliver* training through the Internet, but rather to help trainees to *use* the Internet to obtain material to use in connection with their studies, such as in assignments they are preparing. The following suggestions may help you to help your trainees both to enjoy the Internet and to learn well from it:

- **Play with the Internet yourself.** You need to pick up your own experience of how it feels to tap into such a vast and varied database, before you can design ways of delivering with it to your trainees some meaningful learning experiences.

- **Decide whether you want your trainees to use the Internet or an intranet.** An intranet is where a networked set of computers talk to each other, using Internet conventions, but where the content is not open to the rest of the universe. If you are working in an organization that already has such a network, and if your trainees can make use of this network effectively, there will be some purposes that will be better served by an intranet. You can also have *controlled* access to the Internet via an intranet, such as by using hot-links to predetermined external sites.

- **Use the Internet to research something yourself.** You may well of course have done this often already but, if not, give it a try before you think of setting your trainees 'search and retrieve' tasks with the Internet. Set yourself a fixed time, perhaps half an hour or even less. Choose a topic that you're going to search for, preferably something a little offbeat. See for yourself how best to use the search engines, and compare the efficiency of different engines. Find out for yourself how to deal with 4,593 references to your chosen topic, and how to improve your searching strategy to whittle them down to the 10 that you really want to use!

- **Don't just use the Internet as a filing cabinet for your own training resources.** While it is useful in its own way if your trainees can have access to your own notes and resources, this is not really *using* the Internet. Too many materials designed for use in other forms are already cluttering up the Internet. If all you intend your trainees to do is to download your notes and print their own copies, sending them e-mailed attachments would do the same job much more efficiently.

- **Think carefully about your intended training outcomes.** You may indeed wish to use the Internet as a means whereby your trainees address the existing intended outcomes associated with their subject material. However, it is also worth considering whether you may wish to add further training outcomes, to do with the processes of searching, selecting, retrieving and analysing subject material. If so, you may also need to think about whether, and how, these additional training outcomes may be assessed.

- **Give your trainees specific things to do using the Internet.** Make these tasks where it is relevant to have up-to-the-minute data or news, rather than where the 'answers' are already encapsulated in easily accessible books or training resources.

- **Consider giving your trainees a menu of tasks and activities.** They will feel more ownership if they have a significant degree of choice in their Internet tasks. Where you have a group of trainees working on the same syllabus, it can be worth letting them choose different tasks, and then communicating their main findings to each other (and to you) using a computer conference or e-mail.

- **Let your trainees know that the process is at least as important as the outcome.** The key skills that they can develop using the Internet include designing an effective search and making decisions about the quality and authenticity of the evidence they find. It is worth designing tasks where you already know of at least some of the evidence you expect them to locate, and remaining open to the fact that they will each uncover at least as much again as you already know about!

- **Consider designing your own interactive pages.** You may want to restrict these to an intranet, at least at first. You can then use dialogue boxes to cause your trainees to answer questions, enter data and so on. Putting such pages up for all to see on the Internet may mean that you get a lot of unsolicited replies!

- **Consider getting your trainees to design and enter some pages.** This may be best done restricted to an intranet, at least until your trainees have picked up sufficient skills to develop pages that are worth putting up for all to see. The act of designing their own Internet material is one of the most productive ways to help your trainees develop their critical skills at evaluating materials already on the Internet.

27. Information retrieval from the Internet

The Internet has enormous potential as a source of information for a vast range of tasks. It can also, however, lead to problems and it needs to be used with care. Passing some of this guidance on to trainees will help them avoid pitfalls:

- **Choose your times carefully.** If you plan to give trainees information-retrieval tasks using the Internet during course time, make sure that you plan so that the system will not be too congested at the time. When the system is busy, it becomes very slow and communications can even break down. UK users should use it in the mornings, when the USA is asleep, if possible.

- **Think about the time it might take and what the costs might be for your trainees to find information.** The Internet is generally cheap to use, but costs can mount up. If trainees are using a modem to make their connection, encourage them to do it at weekends or in the evenings to reduce costs. Make sure they have the opportunity to search at these times. You might need to give trainees some hints about where they should search so that they don't waste too much time.

- **Use 'local' sources when possible.** A number of organizations have sites in different parts of the world. If you can find one in the same country (or even continent) that you are working from, communications can be faster at busy times.

- **Use a good search engine to help you find information.** There are quite a few search engines available on the Internet. Choose one that seems to perform quickly and that produces a good range of results. Once again, some search engines have sites in different parts of the world, so using a 'local' one may be faster.

- **Learn to use the advanced facilities of a search engine to refine searches.** Simple searches on almost any single word produce too many matches to be useful. Search engines usually allow you to carry out more refined searches in order to home in more accurately on the information you are looking for. Many of these engines include tutorials that will help you to use them effectively.

- **Be prepared to use the rest of the Internet, as well as the World Wide Web.** Most Internet users are most familiar with the graphical user interface of the World Wide Web (WWW). This is the easiest part of the Internet to use, but some of the other parts make a wider range of information available and (because they don't use graphics widely) are much faster in operation. If the WWW doesn't have the information you need, try to find out about using FTP (File Transfer Protocol), Gopher servers and Veronicas. They may seem difficult to use at first, but they give access to a wide range of information.

- **Be cautious about the quality of the information available on the Internet.** It is very cheap and easy to set up pages, particularly on the WWW. As a result, the quality of the information is very variable. Before relying on it, check out the reliability of the source of the information. The information could have been put there by students as a prank, by a fundamentalist group or by a company for sales purposes. Ideally, you should only use information that provides some means (such as references) for verifying it.

- **Insist that trainees acknowledge their sources of information.** If a source is used, trainees should give the address of the page where it was found. This enables the source to be verified and discourages plagiarism.

- **Be aware that information on the Internet can change or be moved.** It is quite common for links from one page to another page, or another site, to change. A page can also be moved to a different server. Before directing trainees to a source of information, make sure it is still there.

- **Make sure trainees don't drift around on the surf.** It is very easy to follow interesting links around the Internet and to spend a lot of time unproductively. Warn your trainees against this danger and give them some idea how much time should be spent on Internet tasks.

28. Helping trainees to learn from the Internet

The Internet is the electronic highway to the largest collection of information, data and communication ever constructed by the human species. There is information available through the WWW on every imaginable subject. Playing with the Internet is easy, but *learning* from it is not always straightforward. The following suggestions may help you to point your trainees in directions where they will not only enjoy playing with the Internet, but also develop their techniques so that they learn effectively from it too:

- **Consider starting small.** For example, you might be able to download selected information from the Internet on to individual computers, or a locally networked series of terminals. You can then give your trainees specific 'search' tasks, where it will be relatively easy for them to locate specific information.

- **Get your trainees to induct each other.** Learning from the Internet need not be a solo activity. Indeed, it can be very useful to have two or three trainees working at each terminal, so that they talk to each other about what they are finding, and follow up leads together. Encourage them to take turns at working the keyboard, so that they all develop their confidence at handling the medium and are then equipped to carry on working on their own.

- **Give your trainees exercises that help them to improve their selection of search words.** Show them how choosing a single broad search word leads to far too many sources being listed, and makes it very slow and boring to go through all of the sources looking for the information they really want. Get them to experiment with different combinations of search words, so that the sources that are located become much more relevant to their search purposes.

- **Allow your trainees to find out about the different speeds at which information can be found on the Internet.** For example, let them experiment at different times of the day, so they can see when the Internet is heavily used and slower. Also let them find out for themselves how much slower it can be waiting for graphics to be downloaded than for mainly text materials. Help them to become better at deciding whether to persist with a source that is highly relevant but slow to download, or whether to continue searching for sources that may download more quickly.

- **Remind your trainees that finding information is only the first step in learning from it.** It is easy to discover a wealth of information during an Internet search, only to forget most of it within a very short time. Encourage your trainees to download and edit the materials that they think will be most relevant, or even to make conventional handwritten or word-processed notes of their own while they use the Internet.

- **Help your trainees to learn to keep tabs on what they have found.** Entering 'bookmarks' or 'favourites' is one of the most efficient ways of being able to go back easily to what may have turned out to be the most relevant or valuable source of information during a search. Get your trainees to practise logging the sites that could turn out to be worth returning to. Also help them to practise clearing out bookmarks that turn out to be irrelevant or that are superseded by later finds.

- **Give your trainees practice at recording things that they have found during searches.** It can be useful to design worksheets to train them to note down key items of information as they find it, and to train them to be better at making their own notes as a matter of routine when exploring a topic using the Internet.

- **Consider getting your trainees to keep a learning log.** This can be done for a few hours of work with the Internet, and then looked back upon for clues about which tactics proved most successful. It can be even better to get trainees to compare notes about what worked well for them, and where the glitches were.

- **Help your trainees to develop their critical skills.** For example, set them a task involving them reviewing several sources they find on the Internet, and making decisions about the authenticity and validity of the information that they locate. Remind them that it is not possible to tell whether information is good or bad just by looking at the apparent quality of it on the screen. Remind your trainees that information on the Internet may not have been subjected to refereeing or other quality-assurance processes normally associated with published information in books or journal articles.

- **Remind trainees to balance playing with the Internet and learning from it.** It is perfectly natural, and healthy, to explore, and to follow up interesting leads, even when they take trainees far away from the purpose of their searches. However, it is useful to develop the skills to ration the amount of random exploration, and to devote 'spurts' of conscious activity to following through the specific purposes of searches.

29. Getting there early and setting up

There are few worse nightmares for trainers than that of being late arriving at your training venue, and then finding that the equipment you've been depending upon is not there or not working. This is particularly worrying when you are working away from your normal base, and even more so if you're working abroad! The following suggestions may help you to avoid some of your nightmares becoming realities:

- **Make checklists of all the bits and pieces that you will need.** Divide this into two parts: things *you* will have with you and things that need to be on site in the training room. As you prepare for your session, tick off on your list all the things you will be taking with you and, when you get to the venue, tick off the remaining items. This saves the embarrassment of getting midway through a training session and then discovering that there's something missing, and being *seen* to have messed things up!

- **Liaise in advance if you are working in a distant venue.** Book all of the equipment you are likely to need. This is particularly important when you're planning to use a computer to support your presentation. Find out about compatibility with your own equipment, and with your own software. You may be able simply to take along your PowerPoint presentation on disk, for example, if you already know that the software (in the same version as you use) is installed on equipment in your training room.

- **Check up *again* a week or two before your training session.** It is always worth reminding people at the venue about your requirements. Just occasionally, the records of what you wanted will have entirely disappeared!

- **Plan your fallback position.** For example, make sure that there will be an overhead projector and flipchart in the room. This provides peace of mind, and saves you worrying too much about what you will do if the computer side of your requirements does not turn out to be there. Even if you only use the traditional equipment for the first hour or so (while someone sorts out the computing side for you), it means that you can get your session under way on time.

- **Arrive at your training venue in good time.** About an hour early is usually right, especially if travel is involved. Even if the room is occupied by some other session when you arrive, it is better to be having a cup of coffee nearby than to be wondering if you will get there in time to set up.

- **Make full use of local help in setting up.** The people who normally look after the training room may already know only too well any idiosyncrasies or quirks of the equipment that is there. Don't exclude them from your setting-up, even if you're very confident that you know how to get everything working. You may need their help again if anything breaks down.

- **Test out visibility.** Choose the part of your presentation that might be the most difficult to see, and check that it is readable from any part of the training room, adjusting the furniture accordingly if necessary.

- **Get your back-up ready too.** Check the overhead projector, and position it so that you can easily bring it into play if you need it. Get out at least some of your transparencies, in case you need them at short notice if something goes wrong with the other equipment.

- **Make sure that you can't lose anything irretrievably.** For example, if your PowerPoint presentation is on a disk that you are putting into someone else's equipment, have a copy with you, just in case that disk corrupts or gets erased accidentally.

- **Learn from your own disasters!** When something goes wrong, and a session is interrupted or has to be replanned at short notice, it is tempting to try to forget the experience. It is, however, worthwhile to keep a short summary of 'lessons learnt for the future', and to look again at this from time to time, to make sure that you don't make the same mistake twice.

30. What to do if there's a power cut

Loss of electricity is not a frequent occurrence, but it is one of most trainers' nightmares, especially when using computer-aided presentations or demonstrations away from home. The following suggestions may help you to keep your show on the road until normal service is resumed:

- **Check quickly that it's not an emergency!** Power may go off because there's a fire in the building, or because an accident has happened somewhere. Without panicking your trainees or rushing them out of the room, find out whether you need to leave the venue and, if so, forget everything else and concentrate on getting everyone out safely and quickly.
- **Don't panic when the power goes off!** It may well mean that you will need to restructure your training session, but it doesn't mean that you will have to abandon it (unless, of course, there is no lighting at all left in the room). Getting flustered and cross does not help to make your training session a success. Stay cool.
- **Take a break.** If you know that it's going to take you a few minutes to devise a back-up plan for the session, give yourself some time and space to get on with this. Your trainees won't be devastated by the prospect of a few minutes off while you organize some alternatives.
- **Plan some paper-based exercises that could cover some of the same ground as your training session.** You may be using some of these in any case, to add variety to your trainees' learning experience. In particular, have some things ready for your trainees to *do*, so that you can report the power failure and try to get it restored. At such times, it can be really useful to introduce a syndicate task, as this keeps your trainees busy and talking, rather than sitting waiting for the equipment to work again.
- **Switch off projectors, computers and so on at the mains.** There is always the possibility of the power coming back with a surge, and that could cause far more damage than a cut. Some software does not like being shut down unexpectedly, and you may need to be prepared to spend some time setting it up again when the power is restored.
- **If necessary, take your group somewhere else.** If the room is too dark to work in, for example, find somewhere else in the building that has some light, or a lounge area, where you can continue at least in part with your intended session.
- **Continue on flipchart and whiteboard.** Keep the session active, for example by asking your trainees to prioritize options, do brainstorms, make action plans and so on. Make sure that the

products of their activities continue to be available to them, such as by sticking flipcharts round the walls.

- **Consider doing some revision and consolidation.** This is always useful, and it is a productive way of making use of enforced interruptions in your training session. Get trainees to sum up what was the most important thing that they have learnt so far, and get them to work out questions about what they need to find out next.

- **Declare another coffee break when the power comes back on.** Alternatively, give your trainees a few minutes to stretch their legs or look at some other training materials in the room. This gives you the chance to get your equipment switched on and ready for use, and is much more comfortable than trying to do so with everyone's eyes on you.

- **Don't just restart exactly where you left off.** It can be worthwhile to restart at the position a few minutes *before* the power went off, so that your trainees can pick up the threads of what they were thinking when it happened.

31. Replanning your session

Technology is wonderful, when it is all there, all working and all familiar. However, life isn't always so easy! There are times when we all have to go back to blackboards or whiteboards, and overhead projectors. The following suggestions may help you to keep your show on the road when the road seems blocked:

- **Never depend on being able to do a computer-managed presentation.** Most of the time, there will be no problem, but on that occasion where it just isn't going to work, be ready to go ahead using an overhead projector, or even a whiteboard or flipchart if no visual aids are available. Always carry the main part of your presentation on a few carefully chosen overheads, just in case.

- **Keep your back-up resources ready for immediate use.** It could be that you've not used your emergency overheads for months, but it's still worth having them in a sensible order, so that you can locate any one of them at short notice. You will not always need emergency back-up from the beginning of a session, and it looks much more professional if when things break down in the middle of a session you are able to find exactly the right place to pick up in another medium where you were interrupted with the previous medium.

- **Have with you some back-up activities as well as back-up resources.** When there are parts of your planned programme that you just can't do, it is important to be able to fill your trainees' time usefully. Think of some group tasks or exercises that will help them get a firm grip on the basics and that can take place in the time you might otherwise have used to show them some of the finer points about the topic of the session.

- **Don't shoot the messenger.** When things don't work out, it can be tempting to grumble about the facilities at your training venue or about things that were promised turning out to be unavailable. Getting cross with people does not do you any good, and your trainees will be much more impressed if you calmly and cheerfully get on with your training session using other means.

- **Don't spend too long trying to get things working.** Even if you are fairly certain that it will only take another five minutes to get all of the equipment working, five minutes can be a long time for your trainees to watch you trying to sort things out, and there is every chance that it will then take much longer anyway. It is better to get started with your session on time, and to fiddle about with the equipment again (if at all) when your trainees are busy in a task, particularly a group task where they will be much less likely to take any notice of your activities with the equipment.

- **Replan the content of your session.** Don't put yourself in the position of saying, 'Now if we'd had the computer back-up, what we'd have done is…' Your trainees aren't interested in what you would have done. Simply get on with providing as good a session as you can to meet the original aims and objectives. This will often mean missing out altogether some things that you would otherwise have included. It may also mean designing quickly some new task briefings for your trainees, so that they can go ahead even without some of the material you would otherwise have given them or shown them.

- **Make your (revised) objectives clear.** If you can no longer show these on overhead or computer projection, it is well worth writing them up on a marker board or flipchart, so that they remain visible to your trainees throughout your replanned session. It is usually possible to get this done before the session starts. Be prepared to ditch any particular objectives that it would no longer be possible to achieve, and replace these with others that are relevant and useful to your trainees. You may be able to cover the missed ground on a future occasion, but in any case there's not much point talking about things that you are unable to do in the present session.

- **Write up task briefings.** Word of mouth is not usually enough. If you would originally have displayed task briefings on overhead or screen, it is worth writing them up on flipcharts, so that your trainees have no doubt about what you intend them to do for each task in your session. You can write the briefing for the next task while the trainees are working on the present one.

- **Make good use of your handout materials.** For example, you may have planned to give out a handout version of your PowerPoint presentation as a revision aid after your talk. If the technology is not available, it may still be possible to issue your handouts straight away and then talk your trainees through their copies of your slides, getting them to annotate these with their own notes about the most important things as you go along.

- **Use any spare time to find out more about your trainees' learning and experience.** It can be really useful to have the luxury of some time to find out some detail of who knows what, for example about what you may be covering in a future planned session with the same trainees. You may also find time to give them some revision or practice exercises in things that you have already covered with them.

32. Coping with technophobes

In any group of trainees, there will be a few who are convinced that they cannot work with technology. This fear may be very deep-seated and you will have to work very hard to help them overcome it. The following suggestions may give you some ways of starting to overcome their fears:

- **Remind trainees of the difficulties people face in learning new skills.** People are always taking on new challenges that seem impossible at first. If they are persistent enough, they can surprise themselves. Remind your trainees that they have already learnt far more complex topics, such as learning to walk, talk, ride a bike or drive a car. Tasks that seem impossibly difficult at first can become automatic functions with practice.

- **Encourage trainees to think of computers as tools for doing a job.** If the computer is a tool, there is no need to understand how it works. The only knowledge necessary is how to use the tool and how to maintain it properly. If it helps to explain this, use analogies such as a car: there is no need to know exactly how it works in order to drive it. Similarly, there is no need to know how a hammer is made in order to drive in nails.

- **Try to structure learning well so that each stage builds on and reinforces prior learning.** It is important that the trainees' understanding of basic principles is good and that they have plenty of practice before moving on to new topics. If they move on to new areas too soon, the seeds of future confusion can be sown. It is also very useful to incorporate lessons from early work into later stages as well, so that revision is carried out.

- **Make sure that trainees realize that computers do exactly as they are told.** It is common for people to say that 'the computer' did something. This sort of thought can encourage them to believe that the machine is outside their control and acts by itself. It is very important that they should realize that the computer does exactly as it is told. If something unexpected happens, it is as a result of something the computer has been instructed to do, and there is an explanation for it.

- **Be prepared to help trainees carry out a 'post-mortem' when things go wrong.** By talking through what has happened with the trainee and by using 'undo' and 'redo' facilities, it may be possible to illustrate exactly what has gone wrong. Software may also have facilities that show more clearly what is going on; examples are showing spaces and returns in word-processed documents and showing formulae in spreadsheets.

- **Try to relate computer uses to the tasks trainees may need for their work.** If they can see a real point to using computers, trainees will have more incentive to learn. Try to find exercises that will help trainees see how relevant computing can be to them.

- **Make sure that trainees don't worry too much about complex problems during the early stages.** People will often realize that they have been set a simplified task and that the real world is more complex. This may lead them to attempt a more advanced solution than you had planned, leading to difficulties and confusion. Try to word tasks so as to make it clear what level of complexity is involved.

- **Set appropriate challenges. In order for trainees to learn, they must solve problems.** These problems should be hard enough to encourage thought but they must be achievable by the individual. It will take considerable thought to choose tasks that match the needs of each trainee.

- **Review progress regularly, and give praise.** When trainees achieve something, help them realize what they have done. Remind them of all the skills that they used in the task and contrast this with their skill level when they started. It might be useful to make this a formal process, with regular reviews of learning and the filling in of some kind of skills record.

- **Celebrate achievement.** Make sure trainees give themselves credit for their achievements and that they don't compare themselves with others in the group. It is common for people to feel inferior to others who learn faster or who are more technically literate when they start the course. What is important is their own progress, not the achievements of others.

33. Coping with technophiles

People who love computers can become a problem, especially when they know more about IT than you do! It is common for a group to contain some individuals who have considerable IT skills. There are two ways in which they can be a problem: they can become bored and they can be disruptive. It is not an easy job to decide the best way to deal with this and you may need all your tact:

- **Carry out some assessment of prior knowledge at an early stage.** In order to identify those who have good computing skills, you will need to ask questions. You could do this informally, with a few spoken questions. You could also have a form that trainees fill in before the course in order to clarify this. Care should be taken that a form doesn't imply that trainees will need good computing skills, or beginners may be put off.

- **Test that trainees really have the skills that they claim.** People sometimes have an unrealistic view of their skills so you need to check that they can really do all that they claim. Set these people some tasks that will allow them to demonstrate these skills. Avoid any suggestion that you are testing them: say that you are assessing their prior learning in order to help you plan their future work.

- **Don't try to fool them if you aren't sure of the subject.** It can be embarrassing to admit that you don't know something if you are providing training. If you try to bluff somebody who has better knowledge than you, failure is likely. This is even more embarrassing. A better solution is to offer to find the answer to questions or problems for the next session.

- **Remember that training skills are just as important as advanced subject knowledge.** Your confidence may be dented if you find that some of your trainees know more about that subject than you do. Remind yourself that you are multi-skilled: you have computing knowledge and you are skilled as a trainer. Use your training skills in order to help you provide effective computer training. As an analogy, think about world-class athletes. They rely on trainers who help them develop their competitive skills, but these trainers aren't top athletes themselves.

- **See if they can help others who have less knowledge.** If some trainees have skills, they could use them to help those who may be struggling. This can be very helpful to all concerned: your life can be easier, the beginners receive more help and the advanced trainees can crystallize their knowledge by explaining it to someone else. You will still need to supervise this help, however, to make sure it is effective.

- **Ask them to prepare a session on an advanced topic that they could teach to the others.** If you can choose a topic beyond their current knowledge, it will be useful for them to learn it and they can then practise some training skills for the benefit of the rest of the group when they are ready. You can learn from them too!

- **Set them a complex task to keep them quiet.** If you are having trouble because some people are causing disruption, consider setting them a task that will stretch their abilities. This can help keep them occupied but they will still be learning.

- **Ask the trainees concerned what they hope to achieve from attending the course.** This might help focus the disruptive trainees' minds on what they are doing and encourage them to take an active part in it. If nothing else, it might help you to clarify a particular trainee's needs.

- **If it is appropriate, suggest that they consider a more advanced course.** This will need diplomacy, but you could stress that they will not gain anything from the course as they have all the skills already. It would be a more productive use of their time if they were to do a course at a more suitable level.

- **If all else fails, speak to their supervisor.** If you are having problems with one or more trainees being disruptive because they feel superior about their advanced knowledge, you must deal with the problem in order to be fair to the others. If all the techniques above have failed, consider an approach to their supervisor, perhaps suggesting that the course you are presenting is not suitable for these trainees.

34. Looking after yourself when travelling

Travelling trainers are probably as common now as travelling salespeople once were. If your work has you on the road for a significant part of your time, it pays dividends to make sure that the travelling side of things causes you as little stress as is possible. The following suggestions may offer you some low-stress alternatives:

- **Think seriously about using public transport.** If you have long distances to travel and can get to where you need to go by train, for example, this can reduce the strain on you. It means that you can rest on the way home rather than have the strain of driving when you're already tired after a day's training. However, it's worth setting out in good time on your way to your training event, as the strain of the train being late could be even worse!

- **However you travel, aim to arrive at your training venue with plenty of time to spare.** Being late is stressful, but *knowing* that you're going to be late is even more stressful. If there is a distinct possibility of you being late, and you can't compensate for this by setting out early, it can be worth trying to arrange for contingencies, for example with a substitute who can start off your session if you are delayed *en route*, or who can give your trainees a relevant task to do in anticipation of your session.

- **Watch your diary if you're very itinerant!** It's only too easy to see a blank day, and say 'yes' to an engagement in Aberdeen but not to notice that you're in Birmingham the day before or Brighton the day after! Travel takes time, and if you've got long distances to go, you might have to devote some days just to travelling.

- **Try to travel relatively light.** This is particularly important when using public transport and when flying. While it's reassuring to have with you everything you might possibly need for your training event, it is tiring carrying it all around with you. Large collections of overhead transparencies can be surprisingly heavy, as can multiple copies of handout material, or examples of books and manuals.

- **Look after your temperature.** When choosing clothing for training and travel, it's useful to have the option to cope with unexpected heat or cold, and to pack the sorts of clothes that allow you to add or shed a layer when necessary. This can be particularly important if your trip takes in different climates, but even in one part of the world temperatures in training venues can vary quite widely.

- **Look after routine minor ailment possibilities.** It can be a real blessing to have with you small quantities of aspirin or paracetamol for the odd headache or cold, a few throat lozenges for the possibility of a sore voice, something for upset stomach and so on. Even if *you* don't need these emergency supplies, you may be surprised at how often you can help someone else out because of them.

- **Carry some emergency repair materials.** A needle and thread can make all the difference to your composure in the event of a button coming off or a seam coming undone. It can also help to have that spare button, a couple of safety pins, a few tissues for cleaning off spilt food or drinks, and so on. Most hotels have supplies of basic essentials at reception, but not all training centres carry such materials.

- **Keep your toiletries packed if you travel regularly.** It's useful to have a small separate toiletries bag, and to keep it maintained with sufficient supplies for a few days away from home. This can save you having to spend time and energy worrying about packing toothpaste, a toothbrush, shampoo, soap and all the other bits and pieces that you never notice when you have them, but are a pain when you find you haven't got them. Aim just to have to remember to pack *one* thing – the bag – but check that you take the right one!

- **Remember about jet lag if you travel long distances.** Moving to a completely different time zone affects some people much more than others, but it's worth giving yourself a day without meetings or training sessions so that you can catch up on sleep and adjust at least partially. It's not always possible to sleep on long plane journeys, often because of other passengers.

- **Carry some earplugs.** Alternatively, the in-ear phones that connect to portable cassette or compact disc players will do. These can cut down the disturbance to you caused by fellow passengers, or can help you to sleep in hotel rooms where there may be various sounds that, because they are unfamiliar, can keep you awake.

35. Gadgets, leads and grommets

If you travel to deliver training, it is very important that you think carefully about what you need to take with you. If you're taking several of the things listed below, the public transport suggestion in our previous set of tips will be ruled out! If you take too much with you, it will be heavy and at risk of damage or loss. If you forget something, you won't be able to go back for it and you may not be able to borrow or buy it locally. Even if you have asked the people at your destination about their facilities, it is possible to forget something vital; take steps to cover yourself against problems:

- **Think about those who are left behind.** If you need to take equipment away with you to carry out some training, make sure that it won't be needed by other people at your base. If you take it away, leaving others stranded, you will lose popularity!

- **A spare mains lead can be useful.** If your mains adaptor doesn't work, you could ask a technician to put a suitable plug on your extra mains lead. This would ensure reliable operation. If the mains lead incorporates a power supply, this option may not be possible and you might not want to take the risk of having the UK plug cut off your onlv power supply!

- **Take some fuses with you.** Electrical systems abroad will use different sizes of fuses. Take some with you so that you can replace them if they blow.

- **Make sure you have plenty of batteries.** If you want to use equipment while you are travelling or if you want to use batteries to avoid mains problems, you will need enough batteries to operate without interruptions. Be wary of manufacturers' claims for how long their equipment will run on one battery charge.

- **Don't forget your battery charger.** If you foresee a need to charge up large numbers of batteries, you may even need to take an extra charger or one that can charge more than one battery at a time.

- **Make sure you have plenty of ink cartridges if you are taking a printer.** Some printers are very small and light, so taking one with you is not impossible. If you run out of ink, however, it will become a useless dead weight!

- **Take loads of leads with you.** If you think you might want to connect your computer to other equipment, try to think of all the possible variations of leads that might be needed. As an example, you might want to use a modem: take 25-pin and 9-pin serial leads with you.

- **Consider taking a 'palmtop' computer to test this out for future work.** If the thought of taking all this equipment with you is daunting, you might be able to take a very small, light palmtop computer. You would need to be absolutely certain that it would connect up to the system at your destination, however. If you want to try this, take one with you on an early visit to test that it all works.

- **Perhaps you only need a disk or two.** If you don't need a computer on your journey, you might be able to take all the data and software you need on disk. If you need a large amount of disk space, you could take a portable exchangeable disk system. They are very light and can often be connected to the printer port of computers. Again, you should test this before relying on it. A CD ROM can also store a large amount of data, and many systems will incorporate a CD ROM drive.

- **Do you need to carry anything at ail?** As you are a highly sophisticated computer user, why not benefit from modern high-speed data communications? Instead of carrying data with you, e-mail it to your destination. Check that it has arrived safely, however. Perhaps you should take a back-up too!

36. Finding out what they've got at their end

The next pages contain some questions you should ask before setting out to distant parts to deliver training. Most of the questions apply to visiting countries abroad, but some of them are just as important to ask if you're planning some training in a distant venue in your own country:

- **What is the specification of the computers?** It is important to make sure that any software or data that you take with you will work properly. It will be helpful to know the make and model of the computers, what processor they are using and how much memory they have.
- **What operating system do they use?** Again, it is important that you know this for compatibility purposes. Make sure you know what version it is. If it is a version that has been produced specially for that country, it may have important differences from your version.
- **What software is installed on the computers?** You will need to know what versions are available and possibly in what language. Spell-checking with a 'foreign' word processor is not a viable option!
- **Are the computers networked?** If you want to connect your computer to a network, you will need to know details of their system so that you can make sure that you have the hardware and software necessary. This can also be important if you want to add typefaces or software to the system.
- **Will a CD ROM drive be available?** CD writers are cheap nowadays and so CD ROMs are a convenient way of carrying large amounts of data. Make sure that a drive will be available to read your data.
- **Is their some kind of interchangeable hard disk system available?** These can be very useful if you want to take large amounts of data with you. Make sure yours is compatible or, alternatively, check that you can take a portable unit with you to plug into their machines.
- **Will there be technical help available?** If there are problems, you will need help from the local staff to solve them. An important point to note is that systems can be password-protected and you will not be able to alter them without authorization.
- **What sort of printing facilities are available?** You may want trainees to print out their work, or you may want to produce some extra notes and print them. You may want to reprint your presentation on overhead projector transparencies from your back-up on disk. Some knowledge of the printing system will help you plan.
- **What projection systems are there?** You may want to use an overhead projector to show your presentation or to connect your laptop to a large screen or projector. Make sure that you know what will be provided.

- **What voltage and frequency is the electricity supply?** Make sure that your equipment will operate under these conditions. Check your manual or speak to a local service agent to make sure that there will not be problems.

- **What sort of mains outlets are there?** An adaptor may be needed, but check what kind it is. It's useful to get your own adaptor, plus a normal multi-socket outlet so that you can connect more than one of your pieces of equipment to a single foreign socket. This may also be useful for your travel kettle, computer and mobile phone charger in your hotel room!

37. Finding out what you can take elsewhere

You may already be accustomed to training in different countries, or you may have no plans to venture abroad. If neither of these applies, you may find the first time that you take your show abroad rather daunting. We hope that the following suggestions may minimize some of the potential problems that you might encounter:

- **Be careful about customs regulations.** If you take equipment to some countries, you risk having it confiscated or paying duties on it. Find out about regulations and make sure you fill in any forms that you need to use.

- **Make sure that the equipment will work with the power supply in the country you intend to visit.** Some countries have electricity supplies that work at different voltages and frequencies. Make sure that you know what sort of supply is available and that your equipment will cope with it.

- **Check that your equipment will deal with power fluctuations.** Some electricity supplies are liable to fluctuations. These will not upset most electrical items, but computers can have problems with them. There are some simple devices available that will help smooth out minor variations and help your computer to operate properly. These devices can also protect your computer from surges in the electricity supply that could damage your equipment.

- **Battery power can help you if there are electricity problems.** A battery charger is less likely to be upset by electrical mains fluctuations than a computer is. You could recharge the batteries overnight and then use them during the day. You will need to take plenty of batteries with you and make sure that you have adaptors to work the charger.

- **Take suitable mains adaptors with you.** There is a wide range of different mains sockets in the countries of the world. You will need to make sure that you have a suitable adaptor with you. If you have several items of mains-operated equipment, you could take a multi-socket outlet with you so that you can run the equipment from one adaptor.

- **Find out if there is a recognized repairer for your equipment in the places you intend to visit.** Many computer firms have an international network of service agents for their equipment. If you have the details of these, you could contact them if your equipment fails.

- **Check up very carefully on possible compatibility problems.** If you intend to connect your equipment to any other items at your destination, make sure that you have all the adaptors and connectors that will be necessary. If you intend to use any software or data files, you will also need to check that your work is compatible and uses the same operating system.

- **Take back-ups of data and software with you.** It is a good policy to have back-ups of your work all the time, but this is particularly true when you are abroad. Back-ups are light to carry and so won't add much to your load. Carry back-ups in your hand luggage in case the rest of your luggage goes missing.

- **Take back-ups of important leads and connectors too.** Again, these are light so it is easy to carry them. They should also be carried in your hand luggage.

- **Be careful with data held on magnetic disks.** There is a small risk that the X-ray equipment used for security checks could damage data held on magnetic disks. You can protect them in special bags and also ask to have your hand luggage checked by hand.

- **Take data in as many different file formats as possible.** By saving data in different formats, you have as much flexibility as possible to help in overcoming compatibility problems. As an example, you can save word-processed documents in plain text and Rich Text Format (RTF) from many word processors. These formats are widely used and may enable a document to load into a different word processor.

- **Allow plenty of time to sort out compatibility problems.** If there are problems, it can be very difficult to solve them. You may need to seek help from a local expert and it may be hard to find somebody. Even if you can open files, you may find that they need to be edited because of different fonts changing the layout of documents. Word-processed documents may lose some of their formatting because of problems with compatibility.

- **Take a virus-checker.** Viruses are always a danger and you should take all the precautions that you can. Make sure your own computer is virus-protected and check any files before using them.

38. Computing glossary

This glossary has been adapted from one written by Steve Higgins and first published in *500 ICT Tips for Primary Teachers* (Nick Packard, Steve Higgins and Phil Race, 1999, Kogan Page).

Although originally designed for teachers, the glossary has already been found useful, informative and (not least) entertaining, well beyond the classroom. I am grateful for Steve's permission to use a modified version of the glossary to end Chapter 4 of this book.

Most computing terms are deliberately chosen so as to be confusing to the uninitiated. Either their normal everyday meaning refers to something else entirely, or a deliberately archaic word is used in a new and still more unusual way. It is all part of the 'geek-speak' of the computer world. Learning all of these is neither necessary nor helpful. The words and terms below are current educational technology jargon. We have offered what we hope is a helpful definition. Most of them are serious.

Words in italics are mostly defined in the relevant alphabetical place in the list:

address The identification of a specific physical or *virtual* place in a network. On the Internet, this address is called a URL (Universal Resource Locator). For instance, http://www.ncl.ac.uk is the address for Newcastle University. An e-mail address contains the '@' symbol, eg s.e.higgins@ncl.ac.uk is the address of the glossary's author.

adventure program A program that usually puts the player or *user* in an imaginary situation. The player is required to take decisions to control the way the adventure progresses.

application A computer program that is specifically designed for a particular purpose (eg a word processor is an application that handles text).

ASCII American Standard Code for Information Interchange. This is an agreed standard code for letters, numbers and control codes; it is understood by most computers in the same way that US English is understood by other English speakers – or UK English is understood by people from the USA – only imperfectly!

bandwidth A nerd-word used to describe how much data you can send through a connection to the Net. The greater the bandwidth, the faster the rate of transmission. You can think of it as the information-carrying capacity of a connection.

baud rate Geek-speak for the speed of a *modem* (measured in bits per second). It is interesting that the computer world is as obsessed by capacity and speed as car fanatics or train spotters – 56 Kbps (kilobits per second) is currently a fast speed.

bit An abbreviation for BInary digiT. It is the basic unit of information in the computer world. A bit is binary number and has one of two values, 0 or 1. Computers can only count to one as they have no fingers.

browser Software that allows people to access and navigate the *World Wide Web*. Most Web browsers, such as Mosaic, *Netscape* or Internet Explorer, are graphical and use text and pictures (and even sound or video). A few are only text-based such as Lynx. As with most things in the computer world you never have the latest version that lets you hear the latest whistles and bells.

bug An error in a computer program that may cause the computer to 'crash' or behave in an otherwise inexplicable manner. Of course if the computer's behaviour is usually inexplicable it can be difficult to tell.

byte A single computer character, generally eight *bits*. Each letter displayed on a computer screen occupies one byte of computer memory. 1,000 bytes = 1 kilobyte (k), 1,000 k = 1 megabyte (Mb), 1,000 Mb = 1 gigabyte (Gb).

CAI Computer Aided (or Assisted) Instruction.
CAL Computer Aided (or Assisted) Learning.
CBL Computer Based Learning. All of these neat acronyms obscure the fact that the computer is only a tool or a medium to present learning material, albeit in a sophisticated way.
CD ROM Compact Disc – Read Only Memory. A record-like storage medium that uses digital and optical laser technology to store up to about 600 Mb of text, pictures and sound on a single disk. With newer versions (CD ROMXA, CDTV, CD-i), animation and video clips can be stored on the disks.
CD ROM drive A form of disk drive that stores information on optical or compact disks. A CD ROM drive is used for getting the information from the disk but cannot usually be used for writing or storing information (though recordable and rewritable CDs are now widely available too).
clip art A file of pictures specifically prepared for use in other files. Clip-art files contain graphic images (geek-speak for pictures).
commercial online services A company that charges people to allow them to dial in via a modem to get access to its information and services, which can include the Internet. See also *Internet Service Provider.*
concept keyboard An input device (geek alert!) comprising a tablet (A4- or A3-sized) connected to the computer on which overlays can be placed. By pressing different areas of the tablet, actions can be made to happen on the computer (sounds; letters, words, phrases of text; pictures; animations; the control of output devices such as a robot).
content-free software Open-ended programs that permit more control of the computer by the user. A word processor, database and spreadsheet are all 'content-free' in that the person using them decides what the content of the file will be. By contrast, a *drill and practice* program has predetermined content.
control A computer can be made to control a device to which it is connected, such as a disk drive, printer, model or robot. The means by which a computer directs a device is often called control technology.
copy An editing term: the duplication of an item (text, image, sound) to be subsequently *pasted* elsewhere in the same document or transferred to another file.
cursor The flashing mark that appears on the screen to show where text will appear when a key is pressed on the keyboard. A cursor's shape can be changed. Depending on its shape, a cursor is also called an I bar, a caret, an insertion point or a mouse pointer! If all else fails try cursing the cursor; it is guaranteed not to work but may make you feel better.
cut Another editing term: to remove an item (text, image, sound), which can then be *pasted* elsewhere in the same document or file or transferred to another file.

data The 'raw' information that a computer handles. Data can take the form of text, numbers or pictures. If your first thought was Commander Data from Star Trek NG, award yourself two extra nerd points.
data logging A means by which a computer monitors and records events. For example, a computer can be set up to record the temperature in a room at hourly intervals and then 'log' the data over a period of a week. Sorry, no lumberjacks, OK?
database A computer application enabling information to be stored, retrieved and manipulated. The most common form of database is the 'flat file', which is like a card index system in structure. There are also many information databases available now on the Internet for searching.

desktop publishing An application for designing and producing documents that may include text, borders, headings and pictures.
dialogue box A window that appears on screen giving information that requires a response. In fact, no dialogue is possible. You are usually forced to do what the computer requires – a bit like a consultation document in the education world.
dial-up Internet connection Lets a user dial into an *Internet Service Provider* using a modem and telephone line to access the Internet. (See also *SLIP* or *PPP* connections.)
digital camera A camera that captures an image and stores it in electronic form that can be downloaded directly into a computer without the need for film. Despite the derivation this has nothing to do with fingers.
digitizer Geek-alert! A piece of software that transforms a video signal into a digital signal that can be manipulated by the computer. A nerd-word.
dip switch A small switch (usually in a bank of eight or more) usually found on a printer. Setting the dip switches to different positions controls the way the printer behaves. So called because when trainees' little fingers change the position of the switches it makes the printer (and often the trainer) dippier than before.
directory A collection of files is stored in a directory. A directory is usually given a name to help identify the files it contains, eg 'My files' for your files. Online directories are lists of files or other directories on a computer at an Internet site.
disk drive A device used for storing computer information on magnetic or optical disks. There are floppy, hard and optical (CD ROM) disk drives, and even zip and Jaz drives.
domain name The part of the Internet address that specifies your computer's location in the world. The address is written as a series of names separated by full stops. The most common top-level domains are:

- .ac (academic – UK higher education);
- .edu (education – USA);
- .com (commercial – USA);
- .co (company – UK);
- .gov (governmental or public);
- .mil (military);
- .net (network resource).

So http://www.ncl.ac.uk/ is a Web site (http://www) for Newcastle (ncl) University (ac) in the UK.
download The term describing the transfer of information from one computer to another (such as through a modem or from an Internet site). To upload is to send a file to another computer.
drill and practice Low-level educational programs that are designed to provide instruction or practice with specific skills (eg spelling, addition).

e-mail A means of sending (usually) plain text messages between two computers connected via a network.
emoticons 'Smileys' used in e-mail messages to add emotional emphasis:

- :) for happy;
- ;) for a (knowing) wink;
- :(for sad.

Turn the page sideways if you don't see why these symbols are used. Part of the Geek language.

error message A message that the computer sends you to inform you that there is a problem, often caused by a *bug* and displayed immediately prior to a system crash. However, it is usually not you who has made the mistake. These are almost always bad news!
export To transfer information from one application to another. Typically if you export something you will probably not use a *port*. Please remember, if an export fails try a Newcastle Brown instead (a local tip, for inhabitants of north-east England).

FAQ Frequently Asked Questions. Files on the Net that store the answers to common questions. If you are stuck, check the FAQs first, before you ask your own question. The following FTP site is useful and holds most FAQ on the Net.
FTP to: rtfm.mit.edu
Go to the sub-directory pub/usenet/news.answers
file Information that is stored, usually in a folder or *directory* on a disk. A file is usually given a name to help identify it. Most first-time users build up a collection of files either called by their name (eg Steve1, Steve2, Steve3) or 'untitled'. These names are therefore almost completely indistinguishable and it means much time can be fruitlessly spent in locating previously saved work.
filter Hardware or software designed to restrict access to certain areas on the Internet.
flame To send a sharp, critical or downright rude e-mail message to another person.
floppy disk A form of disk used for storing information in electronic form. The plastic case contains a disk of magnetic material, similar to that used in audio and video recorders. Floppy disks store a maximum of 1.6 kilobytes of information. Cunningly, a floppy disk has a hard plastic cover so that it appears neither floppy nor disk-shaped.
FTP Geek-alert! File Transfer Protocol. An application program that uses TCP/IP protocol to allow you to move files from a distant computer to a local computer using a network like the Internet. Non-geeks use sensible computers and programs, which mean they can avoid the technical details.
function key A key (usually labelled F0, Fl, F2, etc) that is used by an application to perform a particular task (eg printing or saving a document). However, in most programs they serve no function or you can't remember which action they are supposed to perform.

gigabyte See *byte* or, if you don't want the detail, it's bigger than a megabyte – 1,000 megabytes in fact.
graphics program An application that enables the user to create or manipulate images on screen. However sophisticated it is, it will not draw graphs.
GUI Graphical User Interface. Software designed to allow the user to execute commands by pointing and clicking on icons or text. It is nerdily pronounced 'gooey'. See also *WIMP*.

hard disk Most modern computers have internal hard disk drives. Like a floppy disk, but a hard disk holds larger amounts of information.
hardware Computer devices such as the computer itself, the printer, the monitor, the keyboard and mouse – the 'kit'.
highlight Marking an area of the screen, usually for editing. Most applications show highlighted areas in reverse colours (eg white on black rather than black on white).

home page The first page you see when visiting a World Wide Web site.
HTML Hypertext Mark-up Language. The programming language of the World Wide Web, HTML software turns a document into a hyperlinked World Wide Web page.
HTTP Hypertext Transfer Protocol. The protocol used to provide hypertext links between pages. It is the standard way of transferring HTML documents between Web servers and browsers. Hence why most Web addresses start http://.
hypertext/hyperlink A highlighted word or graphic in a document that, when clicked upon, enables you to see the related piece of information from elsewhere on the Internet.

icon A small picture (or graphic) that can be selected with the mouse pointer and that visually represents a program or file. Most computers now use icons as part of the way you interact with them. (See also *WIMP*.)
ICT Information and Communications Technologies; used to be just IT (*information technology*).
ILS Integrated Learning Systems. Complex (and expensive) programs offering sophisticated drill and practice for trainees and detailed feedback for trainers.
import See *export*.
infobot (or mailbot) An e-mail address that automatically returns information requested by the user.
Information Superhighway Originally a US idea, the official US government name for the Internet and other computer networks was the National Information Infrastructure but it is more commonly known as the Information Superhighway.
information technology Electronic means for storing, changing and transmitting information.
input device A piece of equipment for entering information into a computer. A keyboard is an input device for entering text into the computer. Nerd-word.
interface A device for connecting equipment to a computer. A modem is a form of interface, as it connects the computer to a telephone line.
Internet No, not World Cup '02 but the global network linking millions of computers around the world. These computers are called hosts, which our dictionary defines as 'an organism on which another lives as a parasite'. Geek-speak would probably define it more as a sort of virtual space in which users can send and receive e-mail, log in to remote computers (Telnet), browse databases of information in text or *hypertext* format (Gopher, World Wide Web, WAIS), and send and receive programs (*FTP*) contained on these computers.
Internet account Purchased through an *Internet Service Provider*, the account assigns a password and e-mail address to an individual or group.
Internet server A computer that stores data that can be accessed via the Internet.
Internet Service Provider (ISP) Any organization that provides access to the Internet. Many ISPs offer technical assistance to organizations looking to become Internet information providers by placing their information online. They also help users get connected to the Net.
Internet site A computer connected to the Internet containing information that can be accessed using an Internet navigation tool such as *FTP*, *Telnet*, Gopher or a Web *browser*.
intranet A local network, for example within a company or organization.
IP address Every computer on the Internet has a unique numerical IP address, which will look something like 123.45.678.9.

IRC Internet Relay Chat. Interactive, real-time discussions between people using text messages. People log into designated Net computers and join discussions already in progress. Some IRC channels even discuss nice things!

joystick An input device that allows control of objects or images on the screen through the movement of a lever, most often used for computer 'arcade' games.
justification The manipulation of text on a line in a word processor. 'Right justify' aligns all lines to end against the right margin, 'left justify' aligns the beginning of lines to the left of the screen and 'fully justified' inserts additional gaps between words to begin and end in line with both margins.

keyword A word or words that can be searched for in documents or menus.
kilobyte (k) See byte.

LAN Local Area Network. A restricted network that connects computers within a building or among buildings for the purpose of sharing voice, data, fax and/or video.
laptop computer See *portable computer.*
LCD screen Liquid Crystal Display screen: a thin form of monitor screen (about the thickness of two pieces of glass). Electrical charges cause different areas of the screen to change colour. Most calculators use LCD display to show the numbers.
load To transfer information from a storage device (such as a disk drive) into the computer's memory.
LOGO A computer programming language whereby instructions are written to control the actions of the computer. LOGO was written by Seymour Papert (among others) to provide a 'low floor, high ceiling' approach to programming – easy enough for infants to use, potentially complex enough to challenge graduates. Professor Seymour Papert now, confusingly, holds the Lego chair!
log on To sign on to a computer system.

mailing lists (or mailbases) There are many thousands of topic-related, e-mail-based message bases that can be read and posted to. People subscribe to the lists they want to read and receive messages from via e-mail. Mailing lists are operated using automatic mailbase (or listserv in the US) software. Thus, many users call mailing lists 'mailbases'. There are two types of lists: moderated and unmoderated. Moderated lists are screened by a person before messages are posted to subscribers. Messages to unmoderated lists are automatically forwarded to subscribers.
megabyte (Mb) See *byte.*
menu A list of options that can be revealed and then selected by the mouse. Like most menus, they never quite seem to have what you want.
menu bar A section of the screen (across the top with PC and Macintosh computers, across the bottom of the screen with Acorn computers) on which menus or the icons of applications are placed. None so far serve alcohol.
merge To bring two different pieces of information together in the same document or file. For example, addresses from a database can be merged with a letter in some word processors to personalize a mailing: hence 'mail-merge'. Geek-speak.

MIDI Musical Instrument Digital Interface – a system (set of agreed guidelines to ensure conformity) for connecting musical instruments to computers. Quite why trumpets might want to browse the Internet we have not yet discovered.
model A representation of a situation that enables predictions to be made. Mathematics is used to model reality (eg when three objects are placed with four objects, there will be seven objects altogether; the model for this is 3 + 4 = 7). A computer uses mathematical patterns and algorithms to model quite complex situations (eg global weather patterns – and gets these wrong too).
modem An electronic device that connects a computer to a telephone line enabling information to be transferred between computers. A modem is required for connection to the Internet. Fax modems enable faxes to be sent and received by a computer. It is an unhelpful abbreviation for MOdulate DEModulate. Modems are available for any computer, can be internal or external, and come in several speeds, known as the *baud rate*. The higher the baud rate, the faster the modem.
monitor Just another word for the thing with the screen showing you what the computer is doing: an output device.
mouse A small plastic box that sits on the table beside a computer and is connected to it or the keyboard by a wire 'tail'. By moving the mouse and pressing its one, two or three buttons, the computer can be controlled. You can now also get tail-less mice, which use infra-red to send signals to the computer. On laptops a variety of trackball, trackpads and what look like little bits of chewing gum are all designed to confuse the uninitiated. Geek-speak plural: 'mouses'. Anorak definition: a computer input device.
mouse pointer See *cursor*.
multimedia An application that makes use of more than one medium, eg words, pictures and noise. Easier than it sounds.

Net surfer Someone who browses the Internet with no definite destination. Now widely regarded as ancient Geek.
netiquette A Geek dialect. The rules of conduct for Internet users. Violating netiquette may result in *flaming* or removal from a *mailing list*. Some service providers (*ISPs*) will even cancel a user's Internet account, thus denying him or her access to the Net, if the violation is severe enough. A fitting punishment indeed!
Netscape Internet navigation software that allows users to access information through a graphical, point-and-click interface rather than text-only screens or menus. Netscape is known as a Web *browser* because it accesses World Wide Web information formatted into special *home pages* using *hypertext*. Other graphical Web browsers include Microsoft's Internet Explorer, Mosaic and Opera.
network A system linking computers. A local network links computers on the same site. The Internet is a global network.

OILS Open Integrated Learning Systems. Even more complex (and still more expensive) programs than *ILS*, offering still further sophisticated drill and practice for trainees and detailed feedback for trainers, with more flexibility than basic ILS.
online/offline When you are logged on to a computer through your modem or via a network, you are said to be online. When you are using your computer but are not connected to a computer through your modem, you're said to be working offline. When teaching with WWW materials you might want to download them so trainees can use them offline.

operating system The internal software that controls the way a computer operates. No matter how new your computer is, you never have the latest version. Technical helplines always ask you which version you have and will reply (with the customary sucking in of breath over the teeth), 'Well, if you'd upgraded to version 9.7.1 you would not have had this problem…'
output device A piece of hardware that enables the computer to represent data for users. A printer is an example of an output device.

palmtop computer See *portable computer.*
paste An editing term meaning to place a previously *copied* or *cut* item in a file or document.
peripheral A piece of equipment connected to the computer by a cable or wire. Most printers are peripheral devices; they are separately plugged into the computer. A scanner or external hard drive is also a type of peripheral. (It is tempting to call them 'ephemerals' because they only work properly when you don't need them to work urgently, and you can never pin down why.)
photo CD A CD on which photographic images are stored. An ordinary colour film can be processed by most high-street chemists into a photo CD (for a small extra charge), enabling photographs to be *imported* directly into the computer.
pirate software Software that has been illegally copied and used on a computer. Tempting and easy to do in most cases, but illegal. Make sure you have the appropriate licence for the software you use.
podule An electronic circuit board that is plugged inside a computer to extend its capabilities. Geek-speak.
pointer See *cursor.*
port A socket on a computer to plug something into.
portable computer A small computer. A laptop computer ranges from about the size of a small attaché case to considerably smaller now. A palmtop or pocket computer is about the size of an adult's hand.
posts E-mail messages sent to a mailing list or Usenet newsgroup to be read by subscribers or others on the Internet. Nerd-word.
printer Dot matrix printers are cheap but are noisy and produce a poor image; inkjets and bubble-jets are relatively cheap, but use water-based inks; laser-jets provide high-quality images but are more expensive.
program A list of instructions to control the operation of a computer; the term is also used as a verb, 'to program', meaning to create such as a list of instructions
programming language A particular vocabulary and syntax of instructions that can be used to give instructions to a computer.

RAM Random Access Memory. The part of a computer's memory that is used for storing loaded programs and files. The easiest analogy is that it is the computer's working, thinking or operating memory.
ROM Read Only Memory. The part of the computer's memory that contains fixed information such as the computer's operating system. Also used for a CD ROM, as the disk can only be read and not written to.

save To transfer information from the computer's operating memory to a storage device such as a disk drive.
scanner A flatbed scanner looks like a photocopier; it takes a picture of what is being scanned and turns it into digital information that can appear and be used by a computer. A hand-held scanner is a smaller device that performs the same function, but it is 'swiped' across a piece of paper-based information.
sensor A device that a computer can use to monitor external events such as temperature or light levels.
shareware Software that does not have to be paid for until it is used. Shareware can be downloaded from the Internet. Most shareware authors deny that they ever receive any money. This is either because anorakish users are too mean to pay for something someone was foolish enough to make available free, or because it is a good tax dodge. Most shareware programs are excellent; some may have unexpected results like a *virus*.
signature file Return address information such as name, telephone number and e-mail address that is automatically put at the bottom of e-mail messages to save retyping basic information.
simulation A computer model of a situation. The user can enter information into the simulation and the computer will respond with an appropriate outcome. Simuiations make it possible to model parts of expensive, difficult, complex, hazardous or impossible situations. However, like most complex things that are simulated, there is always something missing.
SLIP or PPP Serial Line Internet Protocol (SLIP) or Point to Point Protocol (PPP) Internet connections. Both allow a computer to connect to the Internet using a modem and telephone line. Users then navigate the Internet using software on their own computer. This is in contrast to using a *dial-up Internet connection*, where a user is forced to navigate the Net using a text-based set of menus.
software The programs (or procedures) used to instruct the computer.
sort To put items into order (alphabetical or numerical). This process is often used by databases and spreadsheets. Some word processors allow paragraphs and lists to be sorted alphabetically.
spam Slang for posting the same message to multiple newsgroups – frowned on by most people on the Internet.
speech See *voice synthesis*.
spreadsheet A computer application that resembles a large grid of cells. Each cell can be linked to any other by a formula. If information is changed in one cell, all other interlinked cells are changed according to the linking formulae. As might be predicted, you cannot spread it straight from the fridge but it will print out on lots of sheets of paper.
stress sensor All modern technical equipment has a hidden stress sensor. The more stressed you are or the more anxious you become, the more likely the stress sensor will leap into action. On a computer this means that it will perform mundane tasks in a new and creative way, wiping half of your word-processing file as you print it out, for example. Every office photocopier has one attached to the green 'start' button, which ensures a major breakdown the day before all the financial paperwork has to be sent to the tax office.
system software See **operating system.**

Telnet Allows people to access computers and their data at thousands of places around the world, most often at libraries, universities and government agencies. Text-based, but relatively fast.

trackerball An input device that controls the mouse pointer by means of a large ball mounted in a cradle – similar in action to an upturned (or dead) mouse. Can be particularly useful for people with limited fine motor skills.

upload To send information to another computer or network.
Usenet newsgroups More than 17,000 topic-oriented message bases that can be read and posted to. Also called newsgroups.
user One who uses a computer. However, the word clearly has anorakish and addictive connotations.
user group A group of like-minded people who have a similar interest. User groups communicate by e-mail. See also *user.*

VDU Visual Display Unit – see *monitor.*
VGA Video Graphics Array – a standard that specifies the way computers communicate with monitors to ensure conformity.
virtual A much overused term implying something is not quite real. A computer-generated environment.
virus A computer virus is a cunning and occasionally malicious little program that 'infects' a computer's files or operating system. Some viruses can damage a computer by, for example, altering or deleting the contents of files. Viruses are often transferred from one computer to another by floppy disks or over the Internet. All hard-drive-based machines should have some virus protection software installed. It is depressing to consider that they have been created by talented individuals with nothing better to offer the computing community than a widget that weasels its way into your computer and damages it.
voice input Some computers can be controlled by voice. There are also several software programs that can learn to recognize an individual's voice so you can dictate and have your words appear on screen.
voice synthesis A software application that almost, but not quite, unsuccessfully simulates the sound of the human voice. It usually comprises a series of phonemes (phonetic sounds) that are strung together by the computer to form sounds that are almost, but not quite, unlike words. A more accurate description would be a synthetic voice, perhaps polyester or rayon.

WIMP *Windows*, Icons, Menus, Pointers – the environment that is used to interact with most mouse-controlled computers. You move the mouse and point and click. A *GUI* interface is operated through a WIMP environment. There! You can now read Geek!
window A framed area of the computer screen. Several windows can be displayed on the screen. Usually only one window is 'active' at any one time and able to be used. So called because you cannot see through them. They rarely shed any light on the situation and the one you actually want to see is hidden by all the others.
word processor An *application* for displaying and manipulating text. Unfortunately, computers are not yet able to produce appropriate words to process.
World Wide Web (WWW) Part of the Internet that communicates information in text, images, sounds and animation using *hypertext*. By moving the mouse over parts of a World Wide Web page and clicking a button, you are given more information or are transferred to other Web sites. Also know as the 'World Wide Wait' because of long download times over telephone lines.

zoom To magnify part of an image for more detailed work, or to reduce the size of an image to see more of it on screen. Often shown as a percentage of the full size. Zooming to 200 per cent increases the area to four times the original (2×2). When interviewed, most teachers claimed to prefer strawberry Mivvis.

Chapter 5

Evaluating your training

1. Obtaining feedback – and developing your forgettery!
2. First thoughts on questionnaires
3. Some problems with questionnaires
4. Some kinds of structured questions
5. Some ideas for open questions
6. Some ways of using questionnaires
7. Feedback from interviews with trainees
8. Feedback from groups of trainees
9. Following up after a training event
10. More ways of getting feedback!
11. Replanning your training event

The main way we get better at things is by finding out more about what goes right and what goes wrong. It is all too easy to be so busy planning our next training events that we shelve the task of really finding out how our last ones went. We often go as far as collecting feedback, but never really analysing it.

This chapter opens with ideas for **gathering and using feedback** during training events as well as after them. The next sets of suggestions are about **designing and using questionnaires**. Feedback gathered by questionnaire is particularly useful, as it is 'solid evidence' of what people think, and we can sift through the evidence as often as we wish and for as long as we wish, and interpret it in great detail. However, it is all too easy for situations to arise where people fill in questionnaires quickly and 'lightly' without thinking much about the real meaning behind the questions. The suggestions here will help you get the most from questionnaires, and minimize the dangers associated with them. The chapter ends with further advice on **different ways of getting feedback**, both on your training and on your trainees' subsequent performance, and putting it to use.

1. Obtaining feedback – and developing your forgettery!

Just as it is useful to encourage our participants to give feedback to each other, it is vital that we gather feedback from them about us. This can be painful at times! The following suggestions may help:

- **Install a forgettery!** It's all too easy to retain the hurt from negative feedback about our performances as trainers, but it's best consciously to decide to forget the pain and simply to carry forward practical plans for what we will do next time – and what we will avoid doing ever again.

- **Gather feelings in advance when possible.** It is often possible to design a short pre-event questionnaire, including questions to help you to find out in advance what participants already know, and also to find out a little about their existing attitudes and feelings about the theme of the training event.

- **Ask participants how they feel.** It is often worth doing this after a meal break, or at the beginning of a new day in an extended course. All the better if their responses are not confined to their feelings about the training event or course.

- **Put up a 'feelings chart'.** For example, stick up a flipchart in a corner of the room, and place a pad of Post-its on a table. Invite participants to stick Post-its with their feelings or questions on to the chart at any time during the programme. They can choose breaks in the programme to do this, especially if they prefer their feelings to remain anonymous.

- **Ask, 'How are you finding the programme so far?'** Take care to continue smiling (and biting your tongue) when things you hear disappoint you; don't stifle feedback even when it is unwelcome. Bin the pain in your forgettery – carry forward the things you're learning.

- **Try 'stop, start, continue'.** Especially at the middle of your training event, give out Post-its and ask participants to write these three words as headings, and to give you messages about what they would like you to stop doing, start doing and continue to do. You can respond to the 'stop' and 'start' messages during the rest of the training event.

- **Build on positive feedback.** For example, when participants tell you to continue things in a 'stop, start, continue' round, make sure that you build in more of the same things as and when you can.

- **Do a written training event evaluation.** It's useful to design a *short* questionnaire with a few structured questions (for example, tick boxes), so you can get a quick impression of your participants' reactions.

- **Also ask two or three open-ended questions.** For example, ask participants, 'What did you most like about the way the training event was run?' and (if you dare) the corresponding 'least like' question too. Again, put any pain in your forgettery, and carry forward the useful ideas for improvement.

- **Make your own list of feedback points to yourself.** It's well worth spending a few minutes after the close of your training events jotting down notes to yourself about what you learnt, and about what you would or would not try if running the same training event again tomorrow. Don't expect to keep all these thoughts in your head – jot them down, and then you can relax and forget any tensions.

2. First thoughts on questionnaires

Questionnaires can be a really useful source of information and feedback. However, it is essential that you are really clear about the sort of information you want from a questionnaire. Pre-planning and time for analysis are essential features when using them:

- **What are you trying to achieve?** This may seem rather simplistic but it is well worth spending some time thinking about what sort of information you want to receive. It is very easy to get carried away and ask for the world.

- **Keep it simple.** In this way you will be much more likely to get a return. How many times have you started to complete a questionnaire only to find it difficult to understand? Simple words and short sentences are more likely to get responses – and honest ones at that.

- **Avoid jargon or acronyms.** Acronyms like AVA, IT, OHTs and so on may not be understood by everyone. Don't assume that your participants know the special language of your training event topic – or training terminology.

- **Keep it short and sweet.** Decide on the length. Generally speaking, the shorter the better. Psychologically, the greater the length, the more likely we are to put it in the bin or in a place where it will end up buried under a pile of papers. In order to keep the questionnaire to one or two sides of A4 paper, do not reduce the print size so that no one without a magnifying glass or strong spectacles can read it! Instead, reduce the number of questions.

- **Know your audience.** Think carefully about the recipients of this questionnaire. Try to make the questions as relevant and interesting as possible to them.

- **Questionnaire designers do it with a friend.** Always trial your questionnaire first. It does involve extra time, which needs to be built into the planning process, but it is well worth the extra effort. You may just want to check that the questions are understandable to a colleague or neighbour. If, however, your circulation is large and the questionnaire is really important you may need to pilot it with between 10 and 50 people. This will usually lead you towards making some valuable modifications.

- **Use some closed questions.** A closed question is where you ask for a structured response (typically yes/no) or the ticking of an appropriate box. This sort of question is normally very easy to complete, and the responses are easy to analyse. Remember though that participants may make 'instant' or surface decisions – especially if there are too many closed questions.

- **Include some open questions.** There will be occasions when you want a much longer or less structured response than you get just from closed questions. Open questions, such as those including such phrases as 'What is your opinion of...?', 'How have you found...?', 'What would you have liked...?' or 'What do you see happening in the future?' can elicit some very useful information.

- **Consider one or two 'leading questions'.** I've found it useful (for example) to ask participants to tell me, 'The thing I most liked about the way the training event was run was...' and 'The thing that most annoyed me about how the training event was run was...' Sometimes the responses hurt – but are useful feedback nonetheless.

- **Layout – first impressions count.** If the questionnaire looks professional and well set out, you will be much more likely to obtain a good response. Consider whether any of the following would help: a cartoon, different named sections, questions in boxes, answers all to be given in a right-hand column, occasional use of bold and italics, or an unusual font.

- **Are you colour-coded?** How many 'trees' of paper come on to our desks each month, and how will anyone distinguish your questionnaire from the rest of the pile? Think about using a different colour of paper – green, blue or, maybe better, sepia or peach. Pages of different colours seem to 'hit us in the eye' and almost demand our attention.

- **Don't let it degenerate into a 'happy sheet'.** Most questionnaires do end up measuring something that is linked to the happiness of the people who fill them in, but you can make at least some of your questions interesting enough and specific enough to encourage respondents to go well beyond their mood at the time.

- **Give it out at the end, and collect immediately?** This has the benefit that you can get a complete set of feedback, but the drawback that the feedback may be coloured by the feelings of the moment.

- **Provide a stamped addressed envelope.** If you're giving participants (say) a week to reflect on their experience of your training event, the stamp can have quite a pronounced psychological effect. An unreturned questionnaire becomes an unanswered letter!

- **Run a raffle!** Number the questionnaires, and tell participants that the lucky winner will be chosen from all the replies you have by a named cut-off date. The prize could be a relevant learning package or book – or something much more imaginative.
- **Consider using a very short 'instant' questionnaire, and a more spacious follow-up one a week later.** The second questionnaire could include questions about if and how participants' first reactions have changed on second thoughts.
- **Global or selective?** Is it better to send it to fewer but more focused clients or groups, or is it preferable to send it out more widely? This may of course depend on the topic. Will it be sent to specific people, or to a base or office for distribution? If the latter, ensure you have a named contact person who is willing to undertake the distribution and maybe the collection as well. Don't forget to allow reasonable time for people to reply.
- **How is it to be analysed?** This may well depend upon the size of the questionnaire, and the facilities and finance available. It can be analysed by hand, or using an optical mark reader (OMR) for questionnaires where respondents put a pen or pencil mark in between strategically placed brackets. You may even be able to arrange for your questionnaire to be analysed by computer.

3. Some problems with questionnaires

Decide whether or not each of the following potential problems may exist in the processes and instruments you currently use for gathering trainee feedback:

- **The 'ticky-box' syndrome.** People become conditioned to make instant responses to questions. Getting through the questionnaire quickly becomes a virtue. Responses are made on a surface level of thinking rather than as a result of reflection and critical thinking. (This is not a problem on those occasions where instant reaction is what is *wanted*, but the feedback we gather is not usually analysed on that basis.)
- **'Performing dogs' syndrome.** Many people filling in questionnaires tend to want to please! They can usually tell which responses will please the people giving them the questionnaire, and the people whose work is involved in the issues covered by the questionnaire. If they like the people, they are likely to comment favourably on things, rather than use questionnaires to show their real views.
- **Lost learning opportunities.** Questionnaires are often used after an event rather than during it. This tends to minimize any real learning outcomes of the process of completing questionnaires. The sense of ownership is reduced, when trainees don't see how their responses will be of any direct benefit to themselves, and may only help their successors.

- **The 'WYSIWYG' syndrome (what you see is what you get).** Questionnaires produce feedback on the particular issues covered – but often not on other important issues. There is a tendency to design questionnaires that will give positive feedback, and to avoid asking those questions where there is every possibility of critical replies.
- **'Blue, rosy and purple' questionnaires.** A major limitation of most questionnaires is that responses are coloured by how people feel at the moment of filling them in. If the same questionnaire were to be filled in by the same people at two different times, some responses could be completely different. Yet the results are often statistically analysed as though they reflected permanent, considered reactions to questions and issues, rather than fleeting, transient reactions.
- **'Conditioned response' questionnaires.** When the same questionnaire format is used repeatedly, trainees can become very bored, and may revert to answering many of the questions in the same way as they have done previously. Feedback then is not specific to the particular occasion when the questionnaire is being used, and at best represents overall feelings rather than specific responses.
- **'Death by questionnaire'.** This is caused by using too many questionnaires, too often, badly designed and with nothing ever happening as a result of the feedback that is given.

4. Some kinds of structured questions

- **Experiment with ticking boxes or putting marks on scales.** This can be done with contrasting dimensions at opposite sides of a form, such as:

  interesting..boring
  too fast..too slow
  approachable..unapproachable

- **Try out 'usefulness' measures.** Various dimensions mentioned at the left-hand side, with boxes for 'very useful', 'quite useful' and 'not useful' to tick. The dimensions can include such things as handout materials, visual aids and worked examples done in class.
- **Explore 'agreement' measures.** A series of statements can be checked against boxes such as 'strongly agree', 'more or less agree', 'disagree' and 'strongly disagree', for example. The statements can usefully be both positive and negative, to ensure that respondents don't fall into the pattern of agreeing (or disagreeing) with everything they see. Typical statements can be along the lines:

  'I find your presentations usually stimulate me to further work.'

'I remain switched off for most of my time in your presentations.'
'I am clear about the intended learning outcomes of each part of this module.'
'I don't really know what is expected of me in this subject.'

- **Try out number gradings.** Here trainees can be asked to enter numbers to indicate their feelings with regard to a statement or an issue, for example: 5 = most useful, 4 = very useful, 3 = quite useful, 2 = of limited use, 1 = of little use, 0 = of no use.

- **Explore 'more', 'just right' and 'less' boxes.** These could be used (for example) for trainees to record their feelings about the things they do in tutorials, for example:

  practising problem solving;
  seeing worked examples done;
  working through case study materials;
  asking questions of the trainer;
  being asked questions by the trainer;
  having marked homework discussed individually;
  having marked practical work returned and discussed;
  seeing examples of assessment criteria;
  using assessment criteria directly to mark own (or others') work;
  practising addressing previous exam questions.

- **Get trainees prioritizing.** This sort of structure helps overcome the 'ticky-box' syndrome, as it causes trainees to think more deeply about issues. For example, they can be asked to enter '1' against the best features of the training event, '2' against the next-best and so on.. Questions and choices need to be clear and unambiguous.

5. Some ideas for open questions

Open questions allow each trainee to respond freely to set areas. While such questions can overcome some of the limitations we have mentioned regarding structured questions, the fact that trainees are entering their responses in their own handwriting can be a deterrent against them expressing negative or critical views, where they may feel that they could be traced and maybe even penalized as a result. The following examples illustrate the kind of open questions most often used in questionnaires.

The two most useful features of your presentations are:

1.
2.

The two least useful features of your presentations are:

1.
2.
Suggestions for improvement:

The three topics I found it most difficult to make sense of in this course are:

1.
2.
3.

6. Some ways of using questionnaires

- **Consider making the use of questionnaires private to individual trainers.** For feedback about presentations (or tutorials or lab work), I think it best that each trainer should design and use an individual questionnaire, and obtain feedback for his or her own use privately. This doesn't mean, however, that the forms are to be filled in 'privately' by trainees – it may well be better to use them as an agenda for group feedback.

- **Make questionnaires 'short and often, not long and once'.** Any feedback form should be short enough not to bore or alienate trainees. A good guide may be that it should be possible for a group to complete the form in a few minutes or so. This means separate forms for presentations, group work and so on.

- **Use questionnaires for formative rather than summative feedback whenever possible.** Seek feedback during a programme, so that something can still be done about matters emerging. Feedback after completion of a programme is still useful, but is not seen by trainees as so valuable as when they have the chance to suggest changes they themselves will benefit from directly.

- **Employ questionnaires for a wide range of matters to do with your presentation, style and approachability.** These aspects of training can be gathered in the private mode suggested above. Individual questionnaire components can be selected or composed by each trainer to search for comment about issues that may be of particular concern to him or her.

- **Consider 'more-public' questionnaires for general issues and for summative feedback.** These can be used to measure feedback relating to non-personal variables, for example:

  relative workload of different topics or modules;
  perceived relevance of topics, as seen by trainees;
  relevance of practical work to theory, as seen by trainees;
  balance of presentations, group work and other training situations.

  The 'more-public' sort of questionnaire is more likely to have value when used towards the end of a course or module, and to gather summative feedback, which can be used in reviewing the course or module prior to the next time it will be delivered.

- **Structured questionnaires can have the advantage of anonymity.** Even if using a mixed questionnaire containing open-ended questions as well, you may decide to issue the structured and open-ended parts separately because of this factor.

- **Try to avoid surface thinking.** Trainees – and anyone else involved – get bored if they have long questionnaires to complete, and the decisions or comments they make become 'surface' rather than considered ones. Even though trainees may be able to respond to a structured questionnaire of several pages in relatively few minutes, the fact that a questionnaire *looks* long can induce surface response behaviour.

- **Consider the visual appearance of your questionnaires.** Go for a varied layout, with plenty of white space, so that it does not look like a solid list of questions. Use a mixture of response formats, such as deletions or selections from lists of options, yes/no choices, tick-boxes, graduated scales and so on – make it *look* interesting to complete.

- **For every part of the questionnaire, have definite purposes, including positive ones.** Don't ask anything that could prove to be superfluous or of passing interest only. Ask about positive experiences as well as searching for weaknesses.

- **Plan your evaluation report before you design your feedback questionnaire.** It helps a great deal if you know exactly how you plan to collate and use the responses you will get from your questionnaires. Working out the things you hope to include in your report often alerts you to additional questions you may need to include, and (particularly) to superfluous questions that would not actually generate any information of practical use to you.

- **Make each question simple and unambiguous.** If trainees' interpretations of the questions vary, the results of a survey are not valid enough to warrant statistical analysis of any sort. In particular, it's worth ensuring that in structured questions trainees are only required to make decisions involving a single factor.

- **Ask yourself, 'What does this question really mean?'** Sometimes, your reply to yourself will contain wording that will work better in your questionnaire than the original idea you started with.

- **Avoid safe middle ground in scales.** For example, the scale 'strongly agree, agree, undecided, disagree, strongly disagree' may give better results if the 'undecided' option is omitted, forcing respondents to make a decision one way or the other (or to write 'can't tell' on the questionnaire, which then has the validity of a conscious decision).

- **Be aware that some respondents will make choices on the basis of those they think they are expected to make.** Many respondents set out to 'please' the person gathering the feedback, possibly thinking of possible recriminations if critical selections may be traced back to their authors.

- **Keep prioritizing questions short and simple.** For example, if trainees are asked to rank seven factors in order of value (or importance), it may be easy enough to analyse the best and worst choices, but difficult to make a meaningful analysis of 'middle ground'.

- **Pilot your draft questionnaire.** There is no better way to improve a structured questionnaire than to find out what trainees actually do with it! Use short print runs for questionnaires, and edit between each use.

- **Feed back the results to your respondents.** Tell them about the changes that are proposed on the basis of the results from the questionnaire. Otherwise people are likely to become disillusioned about the whole process of giving feedback.

7. Feedback from interviews with trainees

Interviews with trainees can be a valuable source of feedback. However, interviewing trainees is costly in terms of time and effort; the following suggestions may help you to make it a cost-effective process:

- **Prepare your agenda carefully.** To enable you to analyse and collate the feedback you get from trainees, it is important that they are all asked the same questions in the same way. It is all too tempting to develop the agenda on the basis of the replies of the first few trainees, so it is usually worth piloting your question list on a few trainees (not necessarily from the group to be targeted) before starting on a set of 'real' interviews.

- **Link interviews with other means of getting feedback from trainees.** If you are already using (or planning to use) structured or open-ended questionnaires, you may find it worthwhile to work out what *else* you will be particularly looking for in feedback from interviews.

- **Consider the merits of using interviews to follow up questionnaire feedback.** When you have already analysed questionnaire responses by trainees, you may be able to pinpoint a few issues where you want to ask trainees more-detailed or more-personal questions about their experiences with a subject or a course.

- **Consider the alternative possibility of using preliminary interviews to establish the agenda for feedback questionnaires.** This would probably not take the form of interviews with the whole group, but with a representative selection of trainees.
- **You may not be able to interview the whole group.** Decide how you are going to select the trainees you choose to interview. There are many possibilities, each with its own advantages and drawbacks. For example, you could select randomly by name or trainee number, or you could make a representative selection including high performers, middle-range performers and low achievers in related assessments, or you could ask for volunteers (not, however, the most representative of the possibilities).
- **Remember that trainees may be anxious.** Any kind of interview may suggest an assessment dimension to trainees, and this may cause them to be restrained, especially when it comes to expressing dissatisfaction.
- **Ask questions that lead trainees to answer rather than to refrain from comment.** For example, asking trainees 'Was there anything you found unsatisfactory?' may be less fruitful than asking 'What was the thing you liked least about the way this module was taught?'
- **Don't lead your witnesses!** It is one thing to ensure that trainees feel free to answer questions, but another to lead them towards the answers you want or the answers they may think you want. 'Do you like the way I used coloured overheads in my presentations?' is an example of a leading question.
- **It's essential to make good notes!** After four or five interviews, you may have a good idea of the general nature of responses to your questions, but you could have lost a lot of the specific detail. More-recent interview happenings tend to 'drown' earlier ones in your memory.

8. Feedback from groups of trainees

Trainees may be more forthcoming in a group, and you could consider posing the questions (maybe as a handout), leaving the group to come to decisions about how they wish to answer them and then returning to hear their answers. The trainees have the safety of being able to report minority views or controversial views without the trainee who speaks such responses having to 'own' the view reported. Group interviews can save a considerable amount of time compared to solo interviews, and allow trainees to compare and contrast their own perspectives. Trainees in groups can also be helped to prioritize or put in order of importance their responses, making their feedback even more valuable. Group interviews can be used to get trainees to clarify or explain issues or responses that at first may be unclear. Feedback from groups can be more useful than feedback from individuals, for the following reasons:

- **Feedback from groups captures discussion, reflection and debate.** This is more useful than only having the reactions of individual trainees.
- **A group can present negative feedback with less embarrassment than an individual.** Individuals can be more forthcoming in making inputs in a group, when their feedback is then rendered more or less anonymous within the group.
- **Group feedback is likely to range more widely.** Where a questionnaire is used as an agenda for group feedback, the group is more likely to be willing to go beyond the agenda.

9. Following up after a training event

Normally, fatigue and total relief (for most of us, anyway!) follow a training event. Once revived, however, we should ask ourselves, 'What next?'

- **First reflect.** A personal reflective journal is a really useful and essential tool. This may take the form of a notebook that you keep on one side, a file in your container or an audiotape you speak comments on to. The value lies not in the method of reflecting, but in the time taken doing so. Try and build in this time when planning a training event.
- **Follow up on the spot.** Ask your participants how they would like to keep in touch. If they are enthusiastic and feel that the training event was useful, they may ask you to organize a follow-up session, maybe in a month or even in six months' time. Try and set a date and place there and then if possible – you can always confirm or adjust later.
- **Set an agenda.** It is really important that you have a proper agenda for a follow-up meeting. Write and confirm date, place and time as soon as possible. Then a week or two before the follow-up, write to participants with a draft agenda, and involve them as much as possible in fine-tuning it.
- **Be clear about participants' involvement.** The greater the involvement of the group, the more your participants will take on ownership of the event. You may (for example) ask them to do presentations of what they have achieved since you last met. Give them an indication of how long you want these presentations to be, and the format you expect them to use. If you find they are not confident about the prospect of giving presentations, you have a clear pointer to the topic of a future training event!
- **Set up local support or friendship groups.** These may be in one company, or within a geographical area. Think carefully about the purpose of such groups, and how they will function. Do the groups need to establish ground rules, for example the frequency of their meetings?

- **Think technologically.** Many organizations are now already connected (or thinking of being connected) by electronic mail. This is a really quick and easy way of keeping in contact with many people in different places. A network can be set up so that one message automatically goes to every member of the group, allowing them to ask questions or reply individually at any time.

- **Consider videoconferencing.** Almost by the minute, the price of videoconferencing is coming down. A computer, an ISDN telephone connection, special software and cameras are all that you need. At the time of writing, if you already have the computer and telephone connection, the rest costs around £2,000.

- **Consider a newsletter.** If you can produce a newsletter quickly and cheaply, it can provide an excellent way of keeping in touch with a group. With desktop publishing, attractive-looking newsletters can be produced very quickly. Plan the costings: who will pay for the paper, the printing and the distribution? The costs could be small, especially if the newsletter is kept to a single sheet of A4 paper.

- **Don't forget audiocassettes.** These are cheap, quick and easy to produce, and can provide an attractive way for members of a group to catch up with news and progress, for example while driving to work or commuting. They have the advantage of tone of voice and humanity. Also, the tapes can be reused.

- **Offer a qualification.** If your participants can obtain qualifications while attending your training events, so much the better. Can you gain accreditation yourself as an assessor? Link in with local colleges or universities.

10. More ways of getting feedback!

A training event may be said to be successful if skills are developed and improvements are made to workplace performance or participants' personal performance. But how can we find out exactly what changes take place as a direct result of our courses? The more different sources of feedback we can use, the better we can evaluate our courses:

- **How will participants know if they have been successful?** Ask them by what criteria they will know if they have succeeded, and who will be the judge – themselves, colleagues, line managers or a combination. This exercise provides useful information about how we as trainers can follow up the outcomes of our courses.

- **Start a suggestion box.** Encourage participants to ask colleagues at all levels to list one strength, one area for enhancement and one aspect they think participants have improved as a result of participating in your course. Then ask the participants to share this information with you and other group members. Make sensible ground rules for sensitive information.

- **Set aside time for follow-up telephone calls to managers.** Time must be put in your diary if you are to gather feedback properly and reflect on it well. If you intend to follow up by using the telephone, try to provide managers with a choice of times – they can't talk to you if they are busy or away. Suggest how long the conversation is likely to take, and stick to schedule. It can help to design a written checklist before you ring; this helps you to ask the same questions, and keeps you to target when sidetracked.

- **Always allow time for 'Is there anything else you would like to ask me or tell me?'** You'll often get some of the most valuable information in response to this final question in a telephone call.

- **Try to find out about personal satisfaction and confidence.** Your participants may tell you one thing about these, but it's well worth finding out what they may have told other people. Use all opportunities gently to gather second-hand comments about your course from people your participants may have spoken to about it. Be careful not to appear to be 'spying' on your participants though – make it clear that the information you're seeking is for your benefit for future planning.

- **Gain information from appraisal procedures.** For example, during a training event use a 'personal agenda setting' or 'personal action planning' exercise. Give participants time to design their own future targets, and suggest that they share these plans during appraisal interviews. Then ask them (or their managers) how useful the plans turned out to be.

11. Replanning your training event

Sooner or later you may be running the same training event again. The best time to decide exactly how you'll make the next run of a training event better is while you're running your present one:

- **Watch out for how your pre-event publicity really worked.** Look out for things that participants did not expect. Particularly be watchful for expectations your participants have that you had not thought of.

- **Check how your arrangements actually worked.** When things go wrong at the venue, jot down some notes about how you could ensure that these particular things will not happen on a future occasion.

- **Look for what worked well.** Often, things go well without any real planning. Try to ascertain the causes of things that go particularly well, and capitalize on these factors when planning your next similar training event.

- **Ask yourself, 'What would I do differently in a similar situation tomorrow?'** Make notes of the changes you intend to make the next time you're planning to run a similar training session.

- **Ask your participants, 'What should I stop?'** This direct question can provide you with some uncomfortable – but really useful – responses. If anyone thinks that some things you are doing are not useful or productive, it's worth thinking whether you can do something different next time.

- **Ask your participants, 'What should I start next time?'** This can alert you to ways that you may be better able to meet the expectations or wishes of future participants on similar training events.

- **Ask your participants, 'What should I continue doing in future?'** This is the good news! It's always useful to find out the things that your training event participants really appreciate or enjoy.

- **Redraft your training event programme immediately after the present event.** Don't trust that you will remember all the changes you may wish to make on the next occasion.

- **When something just doesn't work, admit it!** Don't dig your heels in and say that it must remain part of your programme. Look for an alternative that may provide the same learning outcomes for your participants.

- **Plan a new draft training event outline after every event.** These draft outlines can be the real ones you use as your event develops and evolves. Never be afraid to make changes. A programme that worked well once may work even better next time with changes.

Index